18· 99

Applying the Dismal S

Also by Iain McLean

THE CONCISE OXFORD DICTIONARY OF POLITICS, REVISED EDITION (*co-author with Alistair McMillan*)

FIXING THE BOUNDARIES: Defining and Redefining Single-Member Electoral Districts (*co-editor with David Butler*)

THE LEGEND OF RED CLYDESIDE

ABERFAN: Government and Disasters (*co-author with Martin Johnes*)

RATIONAL CHOICE AND BRITISH POLITICS: An Analysis of Rhetoric and Manipulation from Peel to Blair

Applying the Dismal Science

When Economists Give Advice to Governments

Edited by

Iain McLean
Professor of Politics Oxford University, UK

and

Colin Jennings
Lecturer in Economics The Queen's College, Oxford, UK

First published in 2006 by
PALGRAVE MACMILLAN
Houndmills, Basingstoke, Hampshire RG21 6XS and
175 Fifth Avenue, New York, N.Y. 10010
Companies and representatives throughout the world.

PALGRAVE MACMILLAN is the global academic imprint of the Palgrave
Macmillan division of St. Martin's Press, LLC and of Palgrave Macmillan Ltd.
Macmillan® is a registered trademark in the United States, United Kingdom
and other countries. Palgrave is a registered trademark in the European
Union and other countries.

ISBN-13: 978–1–4039–9458–5   hardback
ISBN-10: 1–4039–9458–7   hardback
ISBN-13: 978–1–4039–9459–2   paperback
ISBN-10: 1–4039–9459–5   paperback

This book is printed on paper suitable for recycling and made from fully
managed and sustained forest sources.

A catalogue record for this book is available from the British Library.

A catalog record for this book is available from the Library of Congress.

10 9 8 7 6 5 4 3 2 1
15 14 13 12 11 10 09 08 07 06

Printed and bound in Great Britain by
Antony Rowe Ltd, Chippenham and Eastbourne

Contents

List of Figures and Tables

Figures

Table

Foreword

Martin Wolf

Almost every economist would agree on the wisdom of road pricing, while they have disagreed, often violently, over macroeconomics. Yet policy makers have almost always rejected the former and relied on economists for advice on the latter. Why is this? To economists, the answer seems clear. There is no lobby against full employment and low inflation, but there are powerful lobbies against road pricing. The difference then is not whether the ideas of economists are right or wrong, but whether lobbies can be mobilized against them. Whether a policy is introduced depends not on its wisdom, but on the interests at work.

Economists are comfortable with this analysis, because of their assumption of rationality. They assume that not only economists, but everybody engaged in making decisions, understands how the world works. Under that assumption, only selfish interests can explain bad policies.

This approach is not so much wrong as too simple. People are both benevolent and self-interested. They can be well-informed, rationally ignorant or merely ignorant. The ideas of professional economists can be well developed, as in road pricing, incomplete, as in financial regulation, or wrong, as in naïve Keynesianism. Lobbies may be effective at one time and ineffective at another. Governments are neither benevolent maximizers of a well-defined social welfare function nor narrowly self-seeking.

What is needed is a more subtle analysis. The authors call the needed approach 'political economy'. It is a good label.

The studies in this book show that the ideas of economists matter, but in complex ways. That is not surprising. Ideas of how people should behave affect how they do behave. Even ideas about how they behave change how they behave. The more convinced people are, for example, that advice is self-interested the less likely they are to trust it.

The big conclusion is an optimistic one: better economics, more widely understood, can improve policy. It has done so in macroeconomics. It has done so as well in wide areas of microeconomics: attitudes to liberal trade are an excellent example. Interests matter. But so do ideas, even those about the role of lobbies. Economics aims to be a useful social science. By and large, it turns out, it is so.

Preface

This book is based upon the seminar series 'Political Economy in Practice' held at Nuffield College, Oxford between April and June 2004. All of the speakers were academic social scientists who had worked as high-level advisers on government policy in the United Kingdom. Two other authors – Peter Jay and Ed Balls – have contributed chapters on political economy in the UK, respectively on 1964–70 and 1974–9 (Jay); and 1997 to date (Balls). The seminars were very lively. Several of the chapter authors attended all or most, and commented vigorously on one another's presentations. Contributions from students and colleagues who attended were also very helpful.

All of our authors were asked to explore how far economic theory informs actual policy making. The chapters cover a wide range of government policy from macroeconomic policy (Balls, Allsopp), advice to the Treasury (Budd, McLean), monetary union (Robson) to micro policy (auction design (Klemperer), transport (Foster)).

Some chapter authors regard policy making in a positive light, where policy conforms well to expert recommendations (Allsopp, McLean). Others suggest that with improvements in knowledge, policy will also improve (Klemperer, Budd). However, policy often does not follow expert advice (most clearly in Foster, but applies to all the chapters to varying degrees). A recurrent underlying problem (especially in Foster's chapter) is that public attitudes to risk, and therefore sometimes the attitudes of politicians seeking to win elections, are inconsistent.

The divergence between policies that experts would recommend and those that are actually implemented speaks to the difference between *the public finance approach* and *the public choice approach*.

The public finance approach identifies policies to correct for market failures (macro failures as well as the commonly understood micro failures) and to redistribute income efficiently. In this literature, where economists agree upon efficient solutions, implementation follows automatically. In contrast, public choice recognises that political process and institutions matter. During the election campaign, political parties must woo the median voter. After the election, the principal (the electorate) cannot directly control its agents (public officials). Also, the principal may have such an imperfect understanding of relative risks that the voters may put pressures on politicians to implement inconsistent policies – notably in transport. Politics may therefore push policy away from the recommendation of experts. Institutional design to ensure good governance is a central theme in the normative strand of public choice. However, public choice does not necessarily imply the conservative-libertarian 'Virginia school' prescriptions most associated with it. The more recent literature, returning to the venerable label 'political economy', examines optimal policy given self-interested agents, and stresses incentive-compatible institutional design. The book signals a return to the spirit of Adam Smith, who well understood both public finance and what we now call public choice.

Our Introduction surveys public finance, public choice, and political economy. The succeeding chapters are case studies in political economy. In each case, the author has both a high level of economic expertise and inside knowledge of a policy area. This allows each author to comment upon the quality of decision making. Bad policy may arise from lack of prior agreement by experts and politicians (for instance, due to informational constraints or irresoluble disagreement over distributional issues), or from the political process and government institutions. In the latter case, the editors' Review and Conclusion suggests possible institutional reforms.

The book is aimed at policy practitioners, academics and students (undergraduate upwards) in courses in economics, public administration, and public policy; and to anyone who wishes to know where good economic advice does, and does not, improve policy in an advanced capitalist democracy. We hope it may be especially helpful as a series of case studies for a public policy course at MA level. All contributors have tried to write in a way that can be read profitably by both those with a training in economics and those without. Our findings, and stories about how policy was made, are (we hope) relevant to all those interested in both the science of identifying good policy and the art of making it happen. One of the editors, and most of the chapter authors, are economists; the other editor and one chapter co-author are political scientists.

Our authors were there when it happened. 'It' includes the triumphs and disasters of UK and some European public policy, including:

- Non-devaluation of the pound, 1964–7 and its devaluation 1967 (Jay).
- The Budgets of 1972–3, which contributed to the rampant inflation of 1974–6 (Budd).
- Every innovation in transport policy since Barbara Castle was Secretary of State for Transport in the 1960s (Foster).
- Bank of England independence 1997 (Balls, Robson).

- Interest-rate setting at the Monetary Policy Committee of the Bank of England (Allsopp).
- The third-generation mobile telephone spectrum auctions across Europe (Klemperer).
- Chancellor Gordon Brown's regime in HM Treasury (Balls, McLean).

Some of our stories – for example, Peter Jay's principled resignation from the Treasury in 1966, stymied by the loss of his letter in the internal mail; Alan Budd's account of the Treasury in 1972–3, 'seared by' mass unemployment in the 1930s and therefore quite unprepared for its next searing; Paul Klemperer's story of how third-generation (3G) bidders in the US apparently colluded with each other by sending semi-secret signals through their bids – are so vivid that we hope the dismal science may not appear so dismal after all.

William Morris, Viscount Nuffield, the founder of Nuffield College, where the original seminars took place, intended his college to be a meeting place of academics and policy makers. In the rolling phrases of its Royal Charter, the college exists, among other purposes,

> To provide for men and women who are members of Our [i.e., HM the Queen's] University of Oxford a College for post-graduate work especially in connection with the study by co-operation between academic and non-academic persons of social (including economic and political) problems.

Viscount Nuffield was not only the most generous philanthropist in British history, but also the pre-eminent industrialist of his generation, starting as a bicycle mechanic and finishing as the chairman of the largest British motor company. All too often, academics and policy makers have failed to come together in the way that Nuffield intended. There is fault on both sides. Academics are too academic; policy makers too busy; both too self-absorbed. We hope that this book will be a modest contribution to bringing them together again.

IAIN MCLEAN
COLIN JENNINGS

Notes on Contributors

Christopher Allsopp is a Fellow of New College and Reader in Economic Policy, Oxford University. He served a term as a member of the MPC of the Bank of England, and more recently completed a report for the Chancellor and others on the adequacy of statistics for regional policy.

Ed Balls was Chief Economic Adviser to the Treasury, 1997–2004; MP (Lab.) for Normanton since 2005.

Sir Alan Budd was Chief Economic Adviser to the Treasury from 1991 to 1997.

Sir Christopher Foster has been a professor of economics and a special adviser on transport and local government finance. Ministers he has advised include Barbara Castle and Tony Crosland (Lab.) and, in a non-political capacity, Kenneth Baker and William Waldegrave (Cons.).

Peter Jay has been chief economics correspondent for *The Times*, UK Ambassador to the USA and economics editor at the BBC.

Colin Jennings is Lecturer in Economics, The Queen's College, Oxford.

Paul Klemperer is Edgeworth Professor of Economics, Oxford University. He has advised UK, EU, and US government agencies on auctions and competition policy, and designed the UK's £22.5 billion '3G' mobile-phone auction (jointly with Ken Binmore); he is currently a member of the UK Competition Commission.

Iain McLean is Professor of Politics, Oxford University and a fellow of Nuffield College. His recent research has been in UK public policy.

Mark Robson was Economic Adviser to the Board of Inland Revenue 1985–90, Principal Administrator in the Fiscal Affairs Division of the OECD 1993–95, Senior Manager at the Bank of England 1995–2003, and has worked as an IMF Expert Adviser in Thailand and Israel.

1
Introduction: Public Finance, Public Choice, and Political Economy

Iain McLean and Colin Jennings

It was Thomas Carlyle, the violent Victorian essayist, who first called economics the dismal science:

> [T]he Social Science – not a 'gay science,' but a rueful – which finds the secret of this universe in 'supply-and-demand,' and reduces the duty of human governors to that of letting men alone, is also wonderful. Not a 'gay science,' I should say, like some we have heard of; no, a dreary, desolate, and indeed quite abject and distressing one; what we might call, by way of eminence, the dismal science. (Carlyle, 1853, cited by Levy and Peart, 2001, at http://www.econlib.org/library/Columns/LevyPeartdismal.html)

It is generally, but wrongly, believed that Carlyle was attacking the pessimistic forecast of his older contemporary Thomas Malthus that population growth would always outstrip resource growth, so that mankind would continue to starve. Actually he was attacking *laissez-faire* and the campaign to end slavery in the British Empire and the USA (his original essay is called *Occasional discourse on the nigger question*). Most people nowadays rather approve of the abolition of slavery, so economists should wear their badge of dismal science with pride.

There is nothing inherently abject or depressing about economics. Carlyle was part of a long line of thinkers who objected to economics *per se* – to its whole methodology and (what its opponents assume are) its assumptions. Distinguished fellow-Carlyleans include the art critic John Ruskin in the nineteenth century, the eminent sociologist Richard Titmuss in the twentieth, and critics of globalization such as Naomi Klein in the twenty-first. In this book, we aim to show that economics is

1

a science, but that it is not dismal. Economists can actually help governments govern better. Not always, but sometimes.

Another common fallacy is the belief that economists always disagree. Of course, they disagree about the kind of world they would like to see: as do entomologists and etymologists. There are conservative, liberal, socialist, and revolutionary economists (just as, we assume, there are conservative, liberal, socialist, and revolutionary etymologists). Our contributors are certainly not of one mind as to the world they would like to live in. Probably, neither are the co-authors of this chapter (though we have not asked one another). However, economists *do* agree as to methods. There is a body of agreed methods that economists all use to settle questions such as *What is the effect in the increase of supply of widgets?* Or *of a decrease in the demand for wodgets?*

The fundamental basis of economics is that resources are limited, but that our desires for the goods made from these resources are unlimited. Therefore, choices must be made as to how resources are allocated. The motivational assumption that drives economics is that agents within the economy, for instance consumers or firms, wish to maximize whatever goal it is they seek. For consumers this is generally thought to be satisfaction from a bundle of goods and for firms it may be, for example, profits or sales. The problem of scarcity and the motivation of agents are combined with the institutional setting to determine social outcomes.

The institutional setting could be the ideal of a smoothly functioning free market where firms respond to the desires of consumers and prices act to bring demand and supply into equilibrium. More generally, we see free markets alongside government involvement in the economy so that the institutional setting has both a private and public sector. The role of government in implementing the advice of economists is the theme of this book, but the role of government itself is a subject of major debate amongst economists. These can roughly be divided into those who take the line of traditional public finance versus those who follow the more modern public choice. The debate between these two schools of thought has led to the more modern school of political economics (to some extent resurrecting the even older one of political economy) which tries to incorporate aspects of both. We will discuss these three approaches to studying the role of government in the economy shortly.

While microeconomic issues form the subject matter of much of this book, *macroeconomics* features prominently as well. However, while the methodology of microeconomics is basically agreed, until the 1970s agreement on methodology was less true of macroeconomics. The *Oxford*

English Dictionary defines macroeconomics as 'The branch of economics that deals with large-scale economic factors; the economics of a national economy as a whole' as opposed to microeconomics, i.e. the study of individual economic agents. Neo-classical economists complained that the macroeconomic paradigm that dominated professional economics and public life from the 1930s to the 1970s, namely that defined by J. M. Keynes' *General Theory of Employment, Interest and Money* (Keynes, 1936), lacked microfoundations. By this they meant that in the understandable effort to aggregate from the level of individual agents to the level of the economy as a whole, some vital implications for the economy may be missed. Examples of this come from the Nobel Prize-winning work of Lucas and Kydland & Prescott.

The Lucas Critique (1976) suggested that traditional macro models may be highly misleading in predicting the effect of policy changes, since they do not take into account that the behaviour of private agents may itself change in response to policy changes. In particular, much greater understanding of the formation of expectations is required. This approach points to a micro-based macroeconomics, requiring much closer attention to the role of micro-level agents within the economy.

Kydland & Prescott (1977) drew attention to micro issues in macroeconomics, in their analysis of the time-inconsistency argument for rules rather than discretion. To ignore the motivation of agents may be to ignore a major explanation for observed macro outcomes, for example where policy makers may be tempted to renege on their previous policy announcements. An implication is that it may be better to adopt a set of constitutional rules in areas where the policy maker is subject to the time-inconsistency problem. The major example is the government announcing a low inflation target, but then expanding the money supply at a later date. But since agents in the economy rationally know that the government cannot credibly commit to low inflation, they will not believe the inflation target in the first place and by expecting higher inflation will demand higher wages, thereby making the policy ineffective. Once again, attention to micro-level agents may have a major effect on policy recommendation.

So in the 1970s neo-classical economists supplied the microfoundations of macroeconomic policy. This work is often portrayed as ideologically driven. By arguing that government intervention is ineffective or worse, the supposition may be that government intervention should be minimized. However, it was the Labour government elected in 1997 that made the Bank of England independent, thus making an institutional change in favour of rules over discretion.

However, although macroeconomics and microeconomics are now fully integrated, the same is not yet true of *public finance* and *public choice*. Public finance is the study of government spending and taxation to correct for market failures and redistribute income. In this sense it differs from the analysis of government and spending in macroeconomics as it is more specifically concerned with the allocation of resources between the goods that are produced in a society and how these goods are then distributed between individuals, as opposed to achieving a target level of overall output in the economy. Public choice has been defined as 'the economic study of nonmarket decision making, or simply the application of economics to political science' (Mueller, 2003, p. 1). Both of these are branches of an older tradition, *political economy*. Although it violates chronology, we need to discuss them in that order, because the new political economy is beginning to subsume both public finance and public choice.

Public finance

As just mentioned, the study of public finance can be split into an allocative function (to correct for market failures) and a redistributive function (to correct for inequality). It is, therefore, a normative branch of economics as it studies how governments can intervene in the economy to make things better. Markets if left to themselves will lead to socially valuable markets being missing due to problems with public goods, externalities, information and imperfect competition. To the extent that the existence of these markets generate benefits greater than costs then a government though taxation and spending decisions can provide better outcomes in the sense of Pareto efficiency: i.e., such that all can be potentially better off without anybody being worse-off.

Even if markets did work well, an inequitable distribution of resources may be considered unjust and government would have a further role to redistribute from the rich to the poor. Since the process of redistribution will create disincentives to work and thus lost output, the government should only redistribute until the point where the social gain in terms of increased equality just equals the social loss of reduced output. How much redistribution is optimal? This depends on the costs, but also on how distasteful you find inequality. This is a value judgement and people tend to disagree on this issue.

Public finance traditionally bypasses this thorny issue by introducing the concept of the social welfare function. Whether the issue is solving for market failure (the allocative role) or reducing inequality (the distributional function), governments are generally perceived as behaving in the manner of a benevolent dictator maximizing a social welfare function and thus treating society as an organic unit. So in its purest form, public finance proceeds by treating government process as a black box. This could be defended by arguing that the role of public finance is to identify improvements that can be made to society and recommend them to the government.

From this perspective, whether or not government is, in fact, benevolent is not an issue for the economist. However, for many the working assumption of a benevolent dictator is not an innocent one. It may bias analysis towards the identification of areas in need of government intervention, without proper consideration of the costs of intervention. Some of these costs may be transactional, but others may arise because government is (or may not be), in actual fact, benevolent. The government may act in its own interest directly (for example, through excessive taxation that it spends on itself), or indirectly through serving special interests that would be not normally considered worthy of transfers from the rest of society. The design of government now becomes a principal–agent problem and the opening up of the black box of government process to the tools of economic analysis becomes an imperative. It was this recognition that stimulated the positive analysis (as opposed to the normative approach of public finance) of government intervention as developed by public choice scholars.

Public choice

Although it can trace its antecedents to Thomas Hobbes (1588–1679), or indeed according to some scholars to Aristotle (c. 384–321 BC), the public choice school is usually defined by a number of works that appeared in the 1950s, and in particular by one journal and two scholars. The journal is *Public Choice*, which began life as *Papers in Non-Market Decision Making*; the founding scholars are James Buchanan (Nobel laureate in Economics 1986) and Gordon Tullock. Mueller's definition of public choice as 'the economic study of nonmarket decision making, or simply the application of economics to political science' contains a narrower and a broader implication. The narrower implication is methodological; the broader one, more substantive. The economic study of non-market decision making applies the tools of economics to the subject matter of politics – voters, politicians, bureaucrats, and lobbyists, for instance. Each of these is regarded as a utility maximizer. The voter is assumed to vote for the outcome that brings her the maximum utility (if she votes at all); the politician, to maximize the probability of being re-elected (if the incumbent) or of throwing the other lot out (if the challenger) at the next election; the bureaucrat – well, this becomes controversial, but in one strand of public choice she is represented as wishing to maximize the budget of her bureau, in another to shape it to her optimum shape; the lobbyist, to get the most bangs (policy outcomes) per buck (financial input).

These thumbnail sketches already show that public choice has been bedevilled by confusion between science and ideology. Buchanan and Tullock are both scientists and (Tullock especially) ideologues. They nurtured public choice in the scientific sense of applications of economic methodology to politics. Buchanan's Nobel citation explains:

> Traditional economic theory explains in great detail how consumers and entrepreneurs make decisions regarding purchase of goods, choice of work, production, investments, etc. In a series of studies, Buchanan has developed a corresponding theory of decision-making in the public sector. This comprehensive theoretical formulation ... goes under the name, 'The New Political Economy' or 'Public Choice', and lies on the boundary between economics and political science ... Buchanan's contribution is that he has transferred the concept of gain derived from mutual exchange between individuals to the realm of political decision-making. The political process thus becomes a means of cooperation aimed at achieving reciprocal advantages. But the result of this process depends on 'rules of the game', i.e., the constitution in a broad sense. This in turn emphasizes the vital importance of the formulation of constitutional rules and the possibility of constitutional reforms ... For a long time, traditional economics lacked an independent theory of political decision-making. Modern welfare theory often relied on the premise that public authorities could apply relatively mechanical methods to correct different types of so-called market failures. Stabilization policy theory – regardless of whether it was Keynesian or monetarist – appeared to assume that political authorities endeavored to achieve certain macroeconomic or socioeconomic goals regarding employment, inflation or growth rates. Buchanan and others in the public choice school have not accepted this simplified view of political life. Instead, they have sought explanations for political behavior that resemble those used to analyze behavior on markets.
>
> Individuals who behave selfishly on markets can hardly behave wholly altruistically in political life. This results in analyses which

indicate that political parties or authorities that to at least some extent act out of self-interest, will try to obtain as many votes as possible in order to reach positions of power or receive large budget allocations. (cited from http://nobelprize.org/economics/laureates/1986/press.html, accessed 06.01.2005)

So, political agents are 'to at least some extent' self-interested. But to what extent? Tullock has stated *ex cathedra*: 'Everyone is altruistic, 5% of the time.' But being an eminent political theorist, he has not demonstrated his 5 per cent rule empirically. We may distinguish between the ideology of (some) public choice scholars and the science of public choice. Ideologues, including Buchanan and Tullock themselves in their monumental *Calculus of Consent* (1962), draw normative conclusions about the sort of constitution we ought to live under from their analysis. Based on their, certainly correct, observation that 'individuals who behave selfishly on markets can hardly behave wholly altruistically in political life', Buchanan and Tullock propose that constitutional contracts must depend on the unanimous approval of those to be subject to them, and more broadly reject the idea of beneficent government intervention in the economy in the absence of well-specified rules. Less subtle ideologues treat public choice as saying simply that governments are bad and markets are good.

In this book, however, we try to stick to the science, as do the chapter authors. The science of public choice is clear about what voters do and what lobbyists do. It is much less clear about what either politicians or bureaucrats do. Voters, to repeat, maximize their utility by voting (if they vote at all) for the outcome that brings them their maximum utility. This says nothing about their actual political wishes; in particular, it says nothing about whether they are selfish or altruistic. Some people vote for the party that they think will make them richest. Other people vote for the party that will do most to reduce famine and disease in Africa.

Lobbyists are people who are paid to lobby. Therefore public choice assumes that they do what they are paid to do (even that may be a dangerous assumption, because of principal–agent problems, but let us leave that aside for now). As with voters, some lobby on behalf of the self-interest of their paymasters – for example, trade unions are lobbyists on behalf of organized labour; farm organizations on behalf of the landed interest; trade associations on behalf of fractions of capital. Others lobby for things that are not necessarily in the material interests of their employers, such as famine relief or constitutional reform.

With politicians and bureaucrats it is more complicated. For a politician to achieve anything it is usually *necessary* to win the next election; but it may not be *sufficient*. No politician is ever in the lucky position of wanting the same as the average voter in every area of policy. Such a prodigy could win every election. Every other politician must either change her policies, or conceal them, or persuade the electorate to support her. The most interesting sort of politicians are the last. Likewise, a bureaucrat who merely wishes to maximize or shape her bureau is not very interesting. The interesting ones, some of whom appear in this book, are those who believe in, and advocate, a particular policy.

None of this, therefore, assumes that all economic agents are selfish. A lot of people are selfish a lot of the time. But not everyone is selfish all the time (if they were, social life would be impossible). Understood properly, public choice makes no assumptions about selfishness, except that people in different occupations are roughly equally selfish. A notable recent work in social policy – Julian Le Grand's *Motivation, Agency, and Public Policy* (2003) – tries to reconcile political economy with the insights of the Titmuss School. (Le Grand holds the Richard Titmuss Professor of Social Policy, London School of Economics, and is also a policy adviser at No. 10 Downing Street.)

His organizing device is two contrasting pairs: *Knights* v. *Knaves* and *Pawns* v. *Queens*. In days of yore, when knights won their spurs, purveyors of public services were deemed to be knightly figures, who set out on white steeds to rescue helpless damsels (i.e., the population) from ignorance, want, and misery. The damsels, however, in Le Grand's (mixed) metaphor, were pawns, to be moved across the board of social policy at the knights' will. (It is best to try to forget the metaphor before you get hopelessly confused between knights in chess and knights winning their spurs.) 'Knaves' comes from David Hume's famous statement that

> Political writers have established it as a maxim, that, in contriving any system of government, and fixing the several checks and controuls of the constitution, every man ought to be supposed a *knave* and to have no other end, in all his actions, but private interest. (Hume, 1741/1994, p. 24)

This view was a commonplace in Hume's day, shared with Thomas Hobbes and Bernard Mandeville (probably the 'political writers' that Hume had in mind); with Hume's best friend Adam Smith; and with James Madison, a principal architect of the US Constitution of 1787 and co-author of the *Federalist Papers* rushed out in the hope of persuading

New York state to ratify the Constitution. Hume, Smith and Madison were ancestors of the public choice school, whom Le Grand rightly sees as the main intellectual opposition to the Titmuss School (jocularly known as Titmice). The Thatcher revolution in British government brought a thoroughly half-baked perspective to bear on public officials. In a malabsorbed version of public choice theory, it assumed that they were wholly, necessarily, and exclusively concerned with their own interests ('knaves'), and that therefore they should be excluded as far as possible from policy discussion, e.g., by implementing the Poll Tax without consulting anybody in local government finance. To which was added a quarter-baked enthusiasm for consumer sovereignty – treating the consumer as queen. 'Systems run by knights for the benefits of pawns were to be replaced by ones run by knaves in the service of queens' (Le Grand, 2003, pp. 23–4).

Can public policy be designed to get the best of both worlds? If Titmice treat citizens as pawns and service providers as public-interested 'knights', while Thatcherites treat service providers as self-interested 'knaves' and citizens as sovereign 'queens', the trick is to make service providers have a view to the public interest but citizens have genuine sovereignty over the public services. Can we structure institutions so as to encourage pro-social behaviour, by both givers and receivers of public services – to 'align knightly and knavish incentives'? (Le Grand, 2003, p. 64).

Political economy

In a fascinating recent lecture series, the founding fathers of modern public finance (Richard Musgrave) and of public choice (James Buchanan) confronted one another's lives' work (Buchanan and Musgrave, 2001). There are important areas of agreement between them. They agree that the state needs to ensure that public goods are provided (which does not mean that the state must always supply them itself). They agree that public expenditure to fund (re)distribution through transfers differs conceptually from public expenditure to fund public goods provision. They agree that the state should not be treated as a benevolent dictator, but they disagree about the optimal size of the state and the optimal structure of taxation.

Fundamentally, they admit that this may reflect origins and tastes. Buchanan is an American Southerner of Ulster-Scots origin: 'I grew up as a member of a defeated people' (Buchanan and Musgrave, 2001, p. 15). He is therefore an instinctive anti-statist. Musgrave was born and educated in Germany until he emigrated to the USA in the 1930s, and he retains more sympathy for politicians and civil servants as a class than does Buchanan. However, they are both, as Buchanan claimed for them (p. 205), political economists; and they both cite Adam Smith with approval. This encourages us to view political economy as a discipline that subsumes both public finance and public choice, and encourages us to go back to Adam Smith as the fountainhead of both.

Adam Smith (1723–90) is portrayed by some of his admirers, notably the Adam Smith Institute, as the founding ideologue of *laissez-faire* capitalism. This is a one-dimensional view of his work. In *The Wealth of Nations* (*WN*: Smith, 1776/1976) Smith's most persistent theme is his sustained attack on special interests. Smith himself called *WN* a 'very violent attack' on the 'whole commercial system of Great Britain'. But it is a profound misunderstanding to believe that Smith objected to all government interference in the economy. He objected to *rent-seeking* interference in the economy. The term *rent-seeking* was coined by Anne Krueger (1974) to denote any attempt to extract uncompensated value from others by manipulation of the economic environment – notably by shaping regulation or other government decisions in the rent-seeker's interest. The mercantilist economy that Smith attacked was arranged for the benefit of British economic interest groups: a skewed benefit, at that, because the interests of land and capital were heard in politics, whereas those of labour were not. Smith is somewhat more indulgent of landowners (although he attacks their luxurious habits) than of capitalists. People of the same trade seldom meet even for merriment and diversion, he says in one of his biting asides in *WN*, 'but the conversation ends in a conspiracy against the public, or in some contrivance to raise prices'. The whole mercantile system was a conspiracy against the public. So was the entire East India Company, and most other state enterprises.

But that does not make Smith an anti-statist. Far from it. He and Hume worked out what we now call the theory of public goods. A public good is anything characterized by jointness of supply and impossibility of exclusion. National defence is the paradigm case. If anyone gets the benefits of the Royal Navy, everyone does; you can neither practicably exclude anyone from its benefits nor charge anyone in Britain individually for naval services rendered. Public goods are themselves part of a wider class of goods which the market, left to itself, fails to provide. As Hume wrote in 1738,

> Two neighbours may agree to drain a meadow, which they possess
> in common: because ... each must perceive, that the immediate

consequence of his failing in his part, is the abandoning the whole project. But it is ... impossible, that a thousand persons should agree in any such action; ... each seeks a pretext to free himself of the trouble and expense, and would lay the whole burden on others. Political society easily remedies ... these inconveniences. (Hume, 1738/1911, II: 239)

In other words, the market fails to deliver some goods because, left to themselves, people rationally take a free ride. Therefore the state ('Political society') must provide what the market fails to.

Smith sets out the role of the state in Book V of *WN*. It should provide *Defence, Justice, publick Works* and *publick Institutions*. All of these are either non-excludable public goods (defence, a legal system guaranteeing property rights) or goods which, although excludable, are like Hume's meadow. Free-riding inhibits the market provision of public works such as roads and bridges; and of public institutions such as schools and universities. These deliver both a private good to those educated in them and the public good of a more educated and tolerant population. Schools and universities should be part-funded by the state, but independent (as they were in Scotland), not in the service of the established church (as was the case in eighteenth-century England). Their semi-publicness warrants the state in taking a role in their provision.

But public provision does not necessarily imply provision by salaried public employees. Roads and bridges can be financed by turnpike tolls (though that too causes perverse incentives, which Smith discusses). Students should pay fees direct to their professors. Smith himself had collected the fees from his students as Professor of Moral Philosophy at Glasgow and had tried vainly to return them when he left part-way through a year to tutor the Duke of Buccleuch on the Grand Tour. Oxford and Cambridge professors, who drew their salaries whether or not they did any teaching or research, did not impress the young Smith, who spent six years in self-directed study at Balliol College, Oxford.

Smith also laid out some canons of taxation, which the present Chancellor has stated that he had followed in the 2002 Budget:

'All nations' Smith says, 'have endeavoured, to the best of their judgement, to render their taxes as equal as they could contrive; as certain, as convenient to the contributor, both in the time and in the mode of payment, and, in proportion to the revenue which they brought to the prince as little burdensome to the people'. (Gordon

Brown, introducing lecture on Adam Smith, Edinburgh, April 2002, quoting *WN*, V:ii.b)

As Iain McLean explore in more detail in chapter 5, aspects of New Labour are very Smithian. Chancellor Brown has said:

> Every modern generation – since Adam Smith counterposed the invisible hand of the market to the helping hand of government – has had to resolve this question for its time: what are the respective spheres for individuals, markets and communities, including the state, in achieving opportunity and security for their citizens? (Brown, 2003)

Our generation is rediscovering the political economy of Adam Smith. For instance, in the National Health Service, both the Conservatives and New Labour have split purchasers from providers of public services – the very concept to be found in Part V of *WN*. In the speech just quoted Brown called for contestability between public service providers on the basis of cost and efficiency. *Public services are never better performed than when their reward comes in consequence of their being performed, and is proportioned to the diligence employed in performing them.* That is not Margaret Thatcher speaking, nor yet Gordon Brown. It is Adam Smith.

Equally, those on the right who find New Labour dismaying have put their *Wealth of Nations* down before getting to Part V. When Adam Smith recommends that the state should franchise private companies to run canals, collecting tolls and keeping the canal in order, he satisfies neither the left (because it doesn't look like collective social provision) nor the right (who don't think the state should provide canals). But he is cleverer than either. The franchisee's *private interest obliges them to keep up the canal. If it is not kept in tolerable order, the navigation necessarily ceases altogether, and along with it the whole profit that they can make by the tolls.* So Adam Smith is the grandfather of the Private Finance Initiative.

Introduction to the case studies

Political economy, properly understood, therefore embraces both public finance and public choice. The stories told by our contributors begin in the 1960s, when economic policy makers understood public finance quite well but public choice quite poorly. Peter Jay (chapter 2) tells how he was involved in policy making in the Labour governments of

1964–70 and 1974–79. As Jay explains (p. 26 below)

Two big ideas dominated [UK] domestic policy after 1945: to solve the 'crisis of capitalism' manifested in the economic depression of the early 1930s by the application of John Maynard Keynes' concept of demand management; and to combat poverty and inequality with the tripod of the Beveridge revolution in social security, universal free education to the age of 15 based on the 1944 Butler Education Act and Aneurin Bevan's National Health Service.

In the 1960s, policy makers and politicians in all parties believed that these went together. Planners could achieve 'full employment in a free society', which was the title of William Beveridge's second big wartime report (1944). The economy could move from the mass unemployment of the 1930s to full employment by increasing demand when resources were un(der)employed, as Keynes (1933) had advocated. This would enable it to pay for the Welfare State. Social security, covered by Beveridge's earlier report, would become cheaper because, as unemployment dropped, so would the cost of unemployment benefit. Likewise health, in Bevan's vision, would become cheaper as the new National Health Service conquered the killer diseases of the 1930s such as diphtheria and TB. The spirit of wartime cooperation would be carried forward in tripartite cooperation between government, business (representing capital), and the trade unions (representing labour). The planning process that had delivered aircraft during the Second World War would continue to coordinate the economy.

Parts of this vision had started to go wrong before Jay's narrative starts. The idea that social security costs would decline overlooked the increase of life expectancy that was occurring anyhow, and was accelerated by the health and housing improvements of postwar governments. When Old Age Pensions were introduced for 70-year-olds in 1908, very few working-class people survived to that age, and so their implementation would not be costly. This was no longer the case by 1945, and has become less true at an increasing rate. These improvements also ruined the budget projections of the NHS. The old killers such as diphtheria and TB were indeed killed; so people who would otherwise died of these survived to require NHS treatment for some years and then die, more expensively, later, of heart disease or cancer.

Nevertheless, Keynesian demand management seemed to be remarkably successful throughout the 1950s. Unemployment remained at historic lows and inflation was controlled. The worms in the apple were the persistence of economic cycles (known then as 'stop–go') and a belief that Britain's growth was slower than everybody else's, so that the UK was sliding into relative immiseration. Economic management went awry in the 1960s and the situation worsened in the 1970s, for the reasons that Jay relates. He places the break in 1976, with a new Prime Minister, James Callaghan (Jay's father-in-law), expressing some hard truths that had got lost for three decades: *What is the cause of high unemployment? Quite simply and unequivocally it is caused by paying ourselves more than the value of what we produce.*

Peter Jay left the Treasury in 1967; Alan Budd (chapter 3) joined it in 1970. Budd's chapter picks up the story of macroeconomic policy in the 1970s and shows how advances in economic theory fed into policy decisions after the simple Keynesianism of the 1972 and 1973 Budgets had led to disastrous inflation through increases in the money supply. In particular, emphasis has switched from fiscal to monetary policy in order to manage demand, from full employment to price stability as the primary policy goal and much of the neo-classical micro-based thinking on macroeconomic policy has filtered through to influence policy makers. Furthermore, the goals and methods of macroeconomic policy having been highly contended after the postwar Keynesian consensus broke down in the 1960s are once again subject to basically cross-party consensus. Budd is positive about the role that advances in the thinking of economists have had upon the quality of government decisions. In this sense, previous failures were arguably more to do with the inadequate knowledge of economics as opposed to a problem with our political institutions.

Like Peter Jay and Alan Budd, Christopher Foster first worked as a policy adviser in UK government as long ago as the 1960s. In chapter 4 he tells a long and mostly unhappy tale of government transport policy since that date. Foster introduces a Weberian ideal-type model of policy making. A government issues a policy document (a Blue Book in Mr Gladstone's day; a White Paper in Mr Attlee's) explaining what is wrong in some policy area, what it proposes to do about it, how much it will cost, and why the proposal is better than its alternatives, including the alternative of doing nothing. Although the government's proposed course of action must be based on a value judgement – because you cannot derive an 'ought' from an 'is' – it should be based on the best available social science. A modern mantra, not mentioned by Foster but very popular in the contemporary Treasury, is 'evidence-based policy'. Like the slightly earlier phrase 'evidence-based medicine', this leaves the reader wondering if there is any other sort. Public money and support are available for 'evidence-based medicine' and 'evidence-based policy', so is UK policy making in good heart? In the case of UK transport policy, Foster thinks not. Road and rail policy are both in a mess. Comparatively little was spent on road building in the UK in the decades before the 1980s. To begin with, it was simply not a policy priority, and then it was bitterly opposed on environmental grounds. Meanwhile, traffic and congestion were rising very rapidly. A 1984 White Paper proposed to double the roads programme, but that was dropped in 1994, together with any intention to build roads at the same rate as traffic was increasing. Therefore congestion would increase inexorably. In 1994 government announced that it would increase fuel taxation annually in real terms, which would both increase revenue and reduce (the rate of increase of) congestion. This policy continued across the change of government in 1997, but was abandoned in the face of the fuel-price protests and blockades of autumn 2000. Transport White Papers under both the Conservative and Labour governments fail to meet Foster's criteria; he suspects them of being doctored by political advisers. They make reassuring noises, such as 'Public Transport should be improved', but do not say how, or by whom, or at what cost. In the 2002 Spending Review, the Labour government gave as one of the Public Service Agreement (PSA) targets for the Department of Transport: *1. Reduce congestion on the inter-urban trunk road network and in large urban areas in England below 2000 levels by 2010* (http://www.hm-treasury. gov.uk/media/B3039/psa02_ch4t.pdf, consulted on 10.01.05). A PSA is supposed to be something to which a government department is committed, and the department is to suffer some sort of penalty if it fails to meet it. However, by 2004 it was obvious to all that there was no chance of meeting this target by 2010. The corresponding text in the 2004 Spending Review White Paper states: *1. The Department for Transport are developing better measures of inter-urban congestion and will publish a new target by July 2005. They will also publish annual long-term projections of congestion* (Cm 6238/2004, p. 15). Previously, the Department stood to be punished if it failed to reduce congestion. Now it stands to be punished if it fails to publish a target for reducing congestion.

Meanwhile, spending on the rail network was spiralling out of control:

2003 was the first year in which more public money was spent on the railways, which carry less than 7 per cent of passenger-km, than on the roads, which carry 92 per cent. That is planned to continue, though the government has not produced any well-reasoned justification for it. Indeed such rate-of-return calculations as exist suggest that even before the recent doubling and more of rail costs, the expected return from road was much higher than from rail investment. (below, p. 70).

This startling relativity doubtless has many fascinating reasons, which take us far beyond Foster's chapter. One reason is certainly the decision of the newly privatized Railtrack in the mid-1990s to contract out engineering maintenance. Although economic theory since Adam Smith confirms that private contractors *may* deliver public works efficiently, nothing in economic theory – including Adam Smith's – says that *only* private contractors can efficiently deliver public works. Railtrack dissipated its in-house engineering expertise, and contract prices for UK rail maintenance soared. Maybe rail industry contractors had met for a bit of merriment and diversion.

Another reason is rooted in the public's woefully inconsistent attitudes to risk. Rail safety is news; road safety is not news. Every time several people are killed in a rail accident, Something Must Be Done. Sometimes the Something can be well justified; sometimes not. On the one hand, the Kings Cross fire (1987; 31 dead) ended smoking on the Underground and wooden escalators; the Hatfield (2000; 4 dead) and Potters Bar (2002; 7 dead) derailments both cast doubt on the wisdom of having private-sector contractors maintain track. On the other hand, consider the reaction to four crashes: Clapham (1988; 35 dead); Southall (1997; 7 dead); Ladbroke Grove (1999; 31 dead); and Upton Nervet, Berks (2004; 7 dead). Clapham led to a lawyer's (not a rail engineer's) public inquiry report that said that all trains should be fitted with a highly expensive automatic train protection (ATP) which would prevent most accidents caused by a train passing a signal at danger (SPADs in industry jargon). The then government accepted this recommendation, but dropped ATP in 1994 in favour of a cheaper system, TPWS. The train that overran a signal at Southall actually had ATP, but it was defective on the leading car. The train could easily have been turned round at Swansea, its point of origin, where there happens to be a triangle of tracks where trains can be reversed. After Southall, Secretary of State for Transport John Prescott announced that TPWS would be introduced across the network. After Ladbroke Grove, which would probably have been prevented by ATP but not by TPWS, this decision was fiercely criticized, especially by victims' and survivors' support groups. The Upton Nervet crash was caused by a van driver who parked his van on the level crossing in the path of a train, probably in order to commit suicide. It led to calls to close all the level crossings on the rail network.

All of this reflects inconsistent perceptions of risk. Automatic train protection entered the political agenda as a solution to SPADs. But, unnoticed by the mainstream media, Clapham was not a SPAD. It was an instance of a much rarer 'wrong-side failure', when a signal that should have shown red showed green instead. Therefore, *ATP would not have prevented the Clapham disaster.* But rail accidents are news; road accidents are not news. Therefore citizens press for, and politicians propose, inconsistent safety measures. ATP and TPWS may actually cause more deaths than they prevent. This is because they have contributed to the doubling of rail costs to which Foster refers. When passengers bear those costs, they drive people off rail and on to the much more dangerous roads. When the costs fall on the taxpayer, they help to skew the transport budget inappropriately from road (safety) to rail (safety). Speed limits, speed cameras, and preventing drivers from using mobile phones could save many more lives than ATP or TPWS. But you won't learn that from your *Daily Beast.*

Foster distinguishes between *continuous* and *discontinuous* policy. An example of a discontinuous policy is: When, given a fixed exchange rate against other currencies, should you devalue the pound? We know from Peter Jay's chapter how crippling and painful a decision that was in the 1960s, even when it was a non-decision. Move to continuous policy, and life is much easier for policy makers. The exchange rate is determined continuously (by the markets, not directly by politicians); the crises of 1964–7 feel like ancient history. So it is in transport. A decision to raise fuel duty is one-off and painful, as the fuel protests of 2000 showed. Road pricing is a much better idea, for many reasons, one being that, unlike fuel duty, it can be adapted to the degree of congestion. Any decision to introduce road pricing would be so discontinuous that no national politician dared to introduce it and it was left to Mayor Ken Livingstone of London to show that it was not necessarily political suicide. But once road pricing is in position, changes in it are an example of a continuous process which might make it more palatable. Judging by Foster's evidence, it had better, since no other solution to the crisis of UK transport is in sight.

In chapter 5, Iain McLean traces the evolution of New Labour from Old. He argues that Old Labour comprised three strands, which they label as *producerist, egalitarian,* and *internationalist.* New Labour has ceased to be producerist while remaining (in parts) egalitarian and (in parts) internationalist. The Labour Party was by its very origins mainly the creation of the producer-groups of labour, that is the trade unions. In 1900, it became clear that their previous efforts to work within existing parties had become inadequate. They needed a new political party to reverse a damaging court decision (the Taff Vale Case). They got that reversal as one of the first acts of the incoming Liberal government in 1906. The producerist strand in Old Labour remained strong, being at its strongest when the rest of Labour was weak, for instance during the 1930s.

In two notable works, Mancur Olson explored *The Logic of Collective Action* (1965) and *The Rise and Decline of Nations* (1982). In the first, he pointed out that the standard model of political science, called 'pluralism', was broken. Pluralists had argued that there were as many and as strong interest groups as there were interests, and that therefore the interplay of interest groups was democracy in action. But this ignores the differential impact of free-riding. Public policy is a public good. If anybody gets it, everybody does. Therefore, a policy which I want will almost certainly either happen even if I do not lobby for it, or fail to happen even if I do lobby for it. This logic impedes collective action. In an extreme form, it would impede all collective action whatever. However, some groups have very powerful material interests at stake, and/or find it relatively easy to detect and maybe punish the free-riders in their own ranks. Among these strong lobbies are suppliers of the factors of production, especially the two concentrated factors, viz., land and capital.

Thus far Olson's analysis sounds classically Marxist. He supplies an argument, not in Marx, to bolster Marx's belief that politics is class struggle. Because there are more suppliers of labour than of land or capital, however, labour was the last of the factors of production to be organized politically. Trade unions find it harder than trade associations or landowners' organizations to discipline free-riders in their ranks. They were also poorer, and could neither buy seats in the House of Commons nor inherit seats in the House of Lords. From the foundation of the Labour Party, however, the balance of power among organized land, labour, and capital became somewhat more even.

Olson (1982), however, argues that institutional sclerosis crippled old-established democracies. They had become corporatist, meaning that political solutions were determined by the bargaining between organized capital and organized labour. Unorganized interests did not get a look in. The result, he argued, was to depress efficiency and economic growth.

The world has not turned out as Olson predicted in 1982. This may be in part precisely because policy advisers read his work. Not only the UK but also several of the other 'sclerotic' old democracies underwent radical institutional reforms. Australia and New Zealand were two of these, in both of which the Labo(u)r Party moved at least as far from its producerist base as in the UK. In the 1960s and 1970s, the periods covered by Peter Jay's and Alan Budd's chapters, many commentators thought that the cure for the British disease lay not in dismantling corporatism but in making it work. They cited the faster growth in Continental Europe that (with another thirty years of hindsight) may have been no more than postwar catching up. By the 1980s, the opposite argument was heard more often: that the sclerotic economies of corporatist Europe needed a dose of Mrs Thatcher's creative destruction of Olsonian interest groups. McLean argues that both arguments are naïve because they each supposed that an economy could move straight from one equilibrium to another. The UK, they argue, is an instance of a liberal market economy, in which the social (a.k.a. corporate) partners have never truly had the power to run the country. The Trades Union Congress (TUC) has never had the power to deliver a labour-market policy that might be in member unions' long-term interest but incur them a short-term cost. Germany and Sweden are examples of coordinated market economies in which social partners had the power to deliver results that were lacking in the case of the UK. Neither *Modell Deutschland* nor the Swedish model provided a convincing cure for British sclerosis. There needed to be a third way – but what could that phrase mean?

Since the death of John Smith in 1994, the leaders of the British Labour Party have presented themselves as 'new Labour'. Much academic writing on the supposed underpinning of New Labour ('Third Way', 'Stakeholder Society') does not withstand close examination. McLean argues, however, that there is a core set of new (or in some cases very old) Labour policies which they label 'new social democracy'. New social democracy is quietly, but radically, redistributive, and is as closely interested in economic efficiency as in equity. Brown (2003) has recently restated the view of an earlier citizen of Kirkcaldy – viz., Adam Smith – that the proper role of the state is to intervene when the market fails.

Ed Balls (chapter 6) was an economic advisor to Shadow Chancellor Brown from 1992 to 1997, and Chief Economic Advisor at the Treasury from 1997 to 2004. He is widely regarded as the driving force behind the immediate move of the newly elected Labour government, in May 1997, to grant independence over monetary policy to the Bank of England. This decision is analysed from three perspectives in chapters 6, 7, and 8. All three of these chapters deal with the situation since 1997. However, as this book was about to go to press, some remarkable Treasury documents released under the new Freedom of Information (FOI) Act – included one released by mistake – threw a bright light on an economic policy failure that was just as searing as those described in Peter Jay's and Alan Budd's chapters, and which likewise lurks in the background of present-day economic policy making. This failure was the UK's accession to the Exchange Rate Mechanism of the European Monetary System (ERM), and its ignominious withdrawal on 16 September 1992 – known ever since then as 'Black Wednesday'. In response to a request from the *Financial Times*, in February 2005 HM Treasury released ten policy documents analysing the cost of, and the lessons to be drawn from, the UK's expulsion from the ERM on Black Wednesday. Also released, in error to the BBC which promptly put the document on its website, was the internal form on which Treasury officials recorded the sections of the documents that they proposed to edit out, including the names of their authors.

Between about 1986 and 1989, an increasingly sharp disagreement had arisen between Prime Minister Margaret Thatcher and her Chancellor Nigel Lawson about how best to combat inflation. Lawson wanted to control inflation by 'shadowing' the deutschmark, which was thought to be the stablest currency in Europe. Thatcher distrusted this, and as one of the leaked Treasury documents says, the 'open warfare between the Chancellor and the Prime Minister made it especially difficult for the markets to decide what the effective objectives of the government were' (Quoted from http://news.bbc.co.uk/1/shared/bsp/hi/pdfs/09_05_foi_template280105.pdf, accessed 09.03.2005). After Lawson's resignation, the solution, as it seemed to economic advisers in both main parties and to the Treasury, was to join the ERM. But the ERM was not speculator-proof. Speculators who bet on the pound being forced out both made their prediction come true and made a killing in the process. On Black Wednesday, the UK government announced that it would raise interest rates to 15 per cent, but when even that failed to prevent a run on the pound, gave up and withdrew it from the ERM, whereupon its exchange rate against the currencies remaining in the ERM dropped sharply. The Treasury documents show that the official rethink began literally the next day, with a note addressed to Alan Budd arguing that depreciation of the pound 'may well be a blessing in disguise'. Later FOI releases on the Treasury website show that the Treasury had already in 1988 prepared an assessment for Chancellor Lawson of the case for making the Bank of England independent (http://www.hm-treasury.gov.uk/media/7D7/15/boe_autumn1998.pdf, accessed 09.03.2005). This noted that policy had moved a long way from 'the non-discretionary world which Ricardo and others sought' in the early nineteenth century. It goes on:

The general aim of the present proposal is to establish a new counter-inflationary anchor that will limit the authorities' room for discretionary action, by creating a formal duty to secure the value of the currency; and by placing that duty in the hands of agents at one remove from the political process. More specifically, the aim would be, within the limits possible, to take the pursuit of anti-inflationary policies outside the realm of party politics; and to give a degree of insurance against inflationary policies being pursued by future governments.

To achieve this, the report goes on to suggest an independent board remarkably like the Monetary Policy Committee (MPC) created in 1997, one of whose former members, Chris Allsopp, describes its operations in chapter 7. The memo to Chancellor Lawson points out that its proposed MPC, unlike the ERM, posed 'no question of foreigners determining our economic policies'. It also might appeal to 'Labour Party moderates (like the Shadow Chancellor?)' [then John Smith], because, like the ERM, it might 'inhibit the more extreme elements' of their party.

However, the ERM experiment delayed the implementation of Bank independence by nine years. In chapter 6, Ed Balls explains how and why the incoming government made this move, and assesses its effectiveness compared to other possible inflation control regimes. From the vantage point of a former member of the MPC, Chris Allsopp discusses the MPC's role and record since the creation of the current monetary policy regime in 1997. In chapter 8, Mark Robson discusses whether Scotland and/or Northern Ireland could join European Monetary Union and its currency, the euro, even if the rest of the UK did not. Scottish and Northern Irish banks issue their own notes (although some in Northern Ireland may regret this after a £26 million IRA robbery of Northern Irish banknotes in December 2004). However, the main point of Robson's discussion is to use the possibility of devolved euro adoption as a metaphor for the problems and opportunities of a monetary union in a country where economic conditions vary widely in different regions.

In chapter 9, Paul Klemperer, who advised the UK government on the design of its '3G' mobile-phone auction in 2000, explores how some recent national auctions of radio spectrum came to raise far more revenue than others and warns of the danger of trying to apply clever economic theory while forgetting basic economic theory. The UK auction was a runaway success (for government and the UK taxpayer at any rate), raising €650 per head of the UK population. In Switzerland, in the same year, an auction of the same commodity (radio spectrum) raised only €20 per head of the Swiss population. Institutions clearly matter; so does economic advice; so do the actions of politicians and lobbyists in the face of that advice.

In several of the 3G auctions, bidders, or governments, or both, received highly sophisticated economic advice, replete with the latest theorems in auction theory that economists learn in graduate school. One of these results, Klemperer warns, is 'very hard (certainly for the layman)' to understand (below, p. 203). It turned out to be useless. By contrast, factors which are so simple that even non-economists such as one of us can grasp had a huge effect. One of these factors differentiate between the two main forms of auction – sealed-bid and ascending. A sealed-bid auction is what it says. Bidders submit sealed envelopes containing their bids. The highest bid is chosen. An ascending auction is the type conducted by a live auctioneer in loud clothes. Sophisticated theory says that it does not matter which mechanism is chosen, because they yield equivalent revenue. Common sense may suggest otherwise.

In a sealed-bid auction (assuming no criminal collusion) the bidders do not know what one another would be prepared to pay. In an ascending auction, as Klemperer explains, the point at which each bidder (has to) drop out is observed in real time by all those present. A weak bidder (say a company which cannot sustain a loss on this bid by cross-subsidy from another operation, in order to force out weak bidders) will be aware of this difference. Since entering any auction imposes costs which all the unsuccessful bidders lose, a weak bidder will not enter an ascending auction, but may enter a sealed-bid auction. In the Netherlands auction, five licences were offered, and no bidder would be permitted to win more than one of them. There were five incumbents and an ascending auction. The five licenses went one to each incumbent and the total revenue was low, as Klemperer himself and other commentators had predicted in the Dutch press before the event.

Another point that even non-economists can understand is that collusion is easier in an open than in a sealed-bid auction. Collusion involves bidders giving one another signals that are not illegal, but that signal information enabling the bidders in the ring each to do better (and therefore the seller worse) than without collusion. A well-known example is the bridge bidder who says 'Pass' if her hand contains between zero and three points, 'No bid' if it contains between four and eight points, and 'No' if it contains between nine and 12 points. In a footnote, Klemperer gives an example that is hardly any more sophisticated than that:

> Furthermore, auction design is not like computer assembly. It does not take place in a sealed room in hygienic conditions from which all outsiders are excluded. Lobbyists will lobby and politicians will usually take the final decision. That is what they do; what they are there for. Economists who forget these facts, as seems to have happened in Hong Kong, are in for a nasty shock.

Overall, as Klemperer concludes, 'auction designers should remember their industrial economics and political economy (at least) in addition to pure auction theory' (p. 200 below).

Finally, in our Review and Conclusion, we attempt to draw together the lessons of the case studies.

2
1964–79

Peter Jay

This chapter is not an economic treatise. If it can make any contribution to recent history, economic and political, it is only as a sort of witness statement.

There are three reasons for this. First, I am not a proper economist and could not hold down an academic teaching post for five minutes, though at times I may have been guilty of allowing a contrary impression to be entertained by those who did not know better. A little bit of undergraduate economics and half a lifetime of learning on the job can carry one so far, but only so far.

Secondly, by chance my life has been involved at second hand – occasionally at first hand – with the formation and conduct of economic policy in Britain for most of half a century from about 1947. If one of the challenges faced by the historian trying to explain events including the decisions historical characters have made is to capture the intellectual and emotional environment in which such events and decisions evolved, to discover and make vivid how the players felt at the time, then such a recollection as this may be able to help, though of course it can be no substitute for scholarly examination of the facts and the evidence.

The third reason is slightly more complicated. There is a certain economic presupposition of this account; and that presupposition makes it more than ordinarily important to understand the intellectual and emotional climate in which the events were played out.

The presupposition takes the form of an answer to the obvious question which any economic historian looking back at British economic policy since the war is bound to ask, namely why did policy seem to contemporaries to fail so persistently and so depressingly between, say, 1957 (Peter Thorneycroft's 7 per cent bank rate) and 1992 (Norman Lamont's exit from the Exchange Rate Mechanism)?

The presupposed answer divides that period into two quite distinct periods (1957–1976 and 1976–1992). The first we shall call 'the twenty years of the two Harolds' (Macmillan and Wilson), 'nineteen long winters' indeed; and the second we shall call 're-entry', the struggle back to realism pockmarked by winters of discontent and gratuitous blunders by policy-makers (Geoffrey Howe's great inflation of 1979–80, the Lawson boom of 1989–90 and the plunge into the Exchange Rate Mechanism 1990–2).

From 1992 onwards, dominated by Mervyn King's policy model based on inflation targeting, everything suddenly began to go right; and the righter it went the easier it looked. Which left the question, after 12 years of steady growth, falling or low and stable inflation, falling and eventually lowish unemployment and the total disappearance of the periodic economic 'crises' which had previously dominated the political scene, why did they keep getting it so badly wrong before?

The answer proposed here is that until 1976 we ran the economy, or attempted to run it, at what would then have been called too high a pressure of demand and would now be called 'a negative output gap' and that after 1976, when that error began finally to be corrected, we still managed to blunder intermittently, but repeatedly, owing to the amateur, ad hoc and political character of much of the policy making. After 1992 the professionals, led by Mervyn King and powerfully insti-tutionalized by Gordon Brown in 1997, began to take over; and things went better and better, though it remains to be proved that the Monetary Policy Committee, if similarly challenged, could and would avoid the errors of 1987, in response to the shocks of that period, that led to the Lawson boom, the Major bust and the ERM fiasco.

In other words, the answer proposed here to the question why con-temporaries considered economic policies of the period to be such a dis-mal series of failures is that the policy makers of the period failed because their ideas were wrong. If ideas were that important, then it becomes, as suggested above, doubly important to understand what the ideas were and why they were wrong.

This essay is formally concerned with the three Labour governments between 1964 and 1979 (Wilson's first 1964–70, Wilson's second 1974–6 and Callaghan's 1976–9). But to understand the struggles and traumas of that period it is necessary to set the experience in the rather longer time perspective set out above, all the more so since we are looking back from the early years of the twenty-first century when events since 1979 inevitably colour our perceptions.

Since, as stated, this is a personal and therefore inevitably subjective statement, it may be helpful briefly to record the material facts of my involvement as a close and interested observer and, just occasionally, as a participant. I was born on the day my father (Douglas Jay) became city editor of the *Daily Herald*. In my childhood Hugh Gaitskell lived for a while next door and remained for ever my paragon of a political leader.

I became conscious of the world of economic politics from the age of nine, first when I played cricket on Hampstead Heath with the first postwar Labour Chancellor, Hugh Dalton; and then when my father became a junior Treasury minister, sending me – freezing at my prep school – a copy of the Treasury's Economic Survey for 1947, a rather optimistic document. In 1960 in my Oxford finals, being by then a specialist philosopher, I could only answer one question in the PPE history paper – and that the last: 'Explain the dominance of the Conservative Party since 1951'. But on the strength entirely of my father's table-talk I answered it non-stop for three hours – and somehow got away with it.

In 1961 I entered the Treasury as a regular civil servant and served there for six years, seeing in the change of government in 1964 from the vantage point of the Treasury Permanent Secretary's office, where I was the private secretary – and the son-in-law – of the new Chancellor as well as son of the new President of the Board of Trade. We all had a jolly lunch in our flat off the Borough High Street that fateful Saturday, the same day that Harold Wilson, Jim Callaghan and George Brown decided to rule out devaluation of sterling as a solution to the economic crisis they believed they faced.

In 1967 I left the Treasury, joining *The Times* as Economics Editor in response to an invitation from the new editor, William Rees-Mogg. Because his interests also lay that way, though then he was a passionate gold bug (Rees-Mogg, 1974) and Europhile, we joined avidly and prolifically in the coverage of and debate about economic policy, from the devaluation of 1967 to the crisis of 1976, as well as the birth of what at the time I called 'the new realism' thereafter. I viewed the next two years from the embassy in Washington, departing for the private sector shortly after the change of government in 1979.

Two big ideas dominated domestic policy after 1945: to solve the 'crisis of capitalism' manifested in the economic depression of the early 1930s by the application of John Maynard Keynes' concept of demand management; and to combat poverty and inequality with the tripod of the Beveridge revolution in social security, universal free education to the age of 15 based on the 1944 Butler Education Act and Aneurin Bevan's National Health Service. Keynes, Beveridge and Butler had all been embraced by 1944 by the wartime coalition government; and, though the NHS was bitterly debated in Parliament at the time, the Conservatives in power never tried to abolish it – not overtly anyway.

The active involvement of trades unions as partners rather than opponents of government in the nation's life was another bipartisan inheritance of wartime collaboration. Inter-party battles focused instead for a decade or more on such stylised political footballs as nationalization, which did not matter much either way; and even there only one industry – steel – was actually de-nationalized (these were the days before the phrase 'privatization' had been invented). Marxist versions of socialism played a negligible part in the intellectual consensus which dominated economic and social policy, where English empiricism and Whitehall pragmatism responded much more warmly to Keynes and Beveridge.

In macroeconomic policy the bipartisan consensus was so conspicuous that it acquired a name, Butskellism.[1] Its essence was to use the annual budget so to adjust the balance between taxes and government expenditure as to deliver buoyant demand in the economy and thereby continuous full employment, while also – it was hoped – avoiding the perils of inflation and unmanageable balance-of-payments deficits.

Objectively this policy appears in hindsight extraordinarily successful. Postwar employment was never fuller, inflation never lower and the sterling exchange rate never more stable. But, as the 1960s dawned, it had acquired an aura of failure which profoundly affected the politics and policy making of the period. To understand this is to understand so much of what went wrong thereafter.

There were two sources of this pessimism: one was the business cycle and its occasionally dramatic crisis peaks and troughs; and the other was growth, or the perceived lack of it. The late great Christopher Dow, in his magisterial study of postwar economic fluctuations in Britain and the world, describes the business cycles experienced in Britain between 1947 and 1973 as 'in the light of later, worse, recessions, trivial' and as a 'golden age' for demand management (Dow, 1998, pp. 257–60). But this was not how it was perceived at the time, at least on the political left.

The huge beneficial movement in Britain's terms of trade after the end of the Korean War certainly conferred a breathing space on both Treasury policy makers and on formerly hard-pressed, tightly rationed, British consumers which paved the way to Prime Minister Harold Macmillan's later quip in 1959 that 'we have never had it so good', though as with so many famous quotes their author was on the occasion in question actually making exactly the opposite point to that which legend has supposed them to have been making – in this case to point to the dangers of rampant materialism, not to celebrate its triumph.

But in the first five years after the Second World War the public and commentators had grown used to regular economic crises – over convertibility, fuel, wages and prices, devaluation and rearmament. When in 1957 Chancellor Peter Thorneycroft was obliged to raise the Bank rate to a 'crisis' 7 per cent (at a time when inflation was by later standards almost negligible) and when again four years later Chancellor Selwyn Lloyd announced crisis measures, including resort to a form of incomes policy to restrain wage growth, such events were immediately received as evidence of the continuing crisis of capitalism and the threat of a return to the (by now legendary) horrors of the 1930s.

It is important to recognize, even if not now fully to excuse, the strength and moral passion in this period of the conviction that mass unemployment was both the supreme evil and a serious threat. This scourge, it was believed, had been and would again become our lot, unless the utmost vigilance was exercised by the enlightened few, in consequence of the wickedness and stupidity of misanthropes and ignoramuses who neither cared for the sufferings of the poor nor understood the principles of economics, as revealed by Keynes.

This menace was compendiously known as 'deflation'; and deflationists – those who wanted to apply fiscal or monetary brakes to the growth of demand – were regarded and treated rather as someone today who advocates the rights of smokers in the workplace, as fools or knaves. In a world today which congratulates itself every day and twice on Sundays for having unemployment close to 4 per cent it is worth recording that in the 1950s and 1960s when unemployment as then measured was frequently about 1 or 1½ per cent Professor Frank Paish of the LSE was reviled as a figure of loathing and contempt for suggesting that Britain's periodic crises over inflation and the balance of payments would be eased – and its economy made more efficient – by adjusting economic policy to yield a pool of unemployed of about 2½ per cent.

If Montagu Norman himself, the arch bogeyman and governor of the Bank of England in the 1920s and 1930s, had been reincarnate and spoken out, the hostility could hardly have been more vicious than that visited upon the wretched Paish. Likewise, if we had been told by some messenger from the future what would be the history of the 1980s, our reaction would have been, not at all one of surprise that deflation could 'work' as a remedy for inflation (any fool, we would have said, knew that), but of utter horror and disbelief that any government should stoop to such inhuman and intellectually barbarous policies.

I recall vividly a session of the first introduction to economics given to high-flying junior civil servants in about 1963 at Whitehall's brand new

Centre for Administrative Studies in Regents Park. We were visited by the grand vizier of Treasury economic forecasting at that time, Wynne Godley. He posed the question what, in a policy framework geared to the maintenance of full employment via fiscal and monetary demand management, should be the definition of 'full employment', zero not being a practical option.

He suggested a number; and we – including a number of future permanent secretaries and high Bank of England officials – fell upon him with horror and indignation, denouncing what we saw as callous inhumanity and the 'typical' Treasury deflationary mentality. The benchmark Godley suggested was 1¾ per cent; and we, the future Cabinet secretaries, Bank of England directors and heads of the Inland Revenue, considered anything above 1¼ per cent as barbarous.

In 1966, when the Prime Minister Harold Wilson announced an emergency package of economic measures designed to shore up the beleaguered pound, I was so outraged by what I regarded as a deflationary betrayal of the most basic principles of enlightened policy making that I penned my resignation from the Treasury, citing my firm loyalty to a non-political civil service, but explaining nonetheless that in certain cases, when high principle was involved, it could become the duty of an official so persuaded 'to divest himself of the obligations of official reticence' (I rather liked that phrase) and then to carry his dissent into the public domain. Munich and Suez were mentioned to illustrate the point. This missive, though despatched, failed to navigate successfully through the Treasury's internal mail; and a day or two later the moment seemed somehow to have passed.

This extreme hostility to 'deflation', coloured as much by high moral fervour as by technical economic analysis, appeared to me to be widely shared in my generation and among many of the Labour politicians in the new government which came into office in October 1964. It was also widely shared at the beginning of the 1960s in the 'intelligent' press (Andrew Shonfield and Samuel Brittan in *The Observer*, Norman Macrae in *The Economist*, Nigel Lawson – a particularly forceful 'expansionist' – in the *Sunday Telegraph*, William Rees-Mogg in the *Sunday Times*) and even by 'less reactionary' Conservatives, such as the Chancellor from 1962, Reginald Maudling.

The most disastrous and final throw of this outlook was made in Edward Heath's notorious U-turn in 1972 when, horrified by rising unemployment (briefly 3.1 per cent in 1972 Q2[2]) which he saw as a contradiction of everything he had stood for since forming political convictions in reaction to the miseries of the 1930s, he abandoned the management of demand as a weapon against inflation and put all his political capital into a dash for growth combined with an ambitious incomes policy. These failed and ended his political career in February 1974.

Once again to make sense of this history – indeed of the very idea of a political leader risking and losing everything for the sake of a policy conviction – from the more cynical and stony-hearted standpoint of the early twenty-first century one must try to comprehend the overwhelming intellectual and moral revulsion which the idea of unemployment, even in what we would now regard as very small quantities, provoked in every decent breast and in the mind of almost every well-educated graduate of the Keynesian era in economics.

But there was also a second leg to the intense deflation-aversion of this time. In the late 1950s, thanks to the restless inquiries of Nicholas Kaldor in Cambridge and others and thanks also to a flood of improved statistical data from Continental Europe (especially what became the OECD's statistical arm under Christopher Dow), the fact began to dawn on British policy makers and commentators that, give or take the business cycle fluctuations, the British economy was growing more slowly than other economies, notably France, Germany, Italy and before long Japan.

This combined with the procession of regular economic crises occasioned by the peaks and troughs of the business cycle to generate an impression, growing into an almost universal conviction, of economic failure, which could then be blamed on everyone's pet theory of what was wrong with Britain (trades unions, penal taxes, Treasury amateurism, the class system, scientific illiteracy, disregard for engineers, manufacturing decline, loss of empire markets, the Tories, the socialists, whatever). As with the deflation-aversion, so with the growth deficit, it is hard to exaggerate, but vital to grasp, the ubiquity of the belief that the underlying (i.e. from cycle to cycle) rate of real economic growth in Britain was falling disastrously behind that in other comparable economies and that this was proof-positive of a massive policy failure.

The grounds for this belief, apart from its inherent attraction as a novelty moving on from the tedious complacency of the Butskellist consensus, were simple: annual economic growth in Britain during the 1950s was running at less than 3 per cent; and annual economic growth in France, Germany, Italy and Holland was running at between 4 and 6 per cent. Only in Belgium – and, rather inconveniently for glib comparisons, in the United States – was growth similar to Britain's 'miserable' 2–2½ per cent.

An extra turn of the screw was administered by the discovery that Japan was growing at 'double-digit' (i.e. above 10 per cent a year) rates.

The re-discovery by Norman Macrae in the *Economist*, treading in the steps of Herman Kahn at the Hudson Institute in New York, of the laws of compound interest was duly rolled out to induce flesh-creeping nightmares of Britain's prospective backwardness within half a generation. It makes no difference to the historical analysis that we are now in a position to view this evidence very differently, to recognise in the longer experience of mature developed economies – at least until the United States' hypothetical great leap forward in the 1990s – an apparent ceiling on annual economic growth at about 2½ per cent. This may represent some technologically set limit to the ability of even efficient economies to raise productivity once known technologies have been fully applied.

This appears to be the rate at which economic growth in such economies has converged fifty years after the Second World War. Higher rates – as in Continental Europe for the first three decades after 1945, as in Japan until the end of the 1980s, as in Ireland since Garrett FitzGerald's (1991) generation began in the 1970s to throw off the shackles of pre-industrial society and as in the Asian 'tiger' and 'tiger cub' economies (World Bank, 1993) in the last quarter of the twentieth century – appear to be due to the opportunity to catch up on those who have already fully exploited known technologies within whatever limits their cultural and social systems impose.

Thus in retrospect the slow growth in the United States in the early postwar period, frequently glossed over on the grounds that productivity was so much higher in the US than elsewhere, now looks to have been entirely natural rather than some weird quirk of economics. And in this perspective Britain's lame performance, less ravaged by war and with fewer obvious catching-up opportunities, may have been much more normal than it seemed at the time. There were indeed people who made exactly this excuse at the time for low British growth; but they were disregarded as fuddy-duddies and, indeed, as excuse-makers.

As the new fashion for faster economic growth took hold on the policy debate from the late 1950s it fused with the deflation-aversion mood to deliver a belief that deflation was not merely an iniquity in itself, but that it was also the cause – or at least one significant cause – of low growth. When I entered the Treasury in January 1961, I went to work in a 'supply division' where we controlled the expenditure of the War Office. Our work was dominated by the great new thinking embodied in the work of the Plowden Committee (mostly the work of that irascible and tireless genius among Treasury mandarins, Richard 'Otto' Clarke), whose report was published that year.[3]

It was in this report that the phrase 'stop–go' was originally coined, not at first to describe the effects on the economy of the Butskellist economic managers' attempts to steer it between the perils of unemployment and payments deficit, but to describe the use of the investment programmes of the nationalized industries to achieve these short-term purposes, thereby distorting, it was alleged, the smooth evolution of those sectors of the economy. But the phrase was too good to be confined to so narrow an application; and it was soon expanded by politicians (not least Harold Wilson as shadow chancellor mocking the unhappy real chancellor, Selwyn Lloyd) and commentators to indicate the whole business of the four-yearly economic cycle, including periodic 'reflationary' and 'deflationary' budgets and other measures.

This laid the foundation for a new idea, which I associate in retrospect with the name of Donald MacDougall, an exceptionally longaeval Oxford-based economist who played significant roles in economic policy making from 1940 to 1984 and even after that until his death in 2004. The idea took root that it was the negative effects of the business cycle fluctuations on investment confidence which caused the low rate of investment from which Britain was perceived to suffer and which in turn contributed to the low growth of productivity and therefore of the economy.

So, it was argued, if 'deflation' could be resisted, if somehow the economy could be kept going 'full bat' at the moment when the Treasury was suspected of wanting to apply the brakes, then it could burst through into a 'virtuous circle' of high business confidence, high investment, higher productivity, faster growth and a happy life ever after. All that was necessary, it was said, was that the Treasury – and the chancellors it advised – should learn not 'to lose its nerve' when the going (rising prices and soaring imports) appeared to get rough, but instead to keep the economic 'pedal to the metal' long enough for the expected response of booming investment floated the whole contraption into soaring productivity, price stability, international competitiveness and Germanic, if not Japanese, growth.

There were, of course, doubters, easily caricatured as reactionary traditionalists in the Bank of England and as gnome-like Swiss speculators in the foreign exchange markets. And, of course, the Treasury's supposed itch to get its foot on the economic brakes could not be entirely ascribed to the baneful influence of the standard classical education, nor to the overdose of 'iron in the soul' supposedly acquired by sitting too long on the fence. After all, the symptoms of overstrain in an economy with unemployment consistently under 2 per cent,[4] were palpable and becoming more so, as inflation edged up at comparable phases of the economic cycle and as the deficit in our external payments became increasingly troublesome. But fixes for these flaws in the plan were quickly brought forward, at least in intellectual discourse. Restraint should be applied – from both sides of the bargaining table – to pay settlements in return for the promise of sustained expansion leading to faster economic growth. This would control inflationary pressures, which were argued to be mainly 'cost-push' rather than 'demand-pull'. If necessary devaluation of the pound, combined with suitable measures to make room in the economy for the resulting export boom, would restore external balance – and cook the goose of the tiresome speculators, though not until after they had enjoyed one last riotous celebration.

Intellectually this may have had the merits of neatness and of some theoretical plausibility. As a political programme it had all the attractions of a cavalry charge over open ground against massed machine guns.

An incomes policy, as Sir Stafford Cripps had discovered as chancellor in the late 1940s and as successive chancellors such as Selwyn Lloyd, Reginald Maudling, James Callaghan, Roy Jenkins,[5] Tony Barber and Denis Healey found from 1960 to 1979, brings the nation's political leaders into direct head-on conflict with almost each and every home in Britain over the most sensitive item in its entire consciousness, namely the adequacy or otherwise of the income coming into that home. Every privation occasioned by income shortage thus becomes a grievance directly and personally against the chancellor, if indeed not against the prime minister, of the day.

The entire political capital of a government may thus be rapidly consumed in support of one aspect of one branch of that government's policy – and that on an issue, the restraint of pay bargaining, which never formed one iota of the reasons for which any politician ever entered public life. All of which serves to explain why, while some incomes policies have achieved some short-lived results for a year or so, they have never in Britain become a stable and lasting part of any government's peacetime regime.

The political drawbacks of a policy of devaluation are rather different. It is not a subject that the public cares deeply about as such, though skilfully exploited by Opposition or the press it may after the event be effectively used as a stick with which to beat the supposed perpetrators, as happened to the Labour governments in 1949 and 1967 and to John Major's government after 1992. On those occasions the damage was caused by the fact that the governments concerned had failed to sustain the policy to which they had been so firmly committed rather than that the devaluation itself had shocked or hurt the population.

But a proactive policy of devaluation as a cornerstone of an economic policy, however attractive in the seminar room, is almost impossible to sustain on the hustings. The very announcement of it generates a crisis in the foreign exchange markets, if the proposers have any prospect of coming to power; and this crisis is then seen by the public as a demonstration that the policy is irresponsible and impractical. In October 1964 the incoming Labour government could in theory have made a sudden decision to devalue the pretty obviously overvalued pound and blamed it on their shock and horror at discovering the mess bequeathed by their predecessors and revealed to the new government on examining 'the books' in the Treasury.

But after years of Opposition conducted on a different basis and denying any intention to devalue this would have required both a strategic vision, which never distracted Harold Wilson from what was under his nose, and a political suppleness which for once deserted him just when it might have served him best. Anyway, for almost the only time in his prime ministership he allowed his policy to be influenced by his convictions.

He had been opposed to devaluation in 1949; and he was against it now, seeing it as a classical economic device based on the price mechanism far removed from the physical planning which from his wartime experiences onwards he had always much preferred. He ruled it out; and from that moment the whole economic strategy built on faster growth spurred by booming demand and buttressed by an incomes policy to control inflation and devaluation to take care of the balance of payments was in fundamental trouble.

All of this became hideously clear in what was supposed to be the unifying vision and crowing glory of the new high-tech, forward-looking Labour government, the National Plan of 1965. Insofar as it had a serious economic rationale it was founded on the concept of what was called 'indicative planning', a notion associated with Donald MacDougall and the work under him of the economists at the National Economic Development Council which was set up in 1962 (Brittan, 1971, 1975) by the preceding Conservative government of Harold Macmillan as a palliative gesture towards the new preoccupation with economic growth. MacDougall and his team now moved into the new Department of Economic Affairs.

Indicative planning worked, it was said, by inducing a belief that the economy was going to grow at the indicated rate, thereby persuading industrialists and other entrepreneurs to invest on a scale sufficient to meet the level of demand expected on this basis. This investment would then deliver the productive capacity required to validate the growth rate originally indicated – QED. The Treasury, duly horrified by this invocation of the principles of levitation as a basis for economic policy, worked hard between 1962 and 1965 to erode the idea of a 4 per cent – plus growth rate first embraced by the indicative planners; and by the time it saw the light of day in George Brown's National Plan it had been pared back to 3 per cent, still ambitious – not to say fanciful – in relation to Britain's long-established underlying growth rate of 2–2½ per cent.

In retrospect we know that the average annual growth rate over the most recent ten years edged up from 2.7 per cent in 1960 to 3.5 per cent in 1968 before sinking back to 1.1 per cent in 1983 and then resuming the 2–2½ pattern.[6] These fluctuations probably had more to do with the choice of starting and finishing dates in this series than with the true underlying growth rate, which is unlikely by the very nature of the concept to have varied much. In this context ½ a per cent a year is a very large number.

But the National Plan was threatened by a far more lethal and immediate peril than that of any flaws in the theory or practice of indicative planning. At the prevailing exchange rate of the pound, fixed by the devaluation of September 1949 at £1 = \$2.80, there was no prospect that a growth of demand sufficient to induce a 3 per cent annual growth rate in gross domestic product could be reconciled with a financeable deficit in Britain's overseas accounts. Such a rate of expansion required a strong growth of imports which quite simply had no chance of being matched sustainably by comparable export growth.

In the summer of 1965 and again more savagely in the summer of 1966 the government decided to give overriding priority to the exchange rate, after which the whole edifice of the National Plan and its 'indicative' spur to faster growth lay in ruins, a veritable Ground Zero of economic policy (Opie, 1972, p. 177). Hence my own, albeit abortive, urge to resign from my post as a Treasury official in July of 1966.

The rest of the National Plan, those bits which paid lip-service to Harold Wilson's nostalgia for the physical planning of the 1940s in which his skills as a statistician had won him posts first in the Ministries of Fuel and Power and of Works and then in the Cabinet, had from the beginning lacked any effective levers of enforcement, quite apart from their inherent shortcomings as a way of managing a market economy. Without the commitment to a demand management target of at least 3 per cent annual growth the whole thing was – and was seen to be – a dead letter, indeed a dead plan.

Within a couple of years Peter Shore, as George Brown's successor at the Department of Economic Affairs, the sponsor of the National Plan, had produced a new Green Paper entitled 'The Task Ahead', which abandoned all pretence at planning, indicative or otherwise. It coincided with a White Paper from Barbara Castle on the legislative reform of trades unions entitled 'In Place of Strife', which gave me the opportunity in *The Times* to dub this pair of documents as better called In Place of Planning and The Strife Ahead.

In 1967 the inevitable and long-sighed-for devaluation finally came, happily in my case on my wife's birthday; and, as later after Britain's exit from the European exchange rate mechanism, the economy continued to grow quite healthily, at about 3 per cent a year over that decade, largely untroubled by the former curse of the external payments balance. Roy Jenkins presided languidly at the Treasury, permitting the natural effects of the exchange rate change to fulfil themselves, but initiating little – so little indeed that the electors saw no sufficient point in re-electing Labour in 1970 – thereby prefiguring in some detail the similar later lackadaisical Chancellorship of Kenneth Clarke (1993–7).

For a moment it seemed that the growth preoccupation had been dethroned and that Butskellism was back, though this time with a slightly less ambitious definition of 'full employment' and a less optimistic assumption about achievable underlying growth. But by the end of the 1960s it began to dawn on some observant commentators that something else was not quite right with this model, a something else which exploded in the 1970s in a government-toppling series of crises that made the 1960s appear in retrospect an era of decent achievement.

Here, the reader should be warned, we enter into an area of even more acute controversy between rival interpretations and where what is said here represents a point of view at the time which was not and is not established to the satisfaction of all – or even most – economic historians. For an authoritative contrary view, readers are referred to chapters 7 and 8 of Christopher Dow's study (Dow, 1998).

The 'something' which we began to notice – or thought we did – was a degenerative trend in the trade-off between unemployment and inflation, which we had previously supposed to be stable in the long run and described by the celebrated Phillips curve (Phillips, 1958). Each time the economy hunted back and forth between 'crisis' levels of inflation (or its close substitute, unacceptable balance of payments deficits) and 'crisis' levels of unemployment the peaks of both unemployment and inflation seemed to get higher and the troughs became weaker.

This suggested, well before the external shocks of the huge fourfold jumps in oil prices imposed by the Organisation of Petroleum Exporting Countries cartel in 1972–4 (and again later more than doubling in 1978–80), that far from there being a prospect of breaking out of the Butskellist 'stop–go' cycle into sunlit uplands of perpetual 'go–go' growth, we were not even in a position to maintain the performance which we had come to regard as such a miserable failure. Phrases like 'stop–stop' and 'stagflation' appeared in serious publications such as *The Times* and *The Economist*.

This perception became rapidly linked with theoretical arguments put forward in 1967 by Professor Milton Friedman[7] in the United States that there was no such thing as the Phillips curve (or, more technically, that it was straight and vertical), that there was no long-term stable trade-off between unemployment and inflation and that on the contrary unemployment would always tend to gravitate back to its 'natural' level (as set by the structure of the labour market and other supply-side factors) however hard governments tried to reduce it below that level by stimulating demand through fiscal and monetary policy, the only consequences of which must be ever-faster inflation.

These misgivings became further linked by some influential writers to the notion, not embraced by Friedman himself, that the strongly entrenched role of trades unions and therefore of collective bargaining in the British labour market was itself a specific factor working to raise the natural rate of unemployment to an otherwise unnecessarily high level, because unions operated in effect as monopolistic suppliers of labours, thereby posting a price for labour which was systematically above its market-clearing price (Jay, 1976).

If this was true, the only consequences of governmental attempts to return the economy to 'full employment' by stimulating demand would be to drive inflation to ever-higher levels as an irresolvable conflict between the equilibrium, or 'natural', rate of unemployment and the lower target level impelled the economy ever faster round a vicious circle of rising pay settlements (designed by unions to restore the real monopoly price of labour) and rising money incomes (designed by government to restore real purchasing power in the economy sufficient to employ the whole labour force). If this was the model, then the trade-off was not as stated by Phillips between unemployment and inflation, but between unemployment and the rate of acceleration of inflation, with full employment only stably achievable when inflation became infinite, the final *reductio ad absurdum* of the Butskellist approach to economic stability.[8]

By the time Labour returned to power on 1 March 1974, the intervening experiences of Edward Heath's Conservative government appeared to many to have vindicated dramatically this somewhat apocalyptic view of an economic system that was in principle incapable of operating stably, other than in conditions of unthinkably high unemployment. Efforts to control the mild boom at the end of the 1960s led to such a rise in unemployment in 1972,[9] the worst since the war, as to precipitate ministers into a violent U-turn in policy, embracing instead a dash for growth buttressed by an awesomely ambitious attempt to enlist the 'social partners' (government, unions and business) in a policy of statutory prices and incomes restraint as a quid pro quo for the expansion of demand. This had come to a head in a showdown between the prime minister and the National Union of Mineworkers, only resolved when Heath called and just lost a 'who governs Britain' general election in February 1974.

Clearly he did not. Could anyone else? For two years no one did. Nero in the form of the reinstated Harold Wilson fiddled, enfeebled by deteriorating health and plagued beyond human endurance by his secretary Marcia Williams (later Lady Falkender) whose conduct at the time has been definitively recorded by Joe Haines (2003). During 1975 the retail price index rose by 25 per cent.[10] The same year the opportunity to leave the European Economic Community was rejected in a referendum; and in the final quarter of that year unemployment rose above a million[11] for the first time since 1939 (apart from a weather-induced moment during the Arctic winter of 1947).

1976 was the year of fundamental change in British economic policy (cf. Brittan, 1996, p. 186), a change which was the direct consequence of the conviction, born of the events and beliefs described above, that the old approach had come to the end of the road and that something – perhaps even anything – new had to be tried. It was also facilitated by the appointment of a very different Prime Minister and by the mind-concentrating events of that year.

It was during the summer of that year, after a deplorably weak budget, that the basic decision was made to abandon the full employment standard, that is to say not the ideal of high employment, but the working practice of gearing demand management decisions to employment targets. Instead fiscal and monetary policy would be geared to low inflation, not overnight, but degressively over a transitional period, as recommended by Friedman himself at that time. Employment would become the accommodating variable in this model, rather than the goal.

The machinery of concerted pay restraint would continue to be used, but no longer in order to control inflation, but to persuade labour not to price itself out of the labour market by assuming rates of inflation which would not in fact be underwritten by accommodating monetary policies. This historic departure from the generally received understanding of the wartime coalition government's Employment Policy White Paper of 1944,[12] which supposedly established Keynesian methods of demand management for more than thirty years, had in fact been foreshadowed by the chancellor Denis Healey in a speech given in his Leeds constituency in January 1975, though it was only during 1976 that it became reality and even then despite Healey's later denials that he was ever a 'believing monetarist'.

The term 'monetarist' will not be used here, though I am supposed to have played a media-led role in propagating the idea in British policy debates (Parsons, 1989, pp. 180–4), because of what became (thanks to the economic illiteracy of contemporary political commentators) its multiple ambiguity. It has been variously used in the political discourse of this period to refer to: 1. the theory that the money supply, rather than interest rates and fiscal policy, is decisive in determining inflation; 2. the theory described above that there is a natural rate of unemployment which cannot be changed by demand management; 3. belief in the benign influence of free competitive markets and private enterprise; and 4. the bourgeois hunches and class reflexes of the new Conservative leader, Margaret Thatcher – between each and all of which there was and is no logical identity and little connection.

The defining moment of the new policy came at the Labour Party's conference in Blackpool in September when Prime Minister Callaghan himself determined to spell it out in unvarnished language:

> We used to think that you could spend your way out of a recession and increase employment by cutting taxes and boosting government spending. I tell you in all candour that that option no longer exists and that, insofar as it ever did exist, it only worked on each occasion since the war by injecting a bigger dose of inflation into the economy on every occasion followed by a higher level of unemployment as the next step. Higher inflation followed by higher unemployment ...[13]

This coincided with news of the imminent arrival in Britain of a team from the International Monetary Fund to discuss the terms of a large credit drawing which the government proposed to make in order to stem heavy speculative pressures on the pound, which even without a fixed exchange rate was vulnerable on account of what had been perceived to be a feeble budget and what was an over-pressed economy. Some have suggested that the IMF were the real authors of the 'new realism' in British economic policy; but this overlooks the fact that in August the prime minister's mind had hardened on a strategy that included applying to the IMF for a standby credit and cutting the government's swelling borrowing requirement (then the key budget metric).

This strategy in turn flowed from his determination to force his party and the country to face up to economic reality. He wrote later of this moment that 'I had no doubt that if the Labour Party was to fulfil its responsibilities as a Party of Government its leaders must not shrink from telling the truth as we saw it, and then act accordingly' (Callaghan, 1987, p. 424). His biographer later recorded that 'the new Prime Minister subordinated all else to "getting the economy right" ... determined to seize the initiative from the left and to spell out the facts of economic life as he saw them ... his speech was undoubtedly intended to generate a shock effect, ... that the nation should not go on spending what it did not earn and should no longer regard uncontrolled public spending, backed from time to time by foreign creditors, as the recipe for prosperity' (Morgan, 1997, pp. 528–37).

And it took more than the IMF at the door to make a Labour prime minister tell his own party conference

> What is the cause of high unemployment? Quite simply and unequivocally it is caused by paying ourselves more than the value of what we produce ... It is an absolute fact of life which no government, be it left or right, can alter. Of course, in Eastern Europe you cannot price yourself out of your job, because you cannot withdraw your labour. (Callaghan, 1987, p. 426)

That was the voice of conviction, weary of the shallow evasions of his predecessor and angered at the bogus 'alternatives' offered by the Labour left. The IMF, once invited, certainly tried to push the government to make further cuts than it deemed necessary or tolerable; but the final agreement with the IMF in December set the borrowing requirement limit at £8.7 billion (Callaghan, 1987, p. 441), virtually the £9 billion figure which he and his chancellor had wanted back in August.

With unemployment now on a plateau of about 1.1 million[14] and monetary and fiscal policy geared to disinflation, inflation fell from a peak above 25 per cent to 16 per cent in 1977, 8 per cent in 1978 and still below 10 per cent in the year to 1979Q1.[15] By then the 'winter of discontent'[16] – a reaction of militant trade unionism against the tight pay limits adopted by the government in order to mitigate the impact of large pay settlements on jobs – was in full swing; and its political impact was enough to procure the election in May of a Conservative government with a working majority.

Geoffrey Howe became chancellor, conceded the full amount of the pay settlements proposed by Professor Hugh Clegg[17] (who had been appointed by the outgoing government to examine the disputed pay claims that had fuelled the worst strikes of that winter) in substantial breach of the outgoing government's pay ceiling. He all but doubled the VAT to fund an equivalent cut in income tax and threw off the main brakes (including the credit 'corset') on monetary expansion. The result, whether it be attributed to cost inflation spurred by the Clegg settlements and the VAT shock or to monetary accommodation, was that inflation exploded to over 20 per cent.[18]

Thereafter the 'new realism' was resumed, but without the cushioning of an organized attempt to persuade union labour to refrain from pricing itself out of a decreasingly inflationary market. Unemployment peaked at just over 3 million (11.1 per cent) in 1986 before falling back to a low of 1.6 million in 1990,[19] still half a million above the late 1970s plateau.

The big picture revealed by this retrospect on economic policy making between 1964 and 1979 is that for the first 12 years policy was fatally flawed by an unrealistic optimism about the pressure of demand which the economy could stand without inflation (or its short-term substitute large external payments deficits), aggravated in the early 1960s and again in the early 1970s by the beguiling delusion that a faster underlying rate of growth of the economy could be achieved by simply flooring the demand pedal. From 1976 these errors were recognised and rejected.

But a series of less systematic, but still damaging, unforced errors continued to plague the economy – Clegg and Howe's inflation in 1979–80 and the consequent deep recession of the early 1980s, the Lawson boom of 1989 and the consequent deep recession of 1991–2, and the entry into the exchange rate mechanism in 1990. The real benefits of a stable non-inflationary macroeconomic framework only began to become visible from 1993 in much steadier growth – still at the well-tried 2¼–2½ per cent annual rate – and gradually subsiding unemployment, though still at about the level of the 1976 plateau.

As it is, I shall be left with the daydream that this might have happened a quarter of a century earlier had my proposal[20] in 1976 to establish by law an independent Currency Commission to conduct monetary policy on a non-inflationary basis been embraced by Denis Healey. By May of 1979 we might have reached the point we eventually reached in May of 1997, 18 long winters to the good.

Notes

1 Coined by Norman Macrae of *The Economist* after the two chancellors (Hugh Gaitskell and R.A. Butler) who most notably expounded it from 1950 to 1955.
2 CSO 1996, Table 3.2, p. 164.
3 Plowden Report 1961.
4 CSO 1996, Table 3.3, p. 167.
5 Iain Macleod was only chancellor for a few weeks.
6 CSO 1996, spreadsheet gdpa4895x.xls.
7 Presidential Address to the American Economic Association by Milton Friedman, 1967 and Friedman, 1968.
8 The point is exceptionally well explained in Brittan, 1971, p. 274.
9 3.1 per cent UK total unemployed seasonally adjusted 1972 Q2, CSO 1996, Table 3.2, p. 164.
10 1975q4 on 1974q4, CSO 1996, Table 2.1, p. 151.
11 CSO 1996, Table 3.2, p. 158.
12 HM Treasury 1944.
13 Transcribed from BBC video recording of the event. For other accounts of this speech and its genesis see Callaghan, 1987, pp. 425–7 and Morgan, 1997, pp. 535–7.
14 CSO 1996 edition, Table 3.2, p. 164.
15 rpiczbh.xls and CSO 1996, Table 2.1, p. 152.
16 So short and sterile are sub-editorial minds in Fleet Street that the very Shakespearean *cliché* which had been used five years earlier to describe Edward Heath's travails with the National Union of Mineworkers and the three-day week was instantly recycled to describe the challenge by mainly public sector unions to the pay ceiling imposed by the Callaghan government in the winter of 1978–9.
17 Professor of Industrial Relations, University of Warwick, 1967–79.
18 1979Q2–1980Q2, CSO 1996, Table 2.1, p. 152.
19 CSO 1996, Table 3.2, p. 165.
20 'A Solution of Last Resort', *The Times*, 27 April 1976.

3
Fiscal Policy in the United Kingdom

Alan Budd

Introduction

This is an account of fiscal policy making over the past thirty years. During this period I have either been a participant in or an observer of the policy process. I shall discuss the policies and the ideas that shaped them. I shall suggest that there are two sorts of development that influence the path of policy making. The first is changes in economic theory, the second is events. The role of events is crucial. I do not attempt to cover the entire history of the past thirty years but shall concentrate on a limited number of incidents which, I believe, illustrate the points I wish to make. They represent turning-points and, perhaps, paradigm shifts. They are: the Budgets of 1972 and 1973, the Budgets of 1980 and 1981, and the Budgets of 1993 (when there were two Budgets in one year). I also discuss the approach to fiscal policy under New Labour.

Most of my discussion is concerned with the macroeconomics rather than the microeconomics of fiscal policy though I do make some comments about microeconomics towards the end.

The main themes of this account are:

- The abandonment of fiscal activism.
- The shift from fiscal policy to monetary policy as the main instrument of demand management.
- The shift from full employment to price stability as the primary objective of demand management.
- Recognition of inter-temporal budget constraints.
- The use of taxes as a microeconomic instrument.

The 1970s

My account begins in 1970 (when I first joined the Treasury, on second-ment from Southampton University). The Conservatives had won the general election, somewhat against expectations. Edward Heath was prime minister and Anthony Barber had become chancellor of the Exchequer when Heath's first chancellor, Iain Macleod, had died only a month after the General Election. I was working in the part of the Treasury that was involved in producing the annual Budgets. The process worked as follows. The background to the macroeconomic analysis was an economic forecast that looked ahead about 18 months on the basis of unchanged policy. The prospects were then studied to see whether or not they acceptable. The main focus was on the prospects for unemployment and the balance of payments. If they were not thought to be acceptable, fiscal policy was to be changed in the appropriate direction. The menu of changes was provided by what was known as the Brown Book (because its cover was brown). It provided tables of ready-reckoners which showed the effects on unemployment and the balance of payments of changes in taxes and public expenditure. If, for example, the predicted level of unemployment was thought to be too high, and the balance of payments did not act as a constraint, a selection of tax cuts and public expenditure increases could be selected which produced a preferred outcome. The choice of the package involved political judge-ments. The final choice was embodied in the Budget, which was announced in the chancellor's speech on Budget Day. It was accompa-nied by the Financial Statement and Budget Report (the Red Book) which described the economic background, listed the Budget changes and provided forecasts of the economic and fiscal numbers, including the fiscal balance.

The economic theory supporting this process would have been under-stood by anyone who had studied macroeconomics for a term. It could have been represented in the standard 45° diagram (Figure 3.1).

The level of GDP could be varied by shifting aggregate demand. (The multiplier was thought to be about one.) The events which produced this view were, for those with senior positions in the Treasury, the reces-sion and high unemployment of the interwar years. The dole queues of the 1930s wound their way through the corridors of the Treasury. Many in the Treasury had known or been taught by Keynes in the prewar years or had worked with him during or after the war. Keynesian theory had been simplified, but that was equally true of the way in which it was taught in universities. As with the 45° diagram, in theory, there was no apparent limit to the ability of a fiscal expansion to raise GDP. But there

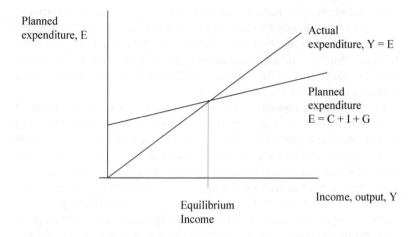

Where, C is consumption, I is investment, G is government expenditure and the economy is assumed closed.

Figure 3.1   Actual vs planned expenditure: the Treasury Model in the early 1970s

were recognised limits in practice. The most important limit was set by the balance of payments. The UK was operating a fixed exchange rate, set at $2.40 to £1 after the devaluation of 1967. The policy objective could therefore be seen as minimizing the level of unemployment, subject to a balance-of-payments constraint, with fiscal policy as the main instrument of fiscal policy.

In general this system appeared to have worked well during the postwar years. For most of the early postwar years the problem had been one of excess rather than inadequate demand; 1958 was the first Budget which had deliberately expanded demand in response to a recession. There had also been a fair degree of confidence that advances in technology and in econometrics would further improve the management of the economy. This confidence had somewhat taken a knock after 1966, when it appeared that a number of well-established relationships had broken down. This might have been the result of the extreme measures that had been introduced in 1966 in the (unsuccessful) attempt to prevent devaluation.

A further feature of policy making was that balance-of-payments problems seemed to have emerged at ever-higher levels of unemployment. It was that observation which had led to the widely held view that the level of the exchange rate was too high and was preventing the economy from growing rapidly enough or from operating at an appropriate level of unemployment. It was hoped that the devaluation of

1967 would remove that constraint. However, the immediate response to the devaluation was the fear that it would create a problem of excess demand. Tough Budgets were therefore introduced in 1968 and 1969 to make room for the expected improvement in the trade balance. The resulting slowdown in the growth of GDP may have contributed to the defeat of the Labour administration in 1970.

By 1971 unemployment was rising and it was feared that it would reach one million, an unacceptably high level. That autumn, Mr Heath demanded that measures be taken to reduce unemployment to 500,000 by the end of 1972. It was a fairly simple matter to estimate the fiscal expansion required to achieve that, but the Treasury argued that an expansion of that order would lead to demand management problems later, as the full effects of the tax cuts or increases in public expenditure came through. The target was changed to reducing unemployment to 500,000 by the end of 1973. It was also agreed that policies would not need to be reversed in the 1973 Budget.

The 1972 Budget was duly introduced. It was the largest fiscal expansion of the postwar period and it was followed by a further fiscal expansion in the Budget of 1973. There were other current developments which were to have a significant effect. The first was that the Conservative government had introduced a series of measures under the heading 'Competition and Credit Control'. They were intended as a background to a move to quantitative control of the money supply as a means of controlling inflation. That move was never made, but Competition and Credit Control led to the removal of the direct controls on the structure of the commercial banks' balance sheets. As a result they greatly expanded bank loans and there was a consequential increase in the money supply, which rose by about 40 per cent over the course of the following two years. The second was a move to a floating exchange rate in June 1972, in the hope that this would remove the balance-of-payments constraint which it was believed had restricted economic growth. The third development was a world boom.

The rapid expansion of the money supply and the world boom added extra impetus to that being provided by the fiscal expansion and the short-run result was that GDP rose by over 7 per cent in 1973, another postwar record.

It might be asked whether this expansionary policy was accompanied by any fears about inflation. The short answer is 'No'. That view was supported by events and theory. I have said that the main constraint, in practice, on expansionary fiscal policy was the fear that rapid economic growth might cause balance-of-payments problems. It was hope that the abandonment of the fixed exchange rate in June 1972 would remove that constraint. During the 1960s, policy makers had recognised that lower unemployment might be associated with a higher rate of inflation. The relationship was embodied in the Phillips Curve. But in 1970 and 1971 inflation and unemployment rose together. In the phrase used at the time, the Phillips Curve had been stood on its head (Phillips, 1958).

The challenge was to explain this mysterious behaviour and a number of theories were produced. One class of theories suggested that inflation was a social rather than an economic phenomenon. The social explanations included the loss of respect for authority that was one of the aspects of the 'Swinging Sixties'. An explanation with slightly more economic content was the belief that, after a long period of acquiescence if not subservience, the workers were beginning to exercise their economic power. Inflation was the outcome of the struggle between capital and labour for the share of GDP. Another related theory emphasized real wage push. The idea was that workers set their pay claims to achieve a target growth of real wages. If they did not achieve the growth in one year they sought to make up the loss in the following year. The significance of this theory was that rapid economic growth, accompanied by rapid growth of real wages, reduced pay claims, since there was no catch-up required. In addition there was the observation that productivity tended to rise in the early stage of an economic recovery, thereby reducing unit labour costs.

The observation that unemployment and inflation had risen together and the theories that were produced to explain it led Mr Barber to say, in his 1972 Budget speech.

> I do not believe that a stimulus to demand of the order I propose will be inimical to the fight against inflation. On the contrary, the business community has repeatedly said that the increase in productivity and profitability resulting from a faster growth of output is one of the most effective means of restraining price increases. (*Hansard*, 21 March 1972, col. 1353, vol. 833).

So it was believed that the fiscal expansion did not carry inflationary risks. Though if such risks did emerge it was assumed that non-economic measures (such as incomes policies) could be used to deal with them.

I should mention two other developments, one an event and the other an idea. The event was the quadrupling of oil prices in 1973–74. The idea was embodied in the work of Wynne Godley and his colleagues at Cambridge who argued that the rapid expansion of the Budget deficit in 1972 and 1973 would be associated with an increase in the balance-of-payments deficit (since the private sector's financial surplus was relatively stable). Thus began a criticism of large fiscal deficits.

There was a more traditional source of criticism (though from outside the mainstream of UK economic thought at the time). A small group of monetarist economists, including David Laidler and Richard Parkin at Manchester University, drew attention to the possible inflationary consequences of the rapid expansion of the money supply. They were joined by Alan Walters who held a post at the London School of Economics, and who became a special adviser to the House of Commons Public Expenditure (General) Sub-Committee, which adopted a role as a commentator on macroeconomic policy and which was, in effect, a predecessor of the Treasury Committee. The monetarists were supported by Peter Jay and Tim Congdon, writing in *The Times*.

The early results of the fiscal expansion seemed extremely favourable. The extraordinary growth of GDP produced a rapid fall in unemployment, which was down to 500,000 by the end of 1973. The longer-term results were not so good. A Labour government was elected in 1974 and inherited the consequences. In 1975 there was, simultaneously, a postwar record for inflation and a postwar record (subsequently broken) for unemployment. Despite a complex series of prices and incomes policies, inflation reached a peak of close to 30 per cent (the threshold pay system introduced in 1973 in attempt to control wage increases actually added to inflation).

As a result of those grim experiences, the following conclusions about policy were (rightly or wrongly) drawn:

- Fiscal policy was ineffective, except possibly in the very short term.
- Monetary policy had powerful effects. The rapid growth of the money supply from 1971 onwards could explain the boom of 1973. The subsequent sharp reduction of real money growth could explain the 1974–75 recession.
- The balance of payments problem was not the result of an inappropriate exchange rate, but rather a sign of supply-side constraints, made worse by legislation that favoured the trades unions and by increases in the replacement ratio, as social security payments were made more generous.

The most noted recognition of these changes was made in the speech by James Callaghan to the Labour Party Conference in September 1976:

We used to think that you could just spend your way out of a recession and increase employment by cutting taxes and boosting government spending. I tell you in all candour that that option no longer exists, and that insofar as it ever did exist, it worked by injecting inflation into the economy. And each time that happened the average level of unemployment has risen. Higher inflation followed by higher unemployment. That is the history of the last twenty years.

Further support for that view was provided after the sterling crisis in the autumn of 1976. Fear that sterling was falling to $1.50 produced the IMF loan and the stringent conditions attached to it. Public spending actually fell in 1977–78. Despite that, the economy recovered in 1978–79.

The Labour government stayed in office until 1979. The experiences of the years from 1972 onwards helped lay the foundation for the approach to fiscal policy adopted by the incoming Conservative government.

Fiscal policy under the Conservatives: the Medium Term Financial Strategy

The Conservative administration, with Geoffrey Howe as Chancellor of the Exchequer, announced that it would use quantitative control of the money supply as its main instrument for controlling inflation and announced targets for monetary growth in its first Budget. At the same time it took steps to reduce the size of the fiscal deficit. Changes in the fiscal deficit were no longer seen as an instrument of demand management. Instead, the new role of fiscal policy was to support monetary policy. One source for this idea was work undertaken at the London Business School. That work suggested that the main consequence of a fiscal expansion was a growth of the money supply. That growth in the money supply caused the exchange rate to fall and prices to rise. The increase in prices caused the savings ratio to rise (as people sought to preserve the real value of their assets). Thus, a fiscal expansion had no little or no effect on aggregate demand and simply caused a rise in inflation. It followed that a successful policy to cut inflation required both a reduction in monetary growth and in the size of the fiscal deficit (or, in particular, a reduction in the public sector borrowing requirement).

These ideas were incorporated, in the 1980 Budget, in the Medium Term Financial Strategy (MTFS) which combined paths for the growth of the money supply and the public sector borrowing requirement (PSBR).[1]

The MTFS evolved through time. In its first version there were paths for monetary growth and for the PSBR, but not for inflation. It set out the idea that fiscal policy supported monetary policy which in turn controlled inflation. The MTFS remained part of the Budget presentation throughout the period during which the Conservative government was in office.

The next year provided a severe test of the approach. The money supply target set in the 1980 Budget was greatly exceeded. In retrospect one can say that there was in fact a severe tightening of monetary policy. The 1980 Budget had raised the rate of VAT to 17.5 per cent, thereby causing a sharp rise in prices, in addition to effects through an increase in oil prices. At the same time, deregulation of financial markets raised the demand for broad money. The unexpected recession raised the PSBR. In the Budget of 1981, the government confirmed its commitment to the MTFS and introduced a significant tightening of fiscal policy in the depths of the recession. Never again was fiscal policy to be used overtly as a tool of demand management.

The 1983 Budget mentioned, for the first time, an inflation 'assumption'. It was to be reduced to 5 per cent by 1985–86. At the same time the PSBR was to be reduced steadily to 2 per cent of GDP. In the 1984 Budget inflation was projected to be 3 per cent by 1998–89 and the PSBR was to be reduced to 1¾ per cent over the same period. The same projections were made in the 1985 Budget.

We may pause for a moment in this account of the policy actions of the time to examine the ideas and events that lay behind them. I have mentioned the disastrous consequences of the Budgets of 1972 and 1973. These experiences seemed to signal victory for the monetarists, who had predicted them. The victors included Milton Friedman and his UK followers. Friedman had not only emphasized the role of the money supply (and warned against the use of active demand management) he had also, in his Presidential Address to the American Economic Association (1968), propounded the idea of the natural rate of unemployment. That could explain the conjunction, in 1971 and 1972, of rising inflation and rising unemployment, which had seemed so mysterious to policy-makers at the time.

Other significant ideas were the development of theories based on rational expectations, associated with Lucas and others. There was also the revival of the ideas of Ricardian equivalence, associated with Barro, Sargent and Wallace, which explained the importance of inter-temporal budget constraints and provided a further explanation for the ineffectiveness of fiscal policy (Friedman, 1968). As the ideas developed, the notion of a simple link between the PSBR and the growth of the money supply became more difficult to justify and emphasis shifted to the relationship between the PSBR, the growth of the money supply and the rate of interest.

What determined the target for the ratio of the PSBR to GDP? Once the link between the PSBR and the growth of the money supply received less attention, emphasis turned to idea of fiscal sustainability. The idea was as follows. The ratio of debt to GDP was about 0.5. If the objective was to get rid of inflation completely and to hold the debt/GDP ratio constant the PSBR/GDP ratio needed to be about 1 per cent of GDP (on the assumption that the sustainable growth of real GDP was about 2¼ per cent). Nigel Lawson, who succeeded Geoffrey Howe as chancellor of the Exchequer in 1983, adopted the 1 per cent target and called it 'the modern version of the balanced budget'.

To return to events, Nigel Lawson, described by Margaret Thatcher as 'my brilliant Chancellor', seemed to have discovered a virtuous circle. A succession of tax cuts seemed to be consistent with a steady reduction in the PSBR. So tax cuts encouraged faster economic growth (presumably through favourable supply-side effects) which in turn allowed more tax cuts. At the same time, since the fiscal numbers tended to work out better than expected, Nigel Lawson was able to replace the 11 per cent target for the PSBR/GDP ratio by a zero balance.

Unfortunately in the early 1990s it became apparent that the favourable fiscal outcomes were achieved by running the economy at an unsustainably high level. There were serious questions about whether the fiscal path was sustainable. As a result the Conservative government introduced a series of very tough Budgets from 1993 onwards. The PSBR was cut first by raising taxes and then by cutting the growth of public expenditure. By the end of the Conservative administration, fiscal consolidation was in place and fiscal surpluses were projected.

Fiscal policy under Labour

The incoming Labour government inherited an extremely favourable fiscal position which it maintained by keeping, for the first two years of office, the same spending totals as projected by the Conservatives. It has not departed radically from the Conservative strategy. (One of the features of the past decade or more is the extent to which there is a bipartisan approach to macroeconomic policy, even if political rhetoric requires politicians to emphasize the differences between them.)

The Labour government has certainly tried to be more transparent about the conduct of fiscal policy. This can be illustrated by the extraordinary increase in the amount of documentation published at the time of the Budget and the pre-Budget Report. It also seeks to incorporate into fiscal policy as much as it can of the features which have made the arrangements for the conduct of monetary policy such a success. One suspects that its dream would be a fiscal equivalent of the Monetary

Policy Committee. That dream can never be realized since fiscal policy cannot be put into commission. The setting of tax rates and decisions about public spending are at the core of the government's actions. But it does rely, as I have said, on voluminous publications, including detailed studies of the long-term sustainability of its fiscal policy. It uses the National Audit Office to vet the assumptions that underlie its fiscal projections and it announces its fiscal rules.

The two fiscal rules are the Golden Rule, which requires that current expenditure should be balanced by current receipts over the cycle, and the sustainable investment rule, which allows the government to borrow to fund investment, provided that the debt/GDP ratio does not exceed 40 per cent. The government justifies the Golden Rule in terms of prudence and inter-generational equity and its investment rule, as its name implies, in terms of fiscal sustainability.

The rules are necessarily practical rather than ideal solutions to extremely complex problems. The Golden Rule is not necessarily optimal and produces scope for disagreement about the precise timing of cycles. The sustainable investment rule produces problems about defining an optimal debt/GDP rule and about drawing a rational distinction between current expenditure and investment.

The Labour government has not only increased the amount of paper it publishes at Budget time, it has also greatly expanded the terms in which it describes the Budget's objectives. A flavour can be provided by the chapter headings from the Budget Report accompanying the 2004 Budget (with the typical flood of present participles):

BUDGET 2004

Prudence for a purpose

A Britain of stability and growth

Maintaining macroeconomic stability
Meeting the productivity challenge
Increasing employment opportunity for all
Building a fairer society
Delivering high quality public services
Protecting the environment

The microeconomics of fiscal policy

This account has concentrated on the macroeconomics of fiscal policy. However, I shall close with some brief comments on the microeconomics of fiscal policy during the period covered by this survey. One way of summarizing the history would be from indifference to activism via neutrality. In the early 1970s, the microeconomic effects of policy were not a major concern, though one exception was the change of the corporate tax system towards the 'classic' system from the previous rules which had favoured retentions (and hence, it was hoped, investment) rather than the distribution of dividends. As described above, the overall balance of the Budget was driven by the needs of demand management and changes in individual taxes were selected as much for their political acceptability as for their effect on the allocation of resources. The replacement of purchase tax by VAT in 1973 was largely for reasons of convergence with the system in the Common Market.

The Conservatives, particularly when Nigel Lawson was chancellor of the Exchequer, emphasized fiscal neutrality, i.e. that the tax system should not favour or discourage particular types of economic activity unless there were a good reason for doing so. Examples of the move to neutrality included the phasing out of the favourable tax treatment of house purchase through mortgage interest rate relief, the removal of married persons' allowances (together with the introduction of separate taxation for married couples) and the increases in the taxation of company benefits, including cars. Tax neutrality remained a guiding principle which was consistent, in the years from 1973 onwards, with increased tax rates on motor and other fuels on environmental grounds.

That move to fiscal activism was accelerated under the Labour government. Environmental taxes have continued to be used and there has been active use of changes in the tax and social security system to encourage people to find jobs and in corporate taxes to encourage research and innovation in the hope of raising the growth of productivity.

A return to fiscal activism?

I have said that fiscal policy has not been used overtly as an instrument of demand management since 1979, if not before. However, one may note the large fiscal expansions in the UK which accompanied US-led economic recession starting in 2001. The justification for these expansions was the over-achievement of the government's fiscal rules. Whatever the justification, it was well-timed and no doubt contributed to the UK's success in sheltering itself from the worst effects of the world recession. (The euro-area economies operated in the opposite direction under the pressures of the Stability and Growth Pact and suffered accordingly.)

As a final irony, the UK may now be returning to macroeconomic fiscal activism. One of the volumes published with the report on the Five Tests for joining the euro describes how fiscal policy could be used to offset movements in monetary policy by the European Central Bank which might have undesirable effects on the United Kingdom economy. There is, of course, a simpler way of avoiding this problem.

Note

1   Terry Burns, who had developed the ideas at the London Business School, became chief economic adviser to the Treasury at the beginning of 1980.

4
The Use and Abuse of Economics and Social Science with Special Reference to Transport Policy[1]

Christopher Foster

My aim in this chapter is to say something about the logic of policy making, its connection with economic theory and some possible consequences of not following that logic.[2] My examples will be drawn mainly – but not exclusively – from UK government transport policy in recent years.

Logic and expression of policy making

The basic logic, as expressed – generally qualitatively – in so many white papers and blue books in the past, can be described simply:

1. Explain the problem which it is thought a change of policy (or law) is needed to solve. Do it in enough detail to show why it is a problem; what are its different aspects; and how it is regarded by various groups it affects. In many instances explanation will be helped by statistics, but not in all: for example, a badly drafted law which has had perverse consequences may need no more than evidence of its perversity.

2. The description of the problem can often be sensibly limited to the here and now. However, generally if the situation is expected to deteriorate, some indication of the future seriousness of the problem may be helpful. That may vary from some description of the anticipated consequences of underlying trends to a formal so-called Do Nothing (or sometimes called Business-as-Usual) forecast.

3. Describe the alternative courses of action which might solve the problem. Of course, these must be a selection since the possibilities are infinite. There are two main defensible principles of selection, the

outcomes of which need not coincide. One is to set down what various people think would solve the problem. However, a substantial part of a good White Paper may consist in showing why even apparently obvious courses of action will not solve the problem. The other amounts to setting out the courses of action which the policy maker – usually a minister – thinks most promising: what they would achieve; how they would affect those concerned. (There is a third possibility to which I will return later.)

4. Again, for example, if the issue is a defective law or regulation, or short-term crisis or other unexpected event in domestic or foreign affairs, no extrapolation into the future may be needed to help make a decision. But there will be other circumstances – usually where the expected consequences are expected to be far-reaching – where an indication of trends or even, as in much transport and other domestic policy, a set of formal forecasts is appropriate, each indicating the predicted future depending on which policy is adopted.

5. The next stage is the evaluation of the chosen alternatives. It requires an evaluation of their pros and cons. In many circumstances this stage, too, can be convincing though done wholly qualitatively and without much formality. Even if some or all the supporting argument is qualitative, the criterion, by which the government or the responsible minister judges between alternatives are to be evaluated, should be unambiguous and otherwise clear. How it operates should be transparent. But there will be more complicated cases calling out for formal cost–benefit analysis (CBA); though in every use of it one has met, there are aspects of the decision which cannot be quantified to the extent they can be subsumed into the CBA.[3] Yet it is reasonable they should influence the decision, but in a way which clarifies the weight the minister has given them.

6. Lastly, the chosen course of action needs to be described fully and shown to be practical. The consequence may be a change in the law or a change in the interpretation of existing law. It should be capable of being shown to be enforceable or otherwise able to work. Invariably there should be the reporting of the outcome of formal discussions and consultations with those directly affected as citizens, consumers of public services and so on, but also with those involved in operating within the policy area in question whose task will be to implement the new policy on the ground.

Similar considerations apply to policy outcomes other than a change in the law. If one were to develop these six points to define a template or check-list by which policy decisions, great and small, might be evaluate, one might add a further four benchmarks:

7. Wherever on the spectrum between qualitative and quantitative, the process of developing a particular policy lies, that process, except in comparatively simple cases, needs to be one of successive refinement, and often of iterative development. Hence, in describing the problem it is natural to draw attention to the criteria by which improvements to the *status quo* will be judged. Moreover the selection of options for further consideration presupposes the deployment of the criteria which later will be used more rigorously to make the final evaluation. At all stages some attention should be given to practicality in making an appraisal, even if the most detailed assessment of the practical details of implementation can only be made for the final option.[4]

8. The output of the social sciences can enter the process in many different forms; and from many disciplines, depending on the subject matter. They may also enter at different stages in its development: as the whole or part of the description of the problem, the choice of options, the various forecasts of the future, during consultation over implementation and in the techniques used for evaluation. While it is theoretically possible for the whole to be a consistent piece of analysis, in which all its parts are logically related, usually it will be fed by many separately undertaken pieces of analysis, often from different disciplines. In many instances many – in many straightforward cases all – will not be social science findings, but put forward as common sense or widely received opinion. In every case someone needs to be capable of being held responsible for the integrity and validity of the whole argument. While under the British system it is formally the responsibility of ministers, every department of state would be better off if it had professional resources, strong and competent enough to test, evaluate and integrate all such evidence, analysis and forecasts as objectively as possible, so as to be able to make parliament and the public aware of its strengths and weaknesses. It hardly needs saying that however good the particular economic and social analyses which are used to underpin aspects of a policy, their use may even be misleading if the logic of the whole and contents of other parts are defective.

9. As David Hume pointed out long ago, one cannot derive 'ought' from 'is' – or from 'will be' (Hume, 1738/1911, Bk 3, pt 1, sec 1). The one element in the process which cannot be derived from evidence is the criterion itself. That must be a political choice. However, the above form of process is consistent with the use of any rational decision-making

criteria: whether well-defined as economic efficiency can be, or economic efficiency modified to achieve a redistributive goal, or a more partial goal to maximize the net benefit to a section of the community; or – as is still most likely in most instances – a more qualitative list of pros and cons to be gone through and evaluated. Whatever the technique chosen, directly or indirectly, the weight given to different considerations is a political decision.

   10. Whatever the exact form of the process, to be intelligible – and arguably to be a democratic process – it needs to be capable at all stages of being summarized objectively so that it may be understood by a wide variety of audiences: by those engaged in developing it within a department of state (or within more than one department where it is a joined-up issue); by other ministers and their departments in Cabinet papers as it goes through the Cabinet system; by Parliament in White Papers and similar public documents; by those directly involved in implementing the law or policy so as to show them how their roles will change; and, through the media, by the general public.

The economics of policy making

However, there is another useful, but distinct, way of classifying forms of policy making by analogy with economics. Policy making, like economics – to revert to what used to be that discipline's classic definition – is about the allocation of scarce resources between competing uses (Robbins, 1932, p. 16). Policy making is never costless and its consequences – one hopes its intention – are to confer (net) benefits on those affected. Moreover there are policy making areas to which macroeconomic techniques most apply insofar as they involve *continuous* changes, and other to which microeconomic techniques – principally the theory of investment – apply more. They are those involving *discontinuous* changes.

Continuous policy making areas

Consider that important area of macroeconomic policy concerned with economic stabilization. Once it involved substantial *discontinuous* policy changes: for the UK, mainly when to devalue and by how much. Because they triggered severe consequences, which were not easily predictable, they were frequently economically and politically a failure, being directly or indirectly among the commonest causes of lost general elections (see chapters by Jay and Balls, this volume). The introduction of floating exchange rates removed one important discontinuity, (temporarily brought back when the UK tried to join the ERM). Gordon Brown, making interest rate determination a potentially monthly responsibility of the Monetary Policy Responsibility of the Bank of England, removed another. There remain fiscal and other actions the government could take which might seriously affect economic stability and growth; but it is now not unreasonable to see macroeconomic policy as largely a continuous process by which economic stability can be sustained by from time to time by altering one price.

There are other areas of the economy which can similarly be dealt with as continuous aspects of market failure. The whole area of monopoly regulation and the promotion of competition is predicated on the desire to make these markets simulate competitive markets as far as possible. The role of economic regulators can be described as generally that of issuing frequent, if not continuous, commands to ensure the market is as near competitive equilibrium as possible. That description of their activity is not fundamentally altered if their decisions also reflect environmental, public health or other relevant externalities, provided they are expressible in economic form.

Similarly, the introduction of efficient road and – even more if at the same time – rail pricing into the transport sector would change it from a policy area where almost endless discontinuities apply into one much more nearly approaching equilibrium; and therefore into one where – more difficult, it has to be said, in urban areas than for the national networks – optimal levels of congestion could be maintained by a host of fairly frequent *localized* price changes – and investments – to reflect changes in circumstances on particular routes.[5] To be economically efficient these price changes and investments should not only reflect changes in congestion levels, but in CO_2 emissions, other pollution and safety impacts, insofar as they can plausibly be regarded as roughly monotonic functions of congestion – i.e., that they increase as congestion increases, and decrease as congestion decreases.

In all the areas reasonably described as *continuous*, the explanation and therefore expression of a particular policy change can be fairly straightforward, though there may be a mass of past and ongoing research on the underlying issues in question. Attempting peer group consensus is a sensible way of determining interest-rate changes. Little further public explanation is needed in each case. The economic regulator may need to put forward a cogent argument when justifying his or her determination on a particular issue; but the context in which it is made will be well understood by those concerned, so simplifying the process. I look forward to a universe of road, rail and other public transport pricing including a few national and a mass of local models – perfectly feasible in the present state of the art – which the public can access, and explain why particular prices are what they are, as well as any proposed changes in them and investments.[6]

Discontinuous policy making

However, most policy changes are discontinuous in the sense we have described. For example – and understandably – no one is prepared to use price – as in the USA – to determine priorities in the NHS, or indeed in education. Nor are they ready to use a proxy for price – for instance the Qaly (Quality-Adjusted Life Year) in the NHS or an analogous measure in law and order issues – to determine priorities and help establish measures of efficiency. So in these areas cost–benefit analysis cannot be used, only measures of cost-effectiveness, and that sometimes with great difficulty. A tenable view is that we will not come within striking distance of making the NHS demonstrably efficient unless a measure like the Qaly is used as a yardstick, though departures from the priorities it indicates may well be authorized on political grounds, which, whatever they are, one hopes will eventually be made transparently.

However, there are many areas, like transport in its present state, energy, employment, many aspects of welfare and land-use policy, where something like a complete battery of quantitative techniques can be used to sort out the main issues. But, as has already been said, many policy issues need nothing like the complete battery of techniques for rational determination; and yet all can and should go through the progression of steps outlined above, if they are to be intelligible.

Transport policy making

With these arguments behind us, let us consider their reference to transport policy. My reasons for doing so are that it is an area in which I have often worked; one of some maturity in the application of science, engineering and social science; for the most part the relevant science and social science is well understood; and the relevant models and other economic techniques – for example, for the purposes of economic evaluation – are available. Policy making would be greatly eased by the adoption of efficient road and comparable rail and other public transport pricing. That so much information and technique exists, ought to make it a not particularly difficult area for rational decision making. Yet transport is in as much a mess as any other microeconomic policy area in the UK.

Recent UK transport policy

To understand one needs to go back. British road building on any substantial scale had virtually stopped from the beginning of the Second World War until the middle of the 1950s. Yet road use was already much higher than in the interwar years. To catch up, the motorway and other road-building programmes were launched. However, every few years, public expenditure crises led to cutbacks. By the end of the 1980s, the road system's inadequacies had become a subject of such public complaint that the White Paper *Roads for Prosperity* promised a doubling of the roads programme (Department of Transport, 1989). The government's own forecasts indicated continuing traffic growth of 2 to 3 per cent a year, but by the mid-1990s the programme was abandoned. By then the environmental campaigners had become effective in putting over the message that immediate and drastic traffic restraint was essential to prevent global warming and air pollution; and that therefore no roads should be improved, let alone built (Foster, 2001, pp. 271–85). With public expenditure again under pressure in 1994, the Conservatives decided to make what they saw as a virtue out of what they were persuaded was an environmental necessity, so they cut road investment and maintenance expenditure while embarking on a policy by which fuel duty rose each year by 5 per cent. Called the fuel duty escalator, it was far too blunt an instrument to approximate to efficient localized road pricing. The escalator had some effect in restraining traffic growth. But because car ownership and road use were still increasing, there was enough traffic growth for congestion to intensify, ironically causing higher CO_2 emissions and more air pollution than if the roads had been built or improved, and demand managed, to let road traffic flow more freely.

The 1997 Labour government

The incoming Labour government in 1997 hardly altered the previous policy, or rather lack of coherent policy. Like the previous government it neither invested in capacity nor managed demand, so that road congestion got worse. In 1998 John Prescott produced a long awaited transport white paper,[7] which met the requirements of none of the stages outlined above. The problems facing the different modes of transport were not satisfactorily described. There were few facts or statistics, no analysis and no forecasts. There was no description of actual travel behaviour or of people's preferences. There was no description or discussion of the alternative policies that might be pursued. No criterion or other basis for choice was put forward. The preferred option was instead simply asserted. Without in any sense demonstrating the assertion, it argued, that the government's own forecasts of traffic growth into the next century were 'unsustainable'. To that end, it asserted that public transport must be improved and dependence on the car reduced. It said more would be invested in public transport, but there was no clarity over how much, or of how much that would be at the expense of road investment. With roads expenditure already at a historically low level, it provided only £22 million extra for transport investment over three years. Several road schemes were abandoned.[8] Since in general its proposals were vague, it is unsurprising that their consequences were not forecast or their implementation shown to be practical.

In September 1998, new methods of investment appraisal were published.[9] The economic appraisal methods of the past had quantified the expected returns from investment in terms of traffic benefits and their impact on road safety. For many years it would have been possible to have extended their coverage so as to quantify and evaluate many environmental impacts of road (and rail) investment: for example, on CO_2 and air pollution.[10] To have done so would have shown that in spite of their inclusion, the returns from many road schemes would have still been highly positive.[11] However, successive politicians had preferred to deploy qualitative environmental factors as an argument against road investment. The new methods took this retreat from rational, and towards political, decision making further. The previous quantified analysis was chopped up into discrete bits. Moreover schemes were not to be appraised, except against the background of a coherent transport policy covering all modes. Schemes should be considered insofar as they increased accessibility, made it easier to travel, increased safety, showed good value for money, facilitated economic activity while allowance should be given for both positive and negative environmental impacts. Actual transport schemes were not only to be better integrated between modes, but to be chosen, bearing in mind their effect on local and regional economies, and on the environment. However, no indication was given of the weight to be given to each element in the appraisal. The need to strike a balance between them promised more political decision-making without transparency or consistency, as indeed occurred.

The 1998 White Paper had some apparently attractive features. It stated there would be more coordinated transport planning at local and regional level. Local authority transport plans and regional transport strategies were to be the engines of change. The principal outcome was a succession of 26 multi-modal studies in which road, rail and public transport solutions to particular local transport corridor bottlenecks were examined. Given the strong preference that the White Paper had shown for public transport, and the greater latitude the new appraisal methods allowed for political decision making, it is unsurprising that many of these studies – which took several years to complete – recommended rail, or other large-scale public transport, schemes far more expensive than their road alternatives, and for which highly imprecise environmental, economic or other counteracting benefits were claimed. By the time these recommendations emerged, rail costs had soared to such an extent that none of the rail schemes have been programmed for implementation. Whatever the intentions of the 1998 White Paper, or of the better-evidenced and more realistic 2000 Transport Plan, there was little increase in actual road expenditure, while the deferment of action to await the outcome of many plans and studies, meant traffic continued to grow as therefore did congestion. In anything approaching the classic sense outlined above, the government did not have a transport policy.

Motoring towards 2050

For that reason, and because government policy relied on a massive increase in rail and public transport use that did not materialize, the RAC Foundation, of which I was then chairman, considered what to do about it. I wrote to the Prime Minister to suggest there should be a proper inquiry into transport policy. He came back and suggested we did it. So the RAC Foundation decided to attempt a classic white paper of the kind the Government might have produced, which, going through the stages outlined above, set out the facts and options as fairly as possible (RAC Foundation for Motoring, 2002). To avoid a report, too easily brushed aside as the biased analysis of a motorists' pressure group, it took three steps:

1. One was to note, and adopt as policy, the fact that many motorists and other road-users too in general gained from an efficient public transport system. Most users of rail and other public transport also used cars. Moreover efficient and well-devised rail and bus services – especially in London and the South-East and elsewhere in many urban areas – provided some relief to road congestion;
2. Another was to choose a steering group in which outsiders were in a majority who between them would effectively stand up for environmental, planning and other transport interests.[12] This group met frequently. It agreed the objectives and structure of the report, and the

work programme. One or more of its members supervised each chapter, overseeing the work done and being responsible for drafts. The chapters were discussed and firmed up by the group as a whole. The report was unanimous.

3. The third was to invite evidence. It subsequently came in from more than 200 academics, other individuals and organisations.

The report

The completed report began by describing the problems that had developed and needed to be addressed.[13] Travel had grown threefold in the last 50 years. In 1950 40 million people in Britain had 2 million cars between them. By 2000 58 million had 24.5 million cars. The geography of the industrial and employment base had become far more decentralized from within city and town centres. Cars meant people could live further from their work. For these and other reasons, while in the 1950s about 30 per cent of passenger-km had been by car, it was now 85 per cent. This huge absolute and relative increase in car travel was despite low investment in new road capacity by the standards of other developed countries. As a consequence, and also because successive governments had failed to restrain demand effectively, the United Kingdom had the worst road congestion in the European Union.

The next chapter contained the group's Do Nothing forecasts. The group decided to look forward for up to 50 years in order to get an indication of the long-term consequences of existing trends, but also because many of the corrective measures needed would take years to develop and implement. The forecasts were carried out by John Bates, one of its members, but on bases consistent with the Department of Transport's own shorter-term forecasts. Despite its rate of increase continuing to decline, as had been recent experience, road traffic was predicted to grow 50 per cent by 2030. It concluded it would be unwise to bank on less traffic growth. It could be more. To continue to rely, as both the Major and Blair governments had done, on worsening congestion to 'solve' the problem would be economically and environmentally damaging. This outcome would not be materially affected by continuing for 30 years the levels of road construction and improvement contained in the 2000 Transport Plan.

The main driver of increased car traffic was higher car ownership. Car ownership in the UK of 439 per 1,000 was among the lowest in the EU (though car use was similar because of higher miles per car). Even in 2030 UK will have fewer cars per head than Italy does today. Any attempt at directly limiting car ownership would affect the poor disproportionately. New car ownership will be concentrated: in the socially excluded as they become more affluent; followed by second and third car owners in households with more than one earner; in addition, there would also be more women drivers and older people continuing to drive. In these circumstances, to try to reduce traffic growth by limiting car ownership would be both operationally and politically difficult.

The report then considered the option which had become the conventional wisdom: shift growth to public transport. It was also the government's stated policy in the 1998 White Paper. After careful consideration the group unanimously decided that it was not feasible. First-class public transport was desirable, but there must be realism about the modal shift it could achieve. As we have seen, 85 per cent of passenger-km were by car or taxi. Outside London, where 76 per cent of commuting journeys were by rail, only 8 per cent travel by public transport. 70 per cent of rail journeys are in London and the Home Counties. 85 per cent of motorists never use buses or coaches. 75 per cent of motorists never use rail or underground. The 2000 Ten Year Plan expected a 50 per cent increase in rail traffic, now unlikely to be realized because of shortfalls in capacity on rail's busy routes and a two to three-fold rise in rail costs.[14] But even if it had been realized, it equals only about one year's traffic growth on the roads. While there was a very strong economic case – coupled with more traffic restraint to reduce congestion – for substantially more reliance on buses in at least the top 20 cities, there was no practical way in which public transport could solve the road traffic growth problem. A 10 per cent fall in car travel would need to be offset by a 65 per cent increase in travel by public transport. To offset the 50 per cent increase in passenger road traffic forecast – or anything approaching it – would require an unimaginable and indeed practically impossible increase in public transport.

If public transport could not provide a solution, what could? The first requirement was to address the environmental issues. The report noted that road transport now accounted for about half of most pollutant emissions and 20 per cent of CO_2 emissions. Moreover while not the largest contributor to CO_2 emissions, it was the only sector where they were expected to increase further. It considered the options by which this sector might meet, and do better than meet, Kyoto requirements into the future. After discussions with the automotive industry, led by one of its members, who had been chief executive of Volkswagen UK, it concluded that improvements in vehicle technology were likely to be the most efficient and least economically damaging possibility, and one that might work in the long term without much of an increase in vehicle costs. By 2030 environmentally acceptable vehicles (e.g., hybrids and hydrogen fuel cells) ought to be capable of being produced at affordable prices. By 2050 the whole vehicle fleet might reasonably be expected to consist of such vehicles, eliminating problems of air quality, climate change, noise (in conjunction with quieter road surfaces), and materials recycling. Some environmental issues would survive – severance of people in different neighbourhoods, visual intrusion, problems with wildlife habitats – but it was agreed that, though important, in detail they were manageable. There would be more problems in handling environmental impacts in cities and many towns, which would require more traffic restraint, but overall these technological developments were likely to be the most cost-effective means of coping with these environmental issues, much more so than trying to restrain traffic growth. Facilitating them through the EU and by other means should be the political priority. Our discussions suggested that the vehicle-making and oil industries were more than ready to rise to the challenge.

If as a consequence it was reasonable to suppose that progressively over time the adverse environmental effects of road – and indeed rail – traffic could be overcome without adverse economic consequences, the government would still have to decide its policy on road investment. What combination of more road-building and more traffic restraint was optimal? The report considered three road-building options:

(1) The lowest postulated no substantial improvement in the road system beyond those provided for in the 2000 Ten Year Plan up until 2010. The resulting congestion would cut traffic growth by about a third. The severe deterioration in network conditions would adversely affect UK competitiveness and personal mobility. Through congestion it would to some extent offset the improving environmental impact of road traffic. Ironically, the model showed that an escalator of about 6 per cent a year – an increase Gordon Brown chose and then dropped because of widespread popular discontent – would be needed to keep congestion no worse than it was in 2002. Therefore there was nothing to be said for this option, either politically or economically.

(2) At the other extreme another possibility would be to build enough extra road capacity to avoid any deterioration in congestion and therefore the need for road pricing to restrain traffic. The cost was predicted to average £20 billion a year or 1 per cent of GDP.[15] It would add 40–50 per cent to the strategic network, but road taxation might have to escalate by, say, up to 4 per cent a year to pay for it. Nevertheless it was likely that overall and in detail the returns on the investment would prove economically worthwhile. Insofar as any road scheme considered

did not do so, it should not go ahead. If road pricing were introduced and used to pay for the investment, it would prove financially profitable as well. The proportion of UK land surface occupied by roads would rise by about 0.1 per cent from its current 2 per cent. In some instances expensive tunnelling and other costly measures would be needed to protect the environment, but even despite these advantages the group doubted whether embarking on such a policy would prove environmentally or otherwise politically acceptable.

(3) Various intermediate options were also considered. They had different mixes of more substantial road improvements than Option (1) and increased road charges. One, at the mid-point between (1) and (2), would have added about 25 per cent to strategic network capacity at annual cost of about 0.2 per cent of GDP or, say, £2½; billion rising to £6 billion a year. It was forecast to need fuel duty, or preferably efficient road prices rising at about 3 per cent a year, which surveys suggested on certain provisos (see below) might be politically tolerable. It was argued that it would probably be acceptable environmentally and would have a positive effect on mobility and the economy. In discussing and deciding between these intermediate possibilities, the key was to undertake sufficient road investment to keep congestion related taxes or charges, *and* congestion down to acceptable levels.

Road taxes and charges

The indications of the model underpinning the report were that some form of demand management would be required after 2010; but the more investment there was in roads the less would be needed. In 1997 Gordon Brown's increasing of the fuel duty escalator to an annual 6 per cent had cut the growth of traffic by about half. However, it was inefficient and unfair in that it had too little effect on congested roads and more effect than was necessary on uncongested ones. It was also a political disaster. The escalator led to the fuel duty protests in 2000, which brought about its abandonment, with the government wrongly claiming that traffic did not respond to fuel prices. If restraining traffic through increasing fuel duty was publicly unacceptable, a flexible charging system, varying charges with levels of congestion, was needed. It might be thought that if Option (2) were adopted there would be no need for efficient road pricing. The report argued that this was not so for three reasons: (i) there would be London and many other urban areas where it would not be feasible – or environmentally or aesthetically desirable – to build enough roads to enable car traffic to flow freely and where road pricing in combination with other measures would be needed to let buses operate reliably instead; (ii) there were enough uncertainties in traffic forecasting and new road provision to make it prudent to develop a nationwide system to manage demand if that proved necessary; and (iii) such a pricing system would be a fair and efficient way of paying for the investment programme.

A survey of public opinion undertaken in conjunction with the report, indeed showed that such a system of road pricing was likely to be acceptable if revenue from these charges was used for transport improvements and reducing fuel duty, rather than providing an additional contribution to general revenue. 69 per cent disagreed with the concept of the fuel duty escalator.[16] Only 22 per cent argue that tax on petrol is a better way of restraining traffic than a charge or toll for using congested roads. 60 per cent felt it would be fairer if motorists paid tax according to the amount of time they drive in congested conditions rather than through tax on fuel and tax discs. 58 per cent think that if charges are introduced for using congested roads there should be concessions for those on low incomes. The survey also suggested that road-users would be more favourable to road charging if national revenue needs were not the criteria for setting charges; if loss of revenue from charges would be ignored when investment proposals for easing bottlenecks are assessed; if the government were to use some revenue from national charges, partly for reducing road taxes, probably fuel duty; and if privacy were to be protected unless a driver fails to pay.

Despite work done in the past,[17] the report concluded more research was required on a number of aspects: the technology needed; the extent of the diversion to be expected to other roads and other modes of travel; the consequences for the socially excluded; and the implications for civil liberties and on the public acceptability of charging. Without charging or very high investment levels, access to the network and to car ownership must be restricted in some other way, all politically difficult. Therefore the government should announce programme of exploratory work on charging. This recommendation it acted on.

A disappointing reaction

The report therefore went through all the stages outlined, except that it was indicated that more work was needed on practicality. We had a 45-minute audience with the prime minister in which to outline our findings. The report received the accolade, or seal of approval, as a contribution to discussion, of a foreword from the prime minister. It was well received and widely commented on in the media. There was continuing interest in it a year later. Yet the government's reaction to it was a disappointing one. There are two aspects to this.

The prime minister, despite his commendation, rightly pointed out that the report could not be government policy. But it was the absence of a government policy, which anywhere near satisfied the requirements given above, that had triggered the report in the first place. There are several reactions the Secretary of State might have had. He might have accepted the report as his policy, possibly with some demurrers, as ministers used to accept and build on the reports of Royal Commissions. Or he might have rewritten it and re-presented its conclusions, so establishing ownership. Or with his access to far more money and resources, he might have improved on our work, perhaps endorsing our conclusions with better evidence than we could provide, especially in urban areas. Or he might have produced a reasoned case which reached different conclusions. In each case he would have provided a rational framework within which he and others – from local authorities to bus companies and the rail industry – could have some chance of being consistent, and even in some cases integrated, with each other. But he has done none of these things. Transport policy has continued *ad hoc* and piecemeal.

A good development is that the government is working with the vehicle manufacturers, the oil companies and other to reduce, and eventually near eliminate, CO_2 emissions; but there is no publicly-explained, coherent policy on how CO_2, air pollution, noise and other adverse environmental impacts are to be reduced to acceptable levels; or which sets out the milestones which it believes should be achievable. Instead it – and many local authorities and others who rely on it for guidance – follow Conservative and Prescott's policies in apparently behaving as if they believed in the canard that the best way of dealing with the adverse environmental impact of traffic growth is to provide no more road (or rail) capacity, despite the additional congestion that causes. Mistakes in government policy and decision making have been among the primary causes of the fact that since 2000 rail operating costs have risen by from 200 to 300 per cent – new project costs by even more – and punctuality has fallen and stayed well below the levels experienced in recent times and probably ever since the Second World War.[18] The eventual outcome in 2004 has been two white papers – on transport and rail – as spun, unquantitative and full of ambiguity – so providing no clear guidance for discussion, let alone action – as John Prescott's.[19] The exception is on road pricing, where some useful follow-up work has been done, but even here there is no sense of urgency, no careful planning and time-tabling of how the problems of implementation are to be overcome and no dispelling of the suspicion that the postponing of the target date until 2015 is any more than a politically convenient kicking into touch.[20] So in practice we are no nearer the position where the introduction of efficient road and rail pricing – together with the use of appropriate investment criteria – turns transport into an area where rationally *continuous* can largely replace *discontinuous* policy making.[21]

The second aspect relates not what has been said or written, but to what has actually happened. Road traffic has gone on rising at about the same rate from 1992 to 2003.[22] It goes on rising with GDP, even if not by as much as it once did. (A 36 per cent increase in GDP over the period has been matched by a 19 per cent increase in traffic.) The mileage of motorways and principal roads available for use has hardly risen since 1993 and of other roads has not risen much. Typically, for several years the government has not published the Highway Agency's stress maps showing the build-up of congestion, but except in the centre of London – because of the introduction of road pricing there – one can be reasonably sure that increased road traffic means growing congestion, as it has always done. It would be straightforward for the government to predict the fuel duty escalator which would be needed in present circumstances to keep congestion no greater than it was in 2000 and also the scale of road programme necessary to catch up on and achieve the congestion levels thought tolerable in *Motoring towards 2050*.[23] But the first can hardly be less than the 6 per cent a year increase in fuel duty which that report said would be required if road building stayed at its current low level, while to achieve the levels of road building postulated in our central Option (3) would require no more public money than the government now uses to subsidize the railways. 2003 was the first year in which more public money was spent on the railways, which carry less than 7 per cent of passenger-km, than on the roads, which carry 92 per cent. This is planned to continue, though the government has not produced any well-reasoned justification for it. Indeed such rate-of-return calculations as exist suggest that even before the recent doubling and more of rail costs, the expected return from road was much higher than from rail investment (Affuso, Masson and Newbery, 2003). So, judged by results, the transport decision making of recent years has done little more than continue that flawed policy of trying to combat traffic growth by increased congestion which it inherited from the previous Conservative government.

Conclusion

Transport policy making is far from the only area from which well-argued *classic* White or Green Papers, or equivalent documents, are absent. The requirements outlined above may seem Counsels of Perfection, but there is nothing wrong with that. However, there are degrees of imperfection. Despite excellent supporting papers in a few cases, it is hard to think of any such public documents in recent years which singly or severally meet the defining characteristics of policy making – qualitative or quantitative – as outlined in this chapter, so as to be capable of being the basis for intelligent discussion in the media or elsewhere.[24] One reason is the new practice of such papers being written or re-written by spin doctors in No. 10 or in departments. But another reason – the third possibility mentioned above – is that the idea that policies should be chosen and developed, which are defensible as in the public interest before Parliament and public opinion, is being replaced by the notion that what matters is the popularity – and therefore the electoral standing – of the government, as registered by the instant reaction of the media or its reception, however poorly explained, by opinion polls and focus groups. In the past the standard dilemma for a minister was how to find policies, large and small, which could both be defended as in the public interest to Cabinet colleagues and parliament in terms outlined as in this essay, and at the same time be politically astute and not unhelpful in winning the next election. The outstanding transport policy success of recent years was Ken Livingstone's introduction of congestion charging into central London. Moreover, it was almost uniquely based on solid research and analysis. However, his suggestions in 2003 and 2004 that the central London congestion pricing should be extended westwards, and later that the charge should be raised from £5 to £8, were not so based, and, if implemented, would almost certainly undermine the benefits of the original scheme. If Livingstone abuses social science and gets it wrong, it is even less likely that other local authorities will take the risk of introducing road pricing.

Some might argue that the political decision making obscure, but inherent, in multi-criteria overlays to cost–benefit analysis – if that is how the present system can fairly be described – only recognises political reality: we have what we have because in some sense politically we must have willed it. But that rationalization echoes F. H. Bradley's amplification of Candide: 'This is the best of all possible worlds and every evil in it is a necessary one.'[25] It reflects a politics which is not and cannot be accountable – neither to Parliament nor to public opinion – and therefore cannot be democratic.

Notes

1   I am grateful for comments on an earlier version to Bill Billington, Christopher Brearley, Stephen Glaister, Edmund King, Peter Mackie, David Newbery, and Robin Pratt and Philip Wood.

2   These arguments directed at economists and more quantitative social scientists are equivalent to arguments aimed at more general and politically-oriented readers in my forthcoming book, Christopher Foster, *British Government in Crisis* (2005).

3   There can be legitimate debate in particular instances how far a minister can reasonably override or otherwise modify the outcome of the formal quantified cost–benefit analysis; but transparent decision making for which ministers can be held accountable to Parliament requires that in any significant instances the formal CBA is publicly available so that ministers can show the impact of any overriding or other modification they have made.

4   One grand review can never resolve all decisions. There will always be discontinuous events and changes in other, but interacting, policies and laws needing ongoing policy monitoring and policy review between the once-in-a-government grand reviews.

5   This possibility is not inconsistent with the view that there must be enough price certainty to avoid destabilizing behaviour, as would happen if prices were constantly changing.

6   A model of this kind was used by Derek Turner and his team at Transport for London to help Mayor Ken Livingstone decide the £5 London congestion charge, Sadly, it was not put in the public domain and not apparently used to underpin suggestions on altering the charge to £8 or extending the charging area to include an area to the west of the original area in 2004. See above.

7   Department of the Environment, Transport and the Regions, 1998.

8   DETR, *A New Deal for Trunk Roads in England*, 31 July 1998.

9   DETR, *A New Deal for Trunk Roads in England: Guidance on the New Approaches to Appraisal*, September 1998.

10   On how it may still be done see Nellthorp and Mackie, 2000.

11   See Newbery, forthcoming.

12   The members were Sir Christopher Foster, chairman; John Bates, consultant economist; Bill Billington, highways economist; David Holmes, formerly in senior positions in the Department of Transport and British Airways; Richard Ide, formerly Chief Executive, Volkswagen UK; David Leibling, formerly of Lex, and author of the Lex (now RAC) Report on Motoring; Prof. Peter Mackie, of the Institute of Transport Studies, Leeds; Richard Mills, Secretary General, National Society for Clean Air; Sir Nick Monck, former permanent secretary at the Department of Employment and second secretary at the Treasury; Prof. Chris Nwagboso, Head of Transport and Automotive System

Research, Wolverhampton University; Prof. Tony Ridley, Professor of Transport Engineering, Imperial College; Robert Upton, Secretary, Royal Town Planning Institute; Joan Williamson, ex-RAC archivist and librarian; and Edmund King, director of the RAC Foundation.

13   As well as the matters discussed here, the report also covered issues by freight, urban transport, walking, motorcycling and cycling, the planning system, and new forms of transport.

14   Rail growth will be much harder and even costlier after 2010. On many of the busiest routes in Birmingham and other cities it is physically and environmentally infeasible to increase capacity, almost whatever the cost. Furthermore making efficient use of the railways is hampered by many unrecognised and unresolved questions about the railways' objectives and priorities. Improvement in vehicle technology will mean the case for public transport on environmental grounds will disappear.

15   And in certain respects less comprehensive, but lower, estimate of the annual expenditure required was Bayliss and Muir Wood, 2002.

16   The polling was done by NOP Automotive.

17   As early as in the Smeed Report (Smeed, 1964).

18   Pollitt and Smith, 2002; Kennedy and Smith, 2004; Foster and Castles, 2004; Glaister, 2004; Foster, 2005, ch 16; Smith, 2004.

19   Department of Transport, 2004a; 2004b.

20   Department of Transport, 2004d.

21   Never completely because of transport impacts – particularly planning and some environmental ones – which cannot easily be quantified. The impact of large-scale planning decisions – e.g. 500,000 more houses in the South-East – will always involve discontinuities, but they can be better managed against a continuous background.

22   These and subsequent figures are from Department of Transport, 2004c.

23   Newbury, forthcoming.

24   On this see Foster, 2005, esp. ch 14.

25   Bradley, 1876.

5
New Labour and New Social Democracy

Iain McLean

The three strands of Old Labour

Until as recently as 1979, the economic and social policy of the Labour Party was indelibly coloured by the circumstances of its formation. Three main strands intertwined to form the Labour Party: we label them the *producerist* strand, the *egalitarian* strand, and the *internationalist* strand.

A fundamental insight due to Mancur Olson (1965, 1982) is that we should expect most of political parties' funding to come from (would-be) *suppliers of the factors of production,* in other words from people and organizations that control land, labour, or capital. We are all consumers, and not all of us are producers. But producers have a more immediate interest in what governments do than consumers. Anyone may lobby government; but most government policy is a public good – that is, a good which everybody gets to the same extent and from which it is hard or impossible to exclude anybody. That applies equally to national defence and to the National Health Service. As an individual I may have strong views on the sort of national defence my country ought to have. I *could* lobby in support of them. But lobbying costs time and money. Almost certainly, the sort of national defence I want will either happen even without my lobbying, or fail to happen even with my lobbying. Therefore it is rational for me, and for most people, to 'free-ride' on the efforts of others, and not to get involved in political lobbying.

It is different for organized suppliers of the factors of production. They have millions of pounds at stake, so the incentive to free-ride is less. Controllers of land and of capital, though not controllers of labour, are relatively few in number, which makes it easier to organize and to detect, and sanction, free-riding by their own members. They not only wish to control government policy, they also wish to supply resources to the government that carries it out. Armaments manufacturers and shipbuilders will certainly lobby the government for their favourite defence policies (respectively, one with lots of guns, and one with lots of ships).

Our view of British political economy before 1900 is therefore essentially Marxist, or Marxist–Olsonian. We do not mean to imply that the class cleavage was the only (or even before 1914 the principal) cleavage in British politics. However, until 1846, Parliament and the executive ran an economic policy that operated principally on behalf of landed interests. The Repeal of the Corn Laws in that year, albeit by a landed parliament for reasons that are still hotly debated (McLean, 2001a; Schonhardt-Bailey, 2003), introduced a class struggle between the interests of land and of (mostly urban) capital. The era of free trade imperialism (1846–1914) saw the interests of capital gradually increasing their ascendancy over the interests of land. However, the UK Parliament never wholly became what Marx called the executive in 1848: 'but a committee for managing the common affairs of the whole bourgeoisie'. Electoral reform gave a voice in the elected House of Commons to the cities and hence to the interests of capital (and, after 1867, labour) within them. But the unelected House of Lords and monarchy continued to reflect the interests of land in the political economy. Their influence was disproportionate to their share of the population because of their control of the unelected parts of the 'King-in-Parliament'; but it was reduced after the Lords' defeat of the 1909 Budget and the consequent Parliament Act 1911, that circumscribes the Lords' veto.

Labour had little lobby power but increasingly it had electoral power. The Reform Acts of 1867 and 1884 gave the franchise to some working-class men (perhaps two-thirds of them after the 1884 Act). Organized labour, in the shape of trade unions, was subject to harsh legal restrictions, whereas organizations of capital and of land were not. Naturally, therefore, the first 'labour' MPs, elected under the Liberal banner in dribs and drabs from 1874 onwards, tried to influence legislation in favour of labour and its organizations. They had some successes, e.g., the Trade Union Act 1876, arising not from their own numbers in Parliament but from politicians' need to placate the median voter (Black, 1958), who was already (probably) a working-class man.

But when capital lost ground to labour in Parliament, it made it up in the courts. In 1900–03 the courts, culminating in the House of Lords, found for the Taff Vale Railway Co. against the Amalgamated Union of Railway Servants. They held the union's officers liable for damages in respect of the business lost by the railway company because the union had picketed it during a strike.

The Labour Representation Committee had been founded just before the start of the Taff Vale case, which galvanized it. It became a campaign to return trade unionists to the Commons in order to reverse Taff Vale. It succeeded brilliantly when the new Liberal Government passed the Trade Disputes Act 1906, a measure that protected unions from actions for damages arising out of strike action. Like the 1876 Act, this one arose not from the voting strength of the 30 LRC (by now Labour Party) MPs, but probably from ministers' belief that the Act would be popular with the median voter.

Thus, without any doubt, the Labour Party arose 'from the bowels of the trade union movement', in the words of one of its later leaders, Ernest Bevin (1881–1951). 'They used to say Gladstone was at the Treasury from 1860 to 1930', said Bevin while Minister of Labour under Churchill during the Second World War: 'I'm going to be at the Ministry of Labour from 1940 to 1990' (Wrigley, 2004). He was out by only 11 years. Old Labour was constitutionally producerist. It came into existence in order to redress the balance of power between capital and labour. As the unions brought it into existence, so they largely determined its constitution. Naturally, they gave themselves most of the votes at the party conference and most of the places on the National Executive. They had founded, and paid for, the party.

But it was not entirely their party. The socialist Independent Labour Party (ILP) antedated the LRC by seven years, and was incorporated into it in 1900. British socialism was predominantly ethical and egalitarian. 'I owe more to Robert Burns than to any man, alive or dead', wrote Keir Hardie (Stewart, 1921, p. 19). A survey of the 30 Labour MPs elected in 1906 found that Henry George, the American land reformer, was their favourite reading. No European socialist featured in their reading lists. Perhaps the true begetter of the Labour Party was neither Karl Marx nor Keir Hardie, but that Col. Thomas Rainborowe of Cromwell's New Model Army who alarmed his superiors by saying in Putney Church in 1647 that 'the poorest hee that is in England hath a life to live as the greatest hee'. The egalitarian, anti-hierarchical tradition was developed in the eighteenth century – soberly by Adam Smith, poetically by Robert Burns, fierily by Tom Paine. It went underground during the French revolutionary wars, but emerged shakily in Chartism, trade unionism, and egalitarian religious denominations such as Primitive Methodism as the nineteenth century wore on.

Religious thinkers also helped to develop the third, internationalist, strand. Quakers and evangelical Anglicans had led the campaign against the slave trade and then against slavery in the British Empire. The moralistic and religious Liberal Prime Minister W.E. Gladstone won the General Election of 1880 with his calls for an ethical foreign policy – although, like Robin Cook under New Labour, he found it easier to demand in opposition than to implement in government.

Until about 1923, the Labour Party shared the egalitarian and internationalist strands of its ideology with the Liberals, or some of them. Between 1908 and 1912, a group of determined Liberal politicians and civil servants – Asquith, Lloyd George, William Beveridge, Sir Hubert Llewellyn Smith, W. J. Braithwaite – laid the foundations of the egalitarian Welfare State, and reduced the powers of the unelected Lords. Labour played almost no part in these events – the role of Sidney and Beatrice Webb has been hugely exaggerated, mostly by themselves. The internationalist wings of both Liberal and Labour were badly damaged by the First World War, where the majority of both parties swung behind the war effort as soon as German troops invaded Belgium in August 1914. The war killed the Liberal Party, but Labour (just) survived. By beating the Liberals, in terms of seats, in the four General Elections between 1918 and 1924, it signalled that it was the only viable home for egalitarians and internationalists. Their lot was cast in with organized labour, like it or not. The crushing defeat of the second Labour government in 1931, when Ramsay MacDonald joined the Conservatives and some Liberals in forming a 'National Government', left the trade unions more than ever in charge of what little remained.

There has always been a snobbish 'labour-aristocratic' side to British trade unionism, or British socialism more generally. Noting in 1915 that the Labour Party failed to win council seats in the poorest parts of Glasgow but won them in 'the better paid, and more comfortably circumstanced, and better read' wards, the local ILP leader Tom Johnston, editor of *Forward*, complained that that 'Neither the bar-tender's pest nor the Sauchiehall Street dude ever spend a penny on the *Forward*'. Instead, he said, they bought the *Daily Record, Weekly Mail*, and *John Bull* (*Forward*, 28 August 1915, quoted by McLean, 1999, p. 177). Less colourfully, the power of trade unionists depends on power in the labour market. The poorest workers, and non-workers, have little or no labour market power. Only those whose threats to strike are credible, because the employer knows that that their skills would be hard to replace, can force the representatives of capital to bargain with them.

Therefore the producerists of Old Labour did not always speak or act for the very poor. That required the socialist egalitarians such as R.H. Tawney, George Orwell (definitely egalitarian, not so certainly socialist), and Richard Titmuss, who were among the leading Labour thinkers between the wars and in the Attlee years 1945–51.

The social democratic consensus, 1940–79

The Labour Party had more power during the coalition governments in both world wars than it enjoyed during its first two single-party (but minority) governments in 1924 and 1929–31. In wartime, the labour power of trade unions really mattered. In both world wars it was corralled into the war effort by bringing Labour Party ministers into government – from 1915 to 1917 and from 1940 to 1945. On both occasions, they introduced a regime of tripartite corporatism. In tripartite corporatism, representatives of government, of capital, and of labour shaped labour market policy together; the outcome had to satisfy all three. The corporatism of the First World War was threatened when Labour pulled its ministers out of government in 1917 because the government would not take Russian peace moves seriously. It collapsed under multiple blows, from the 'Geddes Axe' of 1921 to the General Strike and its aftermath of 1926–7. That of the Second survived the transition to peace; ruled unchallenged under governments of both parties until 1970; came under increasing strain in the 1970s; and collapsed in 1979.

In forming his coalition in 1940 Churchill not only brought in Ernie Bevin as Minister of Labour; he put Labour Party ministers in charge of most of the home front, and leftish Liberals or Conservatives in charge of the rest. The foundations of the second Welfare State were laid during the war. The Beveridge reports on national insurance and on conquering unemployment were published in 1942 and 1944. R. A. Butler (the Conservative part of what the *Economist* later labelled Butskellism, meaning centrist corporatism) enacted the Education Act 1944, creating a tripartite model of secondary education for all English school pupils. There was parallel legislation in Scotland.

The Attlee administration (1945–51) was the most successful Labour government before 1997. It created the National Health Service and the National Insurance system, both of them (but especially the first) high-water marks of egalitarianism. It showed its internationalism by enacting Indian independence and resisting Soviet imperialism (especially by means of the Berlin Airlift of 1949). Its economic achievements were remarkable in the light of the wartime destruction of infrastructure and reserves, but its social policies had hit a hard budget constraint by 1951, when the rising cost of the NHS collided with the Korean War rearmament programme. Since 1918, Labour had been committed to 'the common ownership of the means of production' (and since 1928, of 'distribution and exchange'). This producerist slogan merged socialist and trade union demands. By 1945 a standard pattern of public ownership, due to Peter Mandelson's grandfather Herbert Morrison, was in place. The main utilities and some primary industry (coal and steel) were nationalized, their former private or municipal owners being bought out. The Morrison template put 'workers on the board', but they were not representatives of the industry on whose board they sat. Lord Robens, a former official of the shopworkers' union, ran the National Coal Board for ten years. No representative of the miners' union ever did. Morrison feared that 'workers' control' might degenerate into control of an industry by those who supplied labour to it, in their own interest rather than the public interest. The economic purpose of nationalization was less clear. Nationalized industries were to make a profit 'taking one year with another' (but which with which?). They were to improve working conditions for their staff, and they were to fulfil some ill-defined social objectives.

Nevertheless, the social-democratic consensus continued under the Conservatives from 1951 to 1964. They denationalized nothing except steel and road transport. They continued to favour either generals (Sir Brian Robertson) or trade unionists (Alfred, later Lord, Robens) to run nationalized industries. They preserved the NHS and national insurance. Beginning in 1961, they tried, but failed, to make corporatism more wide-ranging. With a brief interlude between 1970 and 1972, so did all British governments until 1979. They all failed.

They failed because they were trying to convert a liberal market economy (LME, also labelled 'Anglo-Saxon capitalism') into a coordinated market economy (CME, also 'Rhenish capitalism'). Each of these can be a stable equilibrium, which means, unfortunately, that a move from one to the other is a move out of equilibrium (Hall and Soskice, 2001; Wood, 2000, 2002).

In an LME, 'firms coordinate their activities primarily via hierarchies and competitive market arrangements'; in a CME, 'firms depend more heavily on non-market relationships to coordinate their endeavors with other actors and to construct their core competencies' (Hall and Soskice, 2001, p. 8). The implications of this difference spread through the whole of political economy. The role of the state in an LME is to provide a secure legal domain for capitalist competition; to nurture human capital through the public education and health systems; and otherwise to let the market determine what is produced, and where. Industry meets its capital requirements mostly by issuing share capital, which is freely traded. The role of nationalized industries in an LME is uneasy: are they part of the state or of the market?

The role of the state in a CME may be larger, but so is the role of cooperative agreements within and between the social partners. It is the latter rather than the former which coordinate. In Germany, viewed in the 1960s as the model corporatist state, employers band together in trade associations and chambers of commerce, while trade unions are large, 'encompassing' (cf. Olson, 1982) bodies. Between them, the corporations of capital and labour ensure that workers get good training, that firms do not pinch skilled employees trained at their rivals' expense, and that wage claims are moderated. In these matters, firms and workers are in a prisoners' dilemma game with one another. All might recognise that it was in the interests of all that workers not be poached and that wage claims be held down. It remained in the dominant interest of each to poach workers or make inflation-busting wage claims.

In the 1960s, the leading CMEs (most of Continental Europe plus Japan) were growing faster than the leading LMEs (the UK and its Anglophone ex-colonies including the USA). Therefore, Labour ministers in the 1964–70 and 1974–9 governments tried to turn Britain into a CME. On one view, the trade unions were too strong for that. Trade unionists destroyed Labour's industrial relations policy in 1969 and its incomes policy in 1979 (Jenkins, 1970; Butler and Kavanagh, 1980, chs 2 and 7). A truer view is that the trade unions were too weak, and the associations of capital even weaker. Neither of them could actually *coordinate*. The Trades Union Council had little power to persuade individual unions to moderate their wage claims. The Confederation of British Industry had no power whatever to affect employers' training and hiring policies, and nor did chambers of commerce. British banks, unlike (for instance) German ones, did not operate as strong regionally based purveyors of lending to medium-sized industries. The institutions of LME Britain were in equilibrium, however uncomfortable, so that it was not possible to create a CME from an LME – essentially because organizations like the TUC and the CBI could not impose the cooperative solution on the prisoners in the British dilemma.

By the 1980s fashion had moved in the opposite direction. LMEs were showing faster growth than CMEs (Hall and Soskice, 2001, Table 1.1). Germany was trying to become an LME, but failing for the same reason – it was unable to move out of equilibrium to a new (LME) equilibrium. For fuller explanation of this see Wood (1997, 2001).

Some parts of the economic policy of the social-democratic consensus era arose from the unsuccessful attempt to switch the UK from an LME to a CME. Notably, they included successive attempts to restrain inflation through incomes policy, the last of which collapsed in 1979 allowing space for Margaret Thatcher. Other parts depended on a bipartisan belief that Keynesian demand management could deliver macroeconomic stability. The Treasury, whose senior officials had been 'seared' by the failure of effective demand and the consequent mass unemployment in the 1930s, continued to believe in managing demand by fiscal (tax rate) and monetary (interest rate) manipulation until the effects of the 1972 and 1973 Budgets persuaded them otherwise (Budd, this volume).

The breakdown of the social-democratic consensus began with the Conservative victory in 1970. Edward Heath's incoming government set out on a pro-market, anti-state course on election, but felt forced to reverse their policies when unemployment soared to a million and well-known firms (Rolls-Royce, Upper Clyde Shipbuilders) went bankrupt. The Industry Act 1972 was the most generous programme to that date of industrial support, and most of the support went to dying industries, not to weaning ones. It was not sufficient to head off a confrontation with the miners' union over incomes policy, which led to Heath's defeat and the formation of Labour governments under Harold Wilson (James Callaghan from 1976) with first a minority in the Commons (February 1974), then a bare majority (October 1974), then a minority again (1976). Given their parliamentary weakness, these would have been difficult years for Labour in any case, but events crowded in from all sides. The first oil shock (1973–4) led, via massive wage claims, to inflation around 25 per cent – hitting a peak of 26.6 per cent in the third quarter of 1975. With substantial assistance from the leaders of most unions, the government's incomes policy tottered on, but it finally collapsed in the winter of 1978–9. And its flagship policy, of devolution for Scotland in order to head off the Scottish nationalists, collapsed to an English backlash in February 1977. Labour lost a motion of no confidence, nominally over devolution but actually over its entire conduct of government, in March 1979 and the reign of Margaret Thatcher began.

The path-dependence of New Labour

The Thatcher governments immediately destroyed the social-democratic consensus, but did not immediately know what to put in its place. After the deflationary 1980 and 1981 Budgets, enacted as a depression was taking hold, unemployment soared to levels last seen in the 1930s. Mrs Thatcher would have been a one-term prime minister but for the Falklands War and the Labour–SDP split. Not until the third Thatcher term (1987–90) did her ideology of 'a free economy and a strong state' appear coherent (Vickers and Yarrow, 1988; Gamble, 1994; McLean, 2001a).

It was commonplace, said Sir Samuel Brittan at the time, to overestimate Margaret Thatcher's grasp of economics and to underestimate her grasp of politics. However, it was her grasp of politics, combined with collapse and fission on the left, that made 'Thatcherite' economics possible, and set the path on which Labour found itself. It might wish to walk in a different direction, but it must start from the point which economic policy had reached by the fall of Mrs Thatcher in 1990. In a word, New Labour's evolution was *path-dependent*.

Thatcherite economics was anti-producerist and anti-egalitarian. Miners, teachers, local government employees and social workers were regarded as self-interested producer groups, but lawyers and financial advisers were not. Some of Mrs Thatcher's attacks on organized producer groups succeeded, and set the path for New Labour. Above all, her defeat of the miners in 1984–5 was more comprehensive than that of 1926. Never again could a public sector industrial trade union expect to get its demands met by exercising industrial muscle. There were many reasons for Mrs Thatcher's victory. One was the stupidity of the National Union of Mineworkers in starting a strike in spring 1984, when UK coal stocks were at a record high and it was getting warmer. A second was the privatization of publicly-owned trading enterprises, such as the National Coal Board, so that wage-setting in those industries was no longer the government's business. Relatedly, a third was monetarist macroeconomic policy. In her first two terms, Mrs Thatcher, her Chancellors and the Treasury focused macro policy entirely on restraining inflation by restricting the growth in the money supply, irrespective of the consequences for unemployment. The immediate consequence, as already noted, was that unemployment soared to levels last seen in the 1930s. This surge was not planned, for if it had been Mrs Thatcher would have known that the 1983 General Election would have been unwinnable – she could not rationally have anticipated the Falklands War, which delivered that election to her. But mass unemployment had the incidental benefit (for her) of destroying the market power of organized labour.

One Thatcher legacy that survives in part is the culture of inspection and market testing. Where producer groups could not be directly controlled, they should be controlled by inspection. People who delivered public services – teachers, doctors, nurses, police, social workers – could not be directly subjected to market discipline, nor to mass unemployment. In the NHS, the Thatcher administration tried to introduce quasi-markets, with fairly limited results. In the other public services, it had various control mechanisms. One that worked was setting of cash limits, originally a Treasury device to control spending by service departments. If public service growth was measured by cash, not by the volume of services delivered, then managers had to trade wage costs against cuts in services. One that failed was her attempts to curb local authority spending – this led only to tears in the shape of the Poll Tax. One that worked in part was market testing. All public service managers, in both central and local government, were expected (and in some cases forced) to consider market provision of services instead of direct in-house provision. On a parallel track, the government introduced frequent tests and performance indicators, beginning in education under Mrs Thatcher's third Education Secretary, Kenneth Baker (1986–9). By introducing a national curriculum and starting to publish schools' performance tables, the Government began a nationalization of education that partly compensated for its failure to gain direct control over local authorities.

A defensible fiscal and monetary policy took longer. Monetarism did not work for a reason that ought to have warned both parties, and in a wider domain than monetary policy. 'Goodhart's Law' (Chrystal and Mizen, 2001), named after a former chief economist at the Bank of England, C.A.E. Goodhart, states, in the original formulation, that *Any observed statistical regularity will tend to collapse once pressure is placed upon it for control purposes.* Alternatively, *When a measure becomes a target, it ceases to be a valid measure.* Originally formulated in 1975, before government started to try controlling inflation by targeting the money supply, it proved prophetic. Whatever definition of money was targeted, money supply continued to grow under some different definition of 'money'. This has sobering lessons for the control of public service delivery by targeting.

The Conservatives' attempt to run macroeconomic policy by rules rather than discretion had a sound intellectual foundation – they had simply chosen the wrong sort of rule. Beginning in the late 1970s, economists had pointed out that Keynesian macroeconomics lacked a micro foundation (Kydland and Prescott, 1977; Barro and Gordon, 1983a). In the long run, these authors pointed out, a democratic government could not credibly commit itself to any particular monetary policy (or other economic policy such as incomes or labour market policy). The time horizon of a democratically elected government is at most five years. Therefore everybody knows that as it faces re-election the incumbent party is tempted to do whatever maximizes its probability of re-election. Keynesian demand management offers the incumbents the opportunity to let rip just before an election and to close down just after if re-elected (and, if not re-elected, the crash becomes someone else's problem). This is known as the *political business cycle*, and it has been around for two centuries. 'A Government is not supported a hundredth part so much by the constant, uniform, quiet prosperity of the country as by those damned spurts which Pitt used to have in the nick of time', as one Whig wrote to another in 1814 about the Tory William Pitt the Younger, the UK's longest-serving prime minister from 1784 to 1801 and 1802 to 1806. (Henry Brougham to Thomas Creevey, cited by Butler and Stokes, 1974, p. 369.)

But the political business cycle is incredible in the long run. Because economic observers understand that governments have attempted to manipulate the political business cycle since Pitt the Younger, their manipulations are incredible, however sincerely they profess (shortly after a general election) that they will not try to manipulate demand in a way that favours themselves (shortly before the next general election). The only stable solution is for a government to promise to be governed by 'rules rather than discretion' in Kydland and Prescott's title phrase. These rules must themselves be credible. We now know that the Treasury was recommending Bank of England independence as a credible-commitment device to Chancellor Lawson in 1988 (see Introduction), but the idea did not catch on in Mrs Thatcher's Premiership. The first credible monetary rule was the partial cession of control of monetary targets to the Bank of England subject to discussion with the chancellor (known under Prime Minister Major as the '[Chancellor] Ken [Clarke] and [Governor] Eddie [George]' Show). This was given a further impetus by the formal independence for the Bank of England announced within a week of the change of government in 1997 (Balls; Allsopp; Robson, all this volume). Finn Kydland and Edward Prescott were awarded the 2004 Nobel Prize in Economics. Their 1977 paper on rules and discretion features prominently in the Nobel committee's citation.[1] (See http:// nobelprize.org/economics/laureates/2004/ecoadv.pdf).

Restoring Labour's electability, 1983–92

But before Labour could change the path set by the Conservatives, they had first to get on to it. This required Labour to return to electability after the manifold disasters that led it to its worst defeat since 1931 in the General Election of 1983. (There are many accounts of these disas-ters, but see in particular Crewe and King 1995.) Under Neil Kinnock (leader, 1983–92) and John Smith (leader, 1992–94) Labour returned to electability, although it unexpectedly failed to win the 1992 General Election. Under Tony Blair (leader since 1994) Labour has returned not only to electability but to election, with landslide victories in 1997 and 2001 and a slimmer but still decisive victory in 2005. Tony Blair frequently repeats that 'we were elected as New Labour and will govern as New Labour'. To begin with, New Labour defined itself by what it was not – erecting under all three of these leaders a caricature of Old Labour. Kinnock as leader barely went on to sketch an alternative vision of what (New) Labour might be. Smith started to, but his efforts were cut short by his untimely death in 1994. Blair involved many writers, intellectuals, and think-tankers in defining the New Labour 'project' before May 1997, but after getting control of the real levers of government he turned to governing rather than theorizing about government. Nevertheless, in what follows we shall argue that it is possible to discern a 'new social democracy' developed under John Smith, and remaining as a strand in New Labour, and its most intellectually distinctive strand at that.

Dropping producerism and unilateralism

Neil Kinnock had to show that the Labour Party was no longer the captive of particular producer groups, and he had to back the party out of a blind alley into which its version of internationalism had led by 1983. In a way he was lucky in his internal enemies. The demands of the National Union of Mineworkers, whose leadership had launched a national strike without balloting their members, were as impossible for a Labour leader to support as had been their predecessors' in 1926. Therefore, although Kinnock faced the same cries of 'betraying the miners' as had Jimmy Thomas in 1926, in truth neither politician had a realistic choice. The defeat of the miners in 1985 was therefore a blessing in disguise for the Labour Party, though the disguise was so heavy that few saw it that way at the time. Kinnock also defeated the Trotskyite 'entryists' of the Militant Tendency (Crick, 1984). Entryism is the tactic of a clandestine organization (Communist or Trotskyist against Labour; fascist or racist against the Conservatives) taking control of party branches in order to take control of the party itself. In the early 1980s, members of the Militant Tendency (in reality members of a clandestine body called the Revolutionary Socialist League) controlled Liverpool and Lambeth councils. Their tactic of 'revolutionary defeatism' involved making the working class as miserable as possible prior to, and in order to bring forward, the revolution. Or, as Kinnock put it in his 1985 Labour Party conference speech attacking Militant: 'We have the grotesque spectacle of a Labour council – a *Labour* council – hiring taxis to scuttle round a city handing out redundancy notices to its own workers ... And then they talk of victory.'

Labour's 1983 manifesto – described by a marginalized Labour politician as 'the longest suicide note in history' – had promised an 'emergency programme of action' involving withdrawal from the European Union and unilateral nuclear disarmament, the latter 'to be completed within the lifetime of the Labour government'. Unilateralism had deep roots in the internationalist side of Old Labour, but had always been bitterly divisive. Since the UK had ceased to be a great power, the fundamental argument was the same as William Wilberforce had used for the unilateral abolition of the slave trade. Irrespective of what other nations did, the UK should set a moral example, both because it was right in itself and because it was hoped that others would follow. In 1957, however, the greatest figure on the Left of Old Labour, Aneurin Bevan, broke with his unilateralist followers, saying that their policy would send the UK's foreign secretary 'naked into the conference chamber ... And you call that statesmanship. I call it an emotional spasm'. Unilateralism tore Labour apart, and was very unpopular outside the Labour Party. The Conservative politician Michael Heseltine relabelled 'unilateralism' as 'one-sided disarmament'. Some thought this was a dirty trick. But 'one-sided' is the Anglo-Saxon for 'unilateral'.

To make Labour electable, Kinnock had to drop unilateralism, and tone down the producerism of the 1983 manifesto, which had promised import controls, a partnership with trade unions to 'take a view on what changes in costs and prices would be compatible with our economic and social objectives', and threatened to nationalize at least one High Street bank. Most of this had disappeared by the next manifesto in 1987. Labour made modest progress in that election, and its biggest threat – the SDP/Liberal Alliance – suffered a modest decline. In 1989 and 1990 it seemed as if the other parties would handily deliver the next General Election to Labour. The Alliance imploded around the obstinate personality of David Owen. The Conservatives forced out the equally obstinate Margaret Thatcher after the Poll Tax had been revealed as an expensive disaster. The safe but colourless John Major succeeded her, and unexpectedly won the 1992 General Election. Kinnock immediately resigned as Labour leader, to be succeeded, in an almost unanimous vote, by John Smith.

Smith was an egalitarian, pro-European, anti-unilateralist, anti-producerist, Scot. His internationalism took the form of being one of the 69 pro-EU Labour rebels who had followed Roy Jenkins in 1972 to vote in favour of EU entry against the Labour whip, thus outweighing the smaller number of Conservative anti-EU rebels and enacting UK membership. However, he was never tempted to follow Jenkins and the rest of the SDP 'Gang of Four' out of the Labour Party in 1980–81. Smith has been labelled as 'old Labour's last leader, an often eloquent champion of enduring values of equity and social justice that were no longer seen as very relevant to achieving electoral success' (Taylor, 2004). But Smith was not old Labour's last leader; he was New Labour's first (or maybe second). He initiated a distinctive strand in New Labour that we label 'new social democracy'. It shared some traits with the ideology of the Social Democratic Party that Smith refused to join. But in his gritty egalitarianism, he was remote from (most of) the SDP leaders. Asked what differentiated him from them, he 'concluded that it was that he felt at home with trade unionists and they did not' (Naughtie, 1994, p. 39).

Smith did not write much, for a party leader, before his sudden death in May 1994. His ideology has to be pieced together from Commons speeches and occasional journalism. As Shadow Chancellor (1987–92) and then as party leader he moved Labour away from its earlier producerism. He introduced 'one member one vote' (OMOV) for Labour Party internal elections, at the expense of both the unions and the militants. He dropped re-nationalization – ('we need both dynamic markets and active Governments ... Ownership is ... largely irrelevant' – 1993, quoted by Brown, 1994, p. 74). 'In an intelligently organised community', he had written earlier, 'prosperity and social justice mutually reinforce each other' (1987, quoted by ibid., p. 62). Social justice required a return to the 1944 Beveridge aim of full and stable employment. Enrich the (still in 1987) three million unemployed by getting them into work, and greater prosperity would accompany more social justice.

Smith's commitment to egalitarian taxation was held (by instant pundits who lacked his sense of social responsibility) to be the cause of Labour's defeat in 1992. He pointed out that the upper earnings limit on National Insurance contributions creates an anomaly in the UK income tax schedule, whereby both average and marginal rates of taxation go down as taxpayers move above that threshold. To the Conservatives and the tabloids he was therefore a 'tax-and-spend Shadow Chancellor'. It illustrates the old adage that the taxes that are the best economically are the worst politically. The anomaly remains.

Smith's Scots egalitarianism was most marked in education policy. In Ardrishaig, Argyll, where he grew up, 'there was no class-consciousness or divisions and there was a sense of unity about the place', he told Sue Lawley in 1991. He called Dunoon Grammar School, where he boarded for three years, 'a useful reminder that many state schools in Scotland have a prouder history than some more pretentious establishments in the so-called private sector' – an unmistakable dig at Fettes College, Edinburgh, the *alma mater* of his Shadow Cabinet colleague Tony Blair. 'I want to turn the whole of education in the world into the type of education I got' (Brown and Naughtie, 1994, at pp. 151, 121, 65 in that order). Smith's view of Scottish education was highly romanticized but emotionally powerful – for him as for many Scots.

New Labour under Blair and Brown

Smith's death left the two dominant figures of New Labour – Tony Blair and Gordon Brown – in harness. Blair became party leader and Brown continued as shadow chancellor. The Conservatives' reputation for economic competence had been destroyed in a day – 'Black Wednesday' in September 1992, when the pound had been forced out of the exchange rate mechanism of the European Monetary System (see Introduction). Even if the Major government had not been, as it was, torn apart between its Eurosceptic and Europhile wings, Labour always looked likely to win the next General Election, which was accordingly postponed until the last possible date in May 1997. Nevertheless, Blair and Brown, both first elected in 1983, both observers of Kinnock's fight against the hard left, were ultra-cautious. They were, willy-nilly, on the path set by Margaret Thatcher and there was to be no return to Old Labour. In 1994–5 Blair succeeded, where Hugh Gaitskell had failed in 1959, in getting the party to agree to the abolition of Clause IV of its constitution, viz., the commitment to 'public ownership of the means of production, distribution, and exchange'. But they could not merely redefine themselves by what New Labour was not. The search for a positive ideology for New Labour preoccupied its leaders during the remaining years in Opposition. It was part of the understanding between Blair and Brown when Blair became leader that Brown would have a free hand to develop economic policy. His macroeconomic policy is discussed elsewhere in this book (Balls; Allsopp, this volume). His microeconomic policy is discussed below.

In the remaining Conservative years, many groups of Labour sympathizers (or at least of Conservative non-sympathizers) offered possible agendas for New Labour. Three that, for a while, influenced Blair and those close to him were *Options for Britain* (Halpern *et al.*, 1996); *The State We're In* (Hutton, 1995); and *The Third Way* (Giddens, 1998).

Options for Britain emanated from a virtual, electronic, think-tank named Nexus, several of whose members went on to advise New Labour ministers in one capacity or another. Their manifesto for a New Labour government was partly procedural (policy needs to cross departments; needs a central capacity and better think-tanks; should work for whole of government, not emanate solely from No. 10 or the Treasury); partly substantive (Labour should spread opportunity and share risks; run a supply-side not a demand-side economic policy; (prophetically) it should offer income-contingent loans to fund students through higher education). The last of these was enacted, but with great pain, in 2004, by which time several of the *Options for Britain* authors were working for the government.

The State We're In was a surprise bestseller. Its acknowledgements page features several future New Labour movers and shakers. Will Hutton indicated his loyalties by its subtitle: *Why Keynesian Economics is best.* It was an eloquent attempt to persuade New Labour to move the UK from a liberal market economy to a coordinated market economy – equivalently, from Anglo-Saxon capitalism to Rhenish capitalism. Hutton called for an incoming government to facilitate bank rather than equity capital for industry; to rebuild industrial training; more generally to do as Germany did, and 'exploit the stakeholder culture engendered by co-operative capitalism' (Hutton, 1995, p. 301). He also deplored the UK's 'elective dictatorship' – a phrase famously coined by the leading Conservative Quintin Hogg (Lord Hailsham) when the Conservatives were out of government, but not repeated when he became a government minister. Likewise, Labour politicians were more in favour of checks and balances in 1995, when Hutton's book was published, than they proved to be on taking office in 1997.

The incoming Blair administration incorporated some of Halpern *et al.*'s contributors, but did not formally adopt their ideas. Hutton's work remained flavour of a few months but was soon dropped when the impracticality of moving the UK from an LME to a CME became clear. *The Third Way* lasted longer, at least as a slogan, where it was briefly copied by the German Social Democrats (*die neue Mitte*). But it was no more than a set of slogans:

- Socialism is dead.
- Neoliberalism is unacceptable.
- Therefore governments need a third way.
- Globalization exists.
- Many issues crosscut left and right.
- Lots of things need radical rethinking.
- Governments need to reduce social exclusion.

Giddens' wish-list was unexceptionable; but he had no concrete propos-als. If the programme for New Labour were to have any content, it would have to look elsewhere.

New social democracy – Smith and Brown

The mantle of new social democracy fell largely on Gordon Brown, as John Smith's successor in post as shadow chancellor. Brown's back-ground and values are very similar to Smith's. The highlights of Smith's policy had been his linking of social justice with increasing employment; his stern fiscal responsibility; and his commitment to constitutional reform. The last culminated after his death in the devolution settlement of 1998. It is of the first importance, but outwith the scope of this chapter. Apart from devolution, New Labour's constitutional innovations were haphazard and came into effect only late in the second term.

Brown came to office determined to demonstrate the fiscal responsi-bility of New Labour. This took many forms. One was his decision to keep public expenditure within the limits proposed by the outgoing Conservatives for two years. Others showed his careful reading of Kydland and Prescott. No government, according to them, can credibly promise not to distort monetary and fiscal policy. Whatever it says when first elected, everybody knows that when the next election looms it will be tempted to promise things that are good for the incumbents in the short term but bad for the country in the long term. Brown therefore gave the Monetary Policy Committee of the Bank of England complete control over monetary policy within a week of Labour's election victory in May 1997 – a move that had not been in the Labour Party manifesto. On the fiscal side, his credible commitment took the form of two public expenditure rules that he bound himself to follow: the 'Golden Rule' and the 'Sustainable Investment Rule'. Their official Treasury definitions are:

- *the 'Golden Rule'*: over the economic cycle, the government will borrow only to invest and not to fund current spending; and
- *the 'Sustainable Investment Rule'*: public sector net debt as a proportion of GDP will be held over the economic cycle at a stable and prudent level.[2] The 'stable and prudent level' is defined elsewhere on the Treasury website to be 'below 40 per cent of GDP in each and every year of the current economic cycle'.[3]

The phrase 'over the economic cycle' in both rules gives the chancellor of the day wriggle room, as did 'taking one year with another' in the requirement on nationalized industries to balance their books. However, up to the time of writing at least, both the monetary and the fiscal rules have proven to be credible commitments not to manipulate the economy in the short-term interest of the governing party. Accordingly, inflation has come down to, and stayed down at, the MPC's target level; and government has found it cheap to raise money because the markets find the two fiscal rules to be credible.

That macro stability, not achieved by any previous Labour government, has given the new social democrats of New Labour room to develop their social and microeconomic policy. As John Smith had observed, the two are linked. A social policy which gets people into work is good microeconomics, and *vice versa*. Gordon Brown has set out the microeconomics of new social democracy in his 'State and Market: Towards a Public Interest Test' (Brown, 2003). He makes his rejection of Old Labour clearest in talking about industrial policy. Old Labour, he says, believed that 'the state should replace market forces where they fail'; corporatists believed in 'supporting national champions (a policy I also reject)'. Rather, 'the best industrial policy for success in a global economy is to help markets work better' (Brown, 2003, p. 267). He goes on to describe his pro-competition policy as 'a break from a hundred years of Labour history' (p. 271; cf Klemperer, this volume). His argument for keeping health care public goes beyond Bevan and Beveridge. The market provision of health care fails because of asymmetric information and the classic insurance pathologies of adverse selection and moral hazard. 'So even if there are risks of state failure, there is a clear market failure' (p. 278). But to prevent the public interest being hijacked by producer interests, public services must be 'contestabl[e] by providers on the basis of cost and efficiency' (p. 279). How best to do this remains, itself, the most contestable ground of British politics. But these extracts suffice to show that the new social democracy differs radically from the old.

The past and future of new social democracy

If we made, say, R.H. Tawney and Richard Titmuss stand for 'old social democracy' and John Smith and Gordon Brown stand for 'new social democracy', what are their similarities and their differences?

Old and new are both egalitarian. In his youth Tawney noted that

> if men and women were equal in the sight of God, so they must be treated as of equal worth in their dealings with each other. Any social system which discriminated against some of its members, or which allowed some people to be used as a means to others' ends, or which

obscured common humanity by emphasizing the differences between people, was immoral. (Précis from Goldman, 2004)

Titmuss, arguing against means testing in the welfare services, said:

All collectively provided services are deliberately designed to meet certain socially recognized 'needs'... 'Needs' may therefore be thought of as 'social' and 'individual'. (Titmuss, 1963, p. 39)

The 'progressive universalism' of Smith and Brown is closer to this than to the union-oriented producerist tradition of Old Labour.

Egalitarians do not like gongs or fancy dress. Tawney and Titmuss both turned down the offer of a peerage. In 1933 Ramsay MacDonald (by this time regarded by Labour supporters as a traitor) offered Tawney a peerage. Tawney wrote back 'What harm have I ever done to the Labour Party?' Gordon Brown's refusal to wear a dinner jacket at the Lord Mayor's Banquet is utterly Tawneyite.

However, new social democracy diverges from the Tawney–Titmuss tradition in two main respects: it is not morally hostile to capitalism, and it countenances means-tested benefits. For Tawney, a search for increasing productivity was a disagreeable mark of 'the acquisitive society' (Tawney, 1921). Titmuss's great study *The Gift Relationship* (1970/1973) showed conclusively that a voluntary blood donation service with no payment to donors was more efficient as well as more equitable than market supply. To that extent, Brown's study of the state and the market is in the Titmuss tradition. But Titmuss went much too far for modern social democrats when he claimed to have 'dispute[d] ... the philistine resurrection of economic man in social policy' (Titmuss, 1973, p. 18). Actually, he had done something more subtle – more subtle than he realized himself. He had taken the tools of economic analysis and turned them against the conventional American economic view that market supply of anything – including blood – is more reliable and more efficient than voluntary supply.

For Smith and Brown, increasing productivity and GDP per head is necessary, although not sufficient, for achieving progressive universalism. Their attitude goes well with a Scottish Calvinist attitude to work (that Tawney well understood in his famous *Religion and the Rise of Capitalism*). 'Labour is a thing so good and godlike ... that makes the body hale and strong and cures the sicknesses produced by idleness ... In the things of this life, the labourer is most like to God' said Calvin's precursor Zwingli in 1525 (quoted in Tawney, 1922/1938, p. 123).

Hence their stress on increasing the economic activity rate of all sectors of the working-age population and all regions of the UK, as reflected in countless Treasury documents since 1997.

Another component of progressive universalism is substantial redistribution through the tax and benefit system. Here the new social democracy has a lot in common with the old, but one big difference. It was a tradition of old social democracy to be bitterly opposed to means-tested benefits. For this there were many rooted historical reasons – for instance, the Webbs' demands for flat-rate benefits in their Minority Report of the Poor Law Commission (1909) and the folk memory of 'the means-test man' intrusively asking whether unemployed people had any resources that would make them ineligible for benefits. In modern debate, old social democrats call for the basic state pension to be raised in line with earnings, and financed from general taxation. New social democrats retort that this would impose a substantial and growing tax burden, while making universal transfers to a class of people many of whom are not poor. Rather, the 1997 and 2001 Labour administrations have relied on widespread means-tested supplements in the guise of pension and tax credits, to guarantee a minimum income level for all pensioners. This departs from the Titmuss tradition, but is vulnerable to the criticism not only from Titmice but also from those who say that the regime weakens the incentives for relatively poor people in work to save, because the pensions they can earn through their savings are less than they would get without saving under the minimum income guarantee.

Nevertheless, many Labour and trade union activists regard the new social democracy as the most authentically Labour part of New Labour. But parts of the 1997–2001 governments' economic policy seem very remote from Old Labour traditions. Among these are the provision of infrastructure through the Private Finance Initiative and New Labour's robust support of global free trade. In this respect the previous Labour figure closest to New Labour was perhaps Philip Snowden, Labour Chancellor of the Exchequer in 1924 and 1929–31, until he defected with MacDonald, although he and MacDonald had come to detest each other.

Opportunities and threats

If New Labour were a brand of leisure clothing, its marketing consultants would be analysing (for a substantial fee) its strengths, weaknesses, opportunities, and threats. Its greatest strength is to have moved in only 14 years from unelectability to electoral hegemony. It has successfully shifted its focus from the interests of producers (i.e., of some people) to those of consumers (i.e., of everybody). It has preserved the egalitarianism and internationalism of Old Labour, while dropping its producerism.

Nevertheless, New Labour faces threats. Any government must carry the median voter. The median voter frequently tells pollsters that she prefers the bundle of tax and services she gets over paying less tax and getting fewer services. The massive increase of public spending on public services in the Spending Reviews carried out in 2000, 2002, and 2004 should do Labour no harm. But if she believes that public services are not improving, New Labour may be in trouble. People willing to accept that their own school and hospital have got better may yet believe that education and health services have got worse.

Labour has successfully depoliticized both monetary and fiscal policy (Balls, this volume). The old tools of demand management through government manipulation of interest rates and tax and spending measures were not credible. The new ones are, so that inflation seems to have been conquered. But the 'Golden Rule' and the 'Sustainable Investment Rule' may prove hard taskmasters as the UK population ages, and a smaller proportion of people of working age have to support a larger proportion of people past working age. A future government (of any party) may have to raise taxes, perhaps substantially, if it is to satisfy both the fiscal rules and people's expectations.

One of the most difficult areas for new social democracy is securing value for money in public services. About a quarter of the UK's public expenditure goes on services delivered by elected local authorities. A further sixth is delivered by unelected local public bodies – in particular local health trusts (Primary Care Trusts in current jargon, although labels and titles change rapidly). In both cases it is hard for central government to exercise quality control. The New Labour brand has to be sold through myriad local stores that head office does not control. The UK's system of local taxation is in a mess, which an official inquiry (the Balance of Funding Review, 2003–04) failed to unravel, and a further inquiry is sitting as I write.

As noted above, New Labour took over the idea of a culture of inspection from the outgoing Conservatives, and has substantially expanded its scope. All local authorities in England (but not in the rest of the UK, where policy is for the devolved administrations) are subject to 'comprehensive performance assessment', where each of their main services is inspected and the results aggregated to a score on a five-point scale from *Poor* to *Excellent*. English health authorities, likewise, are graded on a scale from zero to three stars. There are bound to be considerable doubts about both the reliability and the validity of these scores. A score is *reliable* if an identical performance will always yield an identical score. It is *valid* if it correctly measures what it purports to measure. As the scores for health authorities in particular have fluctuated very rapidly, their reliability is in doubt. As to validity, we are back with Goodhart's Law: *When a measure becomes a target, it ceases to be a valid measure.* Public service managers know what their targets are. Therefore it is rational for them to concentrate on achieving their targets. Services that are not the subjects of targets will tend to be neglected, and managers are tempted to gamesmanship and even fraud in their attempts to show that they have met their targets.

Nevertheless, the new social democracy has provided New Labour with a robust ideology unavailable to any Labour government before 1997. Unlike the vacuous 'Third Way' it has real content. Unlike earlier Labour ideologies, it accepts that Britain cannot be moved bodily from being an LME to being a CME. It preserves an egalitarian distrust of hierarchy that goes right back to Adam Smith (and maybe even to John Knox). Most important of all, it has accepted that the discretion that politicians used to have to intervene in monetary and fiscal policy was not in their own interest, nor in the nation's. By making the British state weaker, John Smith, Gordon Brown, and their advisers, have paradoxically made it stronger – able to do less, better.

Notes

1 See http://nobelprize.org/economics/laureates/2004/ecoadv.pdf.
2 Source: http://www.hm-treasury.gov.uk./Documents/UK_Economy/Fiscal_
   Policy/ukecon_fisc_index.cfm.
3 Source: http://www.hm-treasury.gov.uk./media/CAE/16/Convergence_
   Programme2003.pdf, p. 3.

6
Stability, Growth, and Labour's Macroeconomic Policy

Ed Balls

Introduction

For Britain in 1997, after the boom–bust economic cycles of the previous twenty or so years, a change of government from Conservative to Labour provided a unique opportunity to learn the lessons of Britain's postwar economic history and establish a modern, pro-stability but post-monetarist macroeconomic framework that responded to the challenges of the global economy.

In this chapter, I want to set out the principles that underpin our approach to both monetary and fiscal policy in the UK, the lessons we have learned in operating fiscal policy in our new fiscal regime and assess its performance so far. I will then show how these principles are relevant first to the debate about the role that UK fiscal policy could play in delivering stability and growth were the UK to join the euro, and second to the ongoing debate about reform of the Stability and Growth Pact.

In establishing our new macroeconomic framework, we knew we had to reject a purely discretionary reliance upon government fine-tuning of the macroeconomy based on an assumed long-term trade-off between unemployment and inflation which had collapsed intellectually and empirically.

And we knew that we needed a credible framework which solved what economists call the problem of 'time-inconsistency' – the temptation to make a dash for short-term growth at the expense of long-term stability.

But in the search for credibility we also had to learn from the failure of monetarism as a macroeconomic doctrine – both domestic monetarism and Europe monetarism in the form of the pre-1993 ERM. Its failure was not its rejection of old-style fine-tuning or its desire to achieve long-term credibility in policy making but its inflexibility in prioritizing low money supply growth as the route to low inflation and growth just at the time when the apparently stable relationship between the growth of the money supply and inflation broke down as capital markets were opened up.

Following Britain's exit from the ERM the government of the day did take some tentative steps in the direction of a more credible regime for monetary policy: the shift to inflation targeting and publication of minutes of a monthly discussion between the Chancellor and the Governor. But that did not constitute a credible and sustainable approach.

Decision making remained highly personalized, the inflation target was ambiguous and deflationary and – as the Treasury concluded in its recent assessment of the old and new systems – 'policy-makers operated behind closed doors and decisions were often made with little or no explanation'. Most problematic, the suspicion remained that policy was being manipulated for short-term motives.

In fiscal policy, if anything, the flaws were greater still in the 1980s and persisted into the 1990s – as set out in the Treasury 1997 paper 'Fiscal Policy: Learning the Lessons from the Last Economic Cycle':

- Fiscal policy objectives were not well specified, and changed frequently. Between the early 1980s and the mid-1990s, at least eight different fiscal policy objectives can be identified – roughly one every two years.
- Even when objectives persisted for some time, they were vague, for example 'back towards balance over medium term'. This continual change and vague nature undermined the credibility of fiscal policy.
- Reporting requirements on government were much more limited, making it more difficult to judge the performance of fiscal policy. This allowed the government to take an incautious approach to the cyclical position of the economy in late 1980s – at a time when the government's view of the output gap was kept secret – leading to errors in the conduct of fiscal policy. This misjudgment arose, in part, because the underlying trend rate of growth of the economy was overstated.

That is why in 1997 we set out to establish a new British macroeconomic framework which could meet three central objectives:

First, Credibility. We needed a policy framework in which the government's commitment to long-term stability – low inflation and sound public finances – commanded trust from the public, business and markets.

Secondly, Flexibility. We needed a framework within which policy makers could take early and forward-looking action in monetary and fiscal policy in the face of the ups and downs of the economic cycle without jeopardizing the credibility of the government's long-term goals.

And thirdly, Legitimacy. The new framework had to be capable of rebuilding and entrenching public support and establishing a new cross-party political and parliamentary consensus for long-term stability – a new consensus about goals and a new consensus about the institutional arrangements needed to deliver those goals.

The new post-monetarist model of macroeconomic policymaking we have put in place to meet these objectives is based on 'constrained discretion'. It is an approach which recognises that the *discretion* necessary for effective economic policy – short-term flexibility to meet credible long-term goals – is possible only within an institutional framework that commands market credibility and public trust with the government *constrained* to deliver clearly defined long-term policy objectives and with maximum openness and transparency.

Central banks cannot cut interest rates in the face of weakening global demand if they face accelerating inflation and have to worry about undermining the credibility of their commitment to their inflation target. Governments cannot use fiscal policy to support growth in a downturn – through automatic stabilizers or discretionary changes – if they already have unsustainable levels of debt. Short-term flexibility and discretion is only possible where policy is credibly constrained to deliver long-term stability.

So to make this constrained discretion model of macroeconomic policy operational, we established three principles for sound policy making:

- Clear and well-defined long-term policy objectives;
- Pre-commitment to sound institutional arrangements which could allow credible and flexible policy responses in the face of shocks;
- and maximum transparency.

Maximal transparency is, in my view, a critical part of the new model. Because combining long-term credibility *and* short-term constrained discretion to respond to shocks is only possible if policy makers are seen in practice to be genuinely pre-committed to delivering long-term stability and take the time to build a track record for doing so.

The new UK monetary framework

Our first task in 1997 was to apply these 'constrained discretion' principles to monetary policy and establish a new model of central bank

independence. That new British model has the following features:
First, sound long-term objectives:

- a single symmetric inflation target: with no ambiguity about the inflation target, no deflationary bias and no dual targeting of inflation and the short-term exchange rate;

Secondly pre-commitment to credible institutional arrangements:

- a strategic division of responsibilities: with the elected government setting the wider economic strategy and the objectives for monetary policy, while monthly decisions are passed over to the central bank, thereby pre-committing the government to long-term stability and the Bank to a pre-emptive and forward-looking approach to making policy;
- monthly decisions to meet the government's inflation target taken monthly by an independent Monetary Policy Committee made up of the Governor, four Bank executives and four outside experts appointed directly by the Chancellor and with a non-voting Treasury observer present for all meetings;
- and built-in flexibility: with the Open Letter system to allow the necessary flexibility so that policy can respond in the short-term to surprise economic events without jeopardizing long-term goals and proper procedures to ensure coordination between monetary and fiscal policy;

Thirdly maximum transparency:

- with, in addition to the Open Letter system, monthly minutes published and individual votes attributed and with a strengthened role for parliament – so that the public and markets can see that decisions were being taken for sound long-term reasons and in order to support the government's wider objectives for living standards and employment.

This division of responsibility between the Treasury and the Bank of England – with the Chancellor responsible for what Governor Eddie George labelled in his 1997 Mais lecture the 'political decision' of setting the target and the MPC responsible for the 'technical decision' of achieving it – was a clear change from the normal model of central bank independence. The Federal Reserve, Bundesbank and the ECB are all 'goal-independent' – charged in legislation with delivering price stability, but also responsible for defining the precise target for policy as well as making monthly decisions to meet that target.

Why did we opt for operational independence? Partly, so that the Chancellor could introduce a new and non-deflationary inflation target. But also to strengthen the legitimacy of the unelected MPC in making monthly interest rate decisions by emphasizing that its pursuit of stability was an important part of the government's wider economic strategy to deliver high and stable growth and employment, as Mervyn King explained in 1999. The rejection of the old-style fine-tuning means recognising that there is no long-term gain to be had either from trying to trade higher inflation for more output or jobs or lower inflation at the cost of output and jobs.

Some feared that this would lead to a less credible central bank. And it is, of course, entirely open to the government of the day to set a higher target for inflation, indeed – with the support of Parliament – to suspend or even reverse independence entirely. But in the absence of a long-term trade-off between higher inflation and higher unemployment, there would be nothing to gain and everything to lose from setting a weaker target.

Far from being a weakening of independence or a failure to be bold, I believe that our decision to have the government set the target was, in fact, a more radical approach which strengthened the independence of the central bank. For having set the target for the central bank, it is very hard for the government to question the decisions of the MPC. To doubt their decisions is either to imply that the target is wrong, which is not their fault, or doubt their expertise, which is hard for the government to do, especially if it has appointed the experts itself. Instead, the incentive for the government of the day is publicly to back the MPC's decisions. And from the central bank's point of view, as well as having the government firmly alongside it in making sometimes controversial decisions, it is able to spend its time each month debating how best to meet the inflation target rather than debating and disagreeing over what price stability should mean in practice.

At no time has the government ever cast any doubt about the wisdom of the MPC's individual decisions. Indeed, while backing their strategy in public speeches, Chancellor Gordon Brown has been careful to avoid ever commenting on individual decisions – although the Treasury publicly reviews the MPC's performance against the target. As Eddie George said in that 1997 lecture, this division of responsibilities 'helps to ensure that the Government and the Bank are separately accountable for their respective roles in the monetary policy process'.

The second reason why we wanted the government to set the target was so that we could move from an asymmetric to a single symmetric inflation target. And that we did in June 1997, changing from the ambiguously defined inflation target we inherited of 2.5 per cent or less to a clearly and symmetrically defined inflation target of 2.5 per cent. A stable and symmetric target is the best guarantee of a pro-stability and pro-growth policy. It requires that deviations below target are taken as seriously as above – removing the old deflationary bias of the '2.5 per cent or less' target which makes 2 per cent better than 2.5 per cent and 1 per cent better than 2 per cent, regardless of the impact on output and jobs. It is the key innovation in the new model which ensures that monetary policy supports the government's goals for high and stable levels of growth and employment.

As the Governor of the Bank of England, Eddie George, said to the TUC Congress in September 1998: 'The inflation target we have been set is symmetrical. A significant, sustained, fall below 2½ per cent is to be regarded just as seriously as a significant, sustained, rise above it. And I give you my assurance that we will be just as rigorous in cutting interest rates if the overall evidence begins to point to our undershooting the target as we have been in raising them when the balance of risks was on the upside.'

In our internal discussion at the Treasury in the Spring of 1997, some feared that dropping the aspiration to lower inflation than 2.5 per cent would damage the credibility of UK monetary policy. However, a symmetric target gives much greater clarity – making it more straightforward for the MPC to justify publicly its decisions and be held to account for its record. And it has ensured that the MPC takes a forward-looking, as well as symmetric, view of the risks to the British economy. If inflation is forecast to fall below 2.5 per cent the MPC does not wait to see how far it will fall but instead responds to get inflation back to target.

The setting of the symmetric target, by the government, as the sole target for monetary policy, with the Treasury also responsible for exchange rate policy and intervention, has also removed any suspicion that the government might be trying to target the exchange rate as well as inflation. For in an open economy like Britain, with open capital markets, successfully trying to run dual targets for inflation and the exchange rate is flawed in theory and has proved destabilizing in practice. Britain's economic history suggests that trying to deliver a exchange rate target can only be achieved at the expense of wider instability – in inflation and the wider manufacturing and service sectors.

There is no doubt that the high levels of Sterling caused serious difficulties for exporters and manufacturers. But any short-term attempt to manipulate the exchange rate, overtly or covertly, would have put both the inflation target and – as in the late 1980s – wider stability at risk. The objective of UK monetary policy was and remains clear and unambiguous – then to meet a symmetric inflation target of 2.5 per cent, now 2 per cent on the common European harmonized basis. The government's objective for the exchange rate was and is a stable and competitive pound in the medium term. But there is no short-term exchange rate target competing with the inflation target.

The role of the Chancellor in appointing the four outside members of the MPC was, in my view, part of the delicate constitutional balance we were striking in moving to a legitimate model of central independence consistent with ministerial accountability to Parliament. Some, I am sure, doubted whether our commitment to appoint genuine and independent experts was real. The quality and independence of all the appointments speak for themselves. Importantly, they have demonstrated that it is perfectly acceptable and desirable for independent experts to disagree in public over difficult monetary policy judgements. Should the outside appointments have had longer terms than three years or, as Willem Buiter argued, serve only one term? Perhaps; although, over the first four years of the MPC's life, it would have made no difference. It is hard enough to get experts to commit to leave their posts for three years. And no issue of appointment or re-appointment has been influenced in any way by past voting behaviour.

This new British model also has a built-in flexibility to allow the MPC to respond flexibly in the face of economic shocks and to allow an effective coordination of monetary and fiscal policy. The Open Letter system is, I believe, one of the most important innovations within the 1997 model of Bank independence: if inflation goes more than one percentage point either side of 2.5 per cent, the Governor is required to write to the Chancellor, on behalf of the MPC, explaining why it has happened, what the MPC has done about it, how long it will take for inflation to come back to target and how the MPC's response is consistent with the government's economic objectives – both for price stability and for high and stable levels of growth and employment.

The Open Letter system has not yet been used, confounding the fears of some that it would be used many times. I believe its importance has not been properly understood. Some have assumed it exists for the Chancellor to discipline the MPC if inflation goes outside the target range. In fact the opposite is true. In the face of a supply shock, such as a big jump in the oil price, which pushed inflation way off target, the MPC could only get inflation back to 2.5 per cent quickly through a draconian interest rate response – at the expense of stability, growth and jobs. Any sensible monetary policy maker would want a more measured and stability-oriented strategy to get inflation back to target. And the Open Letter system both allows that more sensible approach to be explained by the MPC and allows the Chancellor publicly to endorse it. In this way, transparency and accountability have the potential to make it easier for the MPC to be flexible when necessary without risking its long-term credibility.

Nor has the new system led to a less flexible approach to the coordination of fiscal and monetary policy. In fact, monetary and fiscal policy are much more coordinated now than they ever were when the sole decision maker was the Chancellor for both interest rates and fiscal policy. Partly because the Treasury representative explains the fiscal strategy to the MPC regularly, and in particular at the meeting before each Budget, on the basis of clearly defined fiscal rules set over the economic cycle. But more importantly the MPC is free – in a transparent way – to respond with interest rates to fiscal policy. So, in preparing the Budget, the Treasury knows that it will be judged both in terms of its medium-term fiscal rules and what the MPC does and says in its minutes about fiscal policy. There is no way, as in the past, that the chancellor can reward him or herself with an interest rate cut the day after the Budget as happened on numerous occasions in the past.

Central to the discussion of each of these reforms is maximum transparency and accountability. The transparency in published voting records has done much to deepen public understanding of the nature of monetary decisions. The fact that independent experts, publicly accountable as individuals for the decisions, are seen to change their minds when the evidence changes has deepened legitimacy but also demonstrates that the MPC's flexibility and forward-looking approach is in pursuit of a credible commitment to the inflation. This innovation, with the minutes now published two weeks after the meeting – consistent with the within-6-week formulation of the legislation – has contributed greatly to a much more mature debate in Britain about genuinely difficult monthly decisions.

Some have argued that the particular arguments and views in the minutes should be attributed. From the outside, this seems to me mistaken. The strength of the meeting at present is that there is a genuinely open debate which the minutes reflect but which allow MPC members to be persuaded by argument. Attributing argument to individuals would quickly lead to members reading prepared texts in the minutes at the expense of flexibility in decision making and the genuinely deliberative nature of the meeting in which people can change their minds and be influenced by the debate.

The minutes are the most important of an array of transparency and accountability reforms. There is also the quarterly Inflation Report, and press conference, the role for the Treasury committee in cross-examining the MPC, the role of the non-executive directors in scrutinizing, monetary policy arrangements, the annual report and parliamentary debate. As the Treasury Select Committee concluded in its report on Bank of England accountability in July 1998: 'We agree with the conclusion by the Organisation for Economic Co-operation and Development (OECD) in its country survey of the UK that "In international comparisons the United Kingdom's framework is among the strongest in terms of accountability and transparency" ' (House of Commons Treasury Committee 1997–8, para. 6).

The new UK fiscal framework – principles

Eight years on from Bank independence, it is clear that the legitimacy of the UK's new monetary regime has been established with cross-party support. It would be premature to reach the same conclusion in fiscal policy. Since 1997 monetary policy has played the primary stabilization role. Fiscal policy has been primarily medium-term in its orientation. But, for a government seeking to establish credibility, promote economic stability and embark upon on a sustained period of investment in public services, achieving both credibility and flexibility in fiscal policy was equally important. In our reforms to the macro-fiscal policy regime, introduced in 1997 and 1998, we have sought to apply the very same 'constrained discretion' principles that we have applied in monetary policy.

First, sound long-term objectives:

The fiscal counterpart to the symmetric inflation target is the government's two fiscal rules adopted in 1997:

- the Golden Rule, that we shall borrow only to invest over the economic cycle;
- and the Sustainable Investment Rule, that net debt as a proportion of GDP will be kept at a low and stable level over the economic cycle.

These two fiscal rules:

- focus on fiscal sustainability because the Sustainable Investment Rule ensures that while borrowing for capital investment is permitted over the economic cycle, this borrowing does not affect the long-term sustainability of the public finances. We are committed to maintain net debt below 40 per cent of GDP in each year of the economic cycle. But unlike a balanced budget rule, the sustainable investment rule implies a stable rather than a falling debt-GDP ratio;

- focus on intergenerational equity by permitting borrowing for long-term investment, that benefits future generations, but not for consumption – thereby removing the old bias against capital investment;
- take account of the cycle in a symmetric way, allowing – subject to meeting the rules over the cycle – the fiscal balances to vary between years in accordance with the cyclical position of the economy. This means that the government can allow the automatic stabilizers to work in full, and where appropriate use discretionary fiscal policy, so that fiscal policy can support monetary policy in maintaining macroeconomic stability;
- but, unlike monetary policy, the rules are deliberately asymmetric because of deliberately cautious assumptions about, for example, the trend rate of growth. Using cautious assumptions for our key forecast variables, and stress testing our projections against a cautious case of lower trend growth has built a margin against uncertainty.

Some economists have argued that a better way than the golden rule to measure intergenerational fairness would be through a balance sheet approach, monitoring indicators such as net worth. This would provide a more complete picture of the government's finances, looking at assets as well as current and future liabilities. But the current National Accounts measure of net worth is not used in the fiscal framework because of difficulties accurately measuring the government's assets. And while innovations such as Whole of Government Accounts will offer better quality data, there are many technical and methodological issues that still need to be addressed. Experience with other countries has shown problems with a balance sheet or net worth approach to fiscal policy.

A significant advantage of the golden rule is that it is a clear rule based on widely accepted and internationally agreed accounting principles. We define capital spending based on the internationally agreed definition of general government net fixed capital formation to avoid any accusation that we take a deliberately elastic approach to capital. And, we know from previous experience, that it is a lack of clear rules and objectives that poses one of the greatest threats to credibility.

But we also try to analyse more comprehensive – and complex – indicators of the long-term fiscal position and intergenerational fairness. The government's Long-Term Public Finance Report sets down a comprehensive analysis of long-term economic and demographic developments and their impact on the public finances. This includes a variety of indicators, including measures of intergenerational fairness. These indicators show, on a basis of reasonable assumptions, that the UK public finances are sustainable in the longer term and are relatively well placed compared to other countries to meet the challenges of an ageing population.

Some commentators have argued that published borrowing and debt figures understate the level of true liabilities as they ignore expenditure under the Private Finance Initiative. But the total capital value of all PFI deals amounts to only 3 per cent of GDP, and all PFI deals are subject to independent audit against independent accounting standards and are reflected in public sector accounts accordingly. Today almost 60 per cent of total capital investment under signed PFI contracts is already scored on the public sector balance sheet – including the London Underground PFI contracts – and is reflected in the figures for public sector net investment and public sector net borrowing.

The second principle is pre-commitment to credible institutional arrangements:

One option we considered and rejected would have been to replicate the MPC with an independent fiscal committee. The wider political complexity of fiscal policy making – the different impacts that the different levers have on a range of different objectives of which stabilisation is only one – would have implied a politically unsustainable break with UK parliamentary tradition.

Instead, the fiscal counterpart to Bank of England independence is the Code for Fiscal Stability. This code – given legal backing in the 1998 Finance Bill – is designed to enhance the credibility and transparency of fiscal policy. It requires:

- clearly stated objectives and rules for fiscal policy;
- independent audit of key assumptions; and
- regular and open reporting of fiscal issues.

Third, maximum transparency:

The government has, through the Code for Fiscal Stability, and further developments made substantial progress in improving the information available on fiscal prospects. This includes:

- publishing full five-year-ahead forecasts for the public finances – including cyclically-adjusted fiscal aggregates and performance against the fiscal rules;
- twice-yearly setting out the economic and other assumptions under-pinning the public finance projections;
- publishing the government's estimates of the output gap and cyclically adjusted fiscal aggregates so that progress against the fiscal rules can be assessed across the economic cycle;
- ensuring that key assumptions are subject to independent audit by the National Audit Office; and
- publishing full and complete information on the fiscal outturns in the End of Year Fiscal Report and a thorough analysis of the long-term fiscal projections covering the next 50 years in the Long-Term Public Finance Report.

While it is clear that decisions are still a matter for the chancellor and the government, the purpose of the Code is, by combining clear rules, clear procedures and enhanced transparency, to achieve a much greater and more systematic scrutiny of fiscal policy than had been achieved before.

The new UK macroeconomic framework – practice to date

As in monetary policy, so in fiscal policy it is against the three objectives for modern macroeconomic policy making – credibility, flexibility, and legitimacy – that the new system must be judged.

With reforms to Bank independence and the fiscal regime, Britain has – I believe – made a decisive step forward to a credible model of macroeconomic policy making in Britain. And today there is a near-universal support for independence. Back then it was seen as a rather risky step. Many eminent columnists were understandably sceptical given the Bank's history. And, of course, the Conservative Party opposed the change.

The day that we announced Bank independence changed British economic policy in some unexpected ways. As Bill Keegan writes in *The Prudence of Mr Gordon Brown* (2003, p. 193), bank independence removed at a stroke one of the main sources of policy tension between No. 10 and No. 11 Downing Street which caused so much grief for Ken Clarke and Nigel Lawson.

And far from weakening the ability of the Treasury to ensure public spending discipline, the risk that the MPC might respond with a rise in interest rates has proved a useful and effective deterrent to profligate departmental proposals on more than occasion. Fiscal policy has supported monetary policy throughout this economic cycle – far more so than in previous decades.

At the same time, bank independence has freed up Gordon Brown to spend much of his time pursuing the goals that this Labour government was elected to deliver – full employment, tackling child and pensioner poverty, reforming and investing in public services, tackling global injustice.

Yet it has been the MPC's deliberately forward-looking and pre-emptive approach to setting interest rates that, I believe, explains why central bank independence has been an economic policy success since 1997.

The Monetary Policy Committee's first big test came in the autumn of 1998 when the Asian and Russian financial crises, followed by the LTCM Wall Street hedge fund scare, sent world financial markets into a tailspin. The Bank of England responded by cutting interest rates month after month to prevent a UK slowdown and sustain growth.

Later, following the US slowdown in 2000 and the collapse in global trade growth, the Monetary Policy Committee again cut interest rates nine times. While the US, Japan, Germany and France all suffered recessions, the UK continued to grow with employment rising and consumer confidence robust.

Why was the MPC able to act in such a decisive manner? Partly because of the explicitly symmetric inflation target of 2.5 per cent. This symmetry has removed for Britain the deflationary bias which has characterized some other independent central banks.

The other key ingredient is the flexibility and discretion that the constraint of operational independence has allowed. Because as *Guardian* Economics Editor Larry Elliott has written, 'voters no longer assume – fairly or not – that the government will play politics with interest rates and screw up the economy as a result'.

This is a rather more subtle point than it first appears. There is no doubt that, pre-1997, there was a tendency to play politics with interest rates, evidenced by the fact that interest rates were often cut on Budget day or the day after. But the case for independence is not simply that it stops venal policy makers from deliberately manipulating interest rates to fit an electoral timetable.

Imagine back in 1998 if a chancellor of the Exchequer had tried to take a similarly forward-looking and pre-emptive approach to setting interest rates and embarked – rightly – on a series of consecutive monthly rate cuts. After the second cut, the political process would be shouting 'panic' and the old 1970s newsreel dusted off. By the time of the third cut, a full-scale political crisis – and probably a sterling crisis – would have been under way.

No wonder that, pre-1997, the temptation for chancellors and Bank of England governors was not to be forward-looking and pre-emptive but to wait and see in the hope that something would turn up. Yet it was this inflexibility and delay that led repeatedly to sharper rises in interest rates to try to bring inflation back under control and then deeper rates cuts too late as the economy slipped into recession.

Since 1997, with interest rate decisions to meet the politically determined inflation target now in the hands of a group of technical experts, regular pre-emptive rate cuts have twice proved not destabilizing but stabilizing – and showed that central bank independence based on constrained discretion can be both pro-stability and pro-growth.

Less appreciated is how the new fiscal framework has radically changed the way in which UK fiscal policy operates and helped to reduce domestic macroeconomic volatility.

Pre-1997, the consequence of allowing the fiscal objectives to change from year to year was that tax and spending decisions could be made in isolation from each other with the published fiscal balance the residual in the fiscal policy-making process. The issue of what the rules and the framework should be effectively became a choice variable within the annual Budget decision process.

It is striking how, by committing to keep to the same fiscal rules year on year – now the longest period of stability in the fiscal regime in the postwar period – the fiscal rules and the Code for Stability have established a new paradigm in which fiscal policy is made, scrutinized and assessed. Whether the government is on track to meet its fiscal rules has become the key test of the credibility and sustainability of fiscal policy making.

The result is that macro-fiscal policy and the fiscal rules are now central to the Budget-making process.

Internally at the Treasury tax and spending decisions now have to be taken together to ensure that the fiscal rules are met. And the Government's semi-annual fiscal forecast is now as important to the Treasury's fiscal policy-making process as the Bank of England's quarterly inflation forecast is to monetary policy. Both fiscal and monetary policy are now subject to a high degree of public scrutiny, whether it be publishing minutes of the MPC's meetings or the open way in which assumptions underpinning the fiscal projections are independently audited and forecasts debated.

From the outset in 1997 the government has acted to ensure that its fiscal rules will be met. The two-year public spending freeze, tax decisions taken in 1997 and 1998 and, in particular, the decision to use the proceeds from the 3G mobile auction – £22 billion – to repay debt – all helped to establish the credibility of the government's commitment to meeting the fiscal rules – and to strengthening the fiscal position and cutting net debt to a lower level than any other G7 country.

Over the period 1996–97 to 2000–01, the fiscal stance was tightened by nearly 4 per cent of GDP. This contrasts with previous periods when the economy moved above trend. Between 1985–86 and 1990–91, the fiscal stance was loosened by nearly 2.5 per cent of GDP; and between 1971–72 and 1974–75 the fiscal stance was loosened by over 7 per cent of GDP. Having the key assumptions that underpin our fiscal projections independently audited combined with comprehensive and transparent fiscal reporting and thorough parliamentary scrutiny has helped to ensure that the government's forecasts remained cautious and prudent. Even though during the recent global downturn net borrowing has overshot the government's fiscal forecasts, as has happened to governments all round the world, the Treasury's forecasting record shows that since 1997, our forecasts for the public finances have been on average cautious – and more cautious than in the past. The 2003 End-Year Fiscal Report examined the differences between forecasts and for borrowing and outturn for the 15 EU countries over the last five years. It showed that the UK has tended to be one of the most cautious forecasters, overestimating the level of borrowing by 0.7 per cent of GDP on average. In fact the UK has been the third most cautious forecaster in the EU with only Finland and Luxembourg tending to overestimate borrowing by more (HM Treasury, 2003, Table 2.9).

Some commentators have argued during our first Parliament that it was a mistake during the above-trend phase of the cycle for the Treasury, using cautious assumptions, to deliberately over achieve its fiscal rules. But the reason for building up a margin for error in the early phase of the economic cycle was precisely to guard against an asymmetric fiscal cycle and the kind of upward revision to borrowing that the UK – like other countries – has seen over recent years. The fact that we are on track to meet the golden rule is a direct consequence of the deliberately cautious approach we have taken.

The scrutiny of the Bank of England's Monetary Policy Committee has also helped establish the credibility of the government's commitment to meeting the fiscal rules. Some in 1997 feared that Bank independence would lead to less coordination of fiscal and monetary policy. In fact, monetary and fiscal policy are much more coordinated now than they ever were when the sole decision maker was the Chancellor for both interest rates and fiscal policy.

This is partly because, as stated above, the Treasury representative explains the fiscal strategy to the MPC regularly, and in particular at the meeting before each Budget, on the basis of clearly defined fiscal rules set over the economic cycle. But more importantly the MPC is free – in a transparent way – to respond with interest rates to fiscal policy. As a result of these monetary and fiscal reforms, long-term interest rates – the simplest measure of monetary and fiscal policy credibility – are around their lowest levels since the 1960s. At the same time, inflation expectations in the financial markets 10 years ahead have averaged around 2.5 per cent since May 1997 compared to 4.6 per cent in the period between October 1992 and May 1997.

This greater credibility is laying to rest the myth that a left-of-centre government, with ambitions for full employment, to cut poverty and to deliver sustained investment in public services, cannot run a successful and prudent long-term economic policy.

But the credibility that the government has built up through these new arrangements in fiscal and monetary policy and its track record for economic management has also allowed it to respond flexibly to unexpected global events.

It has been possible to allow the automatic stabilizers to work in full and for fiscal policy to play its full part in supporting monetary policy during a period of below-trend growth, while maintaining sound public finances. With debt low, in recent years fiscal policy has been able to support monetary policy during a period of below-trend growth and help ensure Britain avoided the recession that hit many other countries.

By contrast, in both the early 1980s and early to mid-1990s, the fiscal stance had to be tightened when the economy was below trend.

Seven years on from Bank independence, is clear that the legitimacy of the UK's new monetary regime has been established with cross-party support. It would be premature to reach the same conclusion in fiscal policy. But progress has been made – and the combination of the Code and the transparency of the system mean that it would now be very difficult for any government to drop the current fiscal rules without a credible alternative.

The high level of transparency in the UK's fiscal framework has also attracted growing support. The IMF has 'welcomed the high standards of transparency in fiscal policy'. These features of the framework have helped to build a consensus that openness and transparency are essential features of a credible fiscal framework.

Some argue that we would have established greater credibility and legitimacy if we had gone further in institutional reform – by getting independent experts, if not to set the fiscal policy stance, at least to give a public view or date the economic cycle.

I am not sure, myself, whether in practice such changes would have made any difference. It is hard to see how public scrutiny or commentary could have been more intense over the past few years. And I have always also been sceptical about the role of government-sanctioned public commentators. Some people may believe that the role of the Chancellor's 'Wise Men' between 1993 and 1997 was to hold the Treasury to account. In practice because the 'Wise Men' could never agree, the resulting cacophony if anything reduced the scrutiny of the Treasury's decision making.

But legitimacy comes, above all, from building the successful track record described above. Building a reputation for economic stability requires a continued commitment to vigilance. It is precisely at this stage when past British governments have resorted to short-termism. We will not repeat those mistakes.

That is why we have backed the MPC in the decisions it has taken to lock in stability as the British economy strengthens. Internationally, too, I believe there is a growing recognition that, in the face of a series of large and destabilizing shocks to the global economy, those countries where monetary and fiscal policy have been flexible, forward-looking and supported growth, with automatic stabilizers allowed to operate fully, have had shallower downturns and are leading the recovery.

By contrast, where monetary policy has been sluggish and inflexible or fiscal policy still based on the old-style annual incrementalism, blind to the economic cycle, then economies have tended to fare worse in terms of growth and inflation. Indeed, where there is no credible long-term commitment to fiscal stability over the economic cycle, economies can find themselves in the perverse position of cutting spending or raising taxes at the wrong time of the economic cycle to meet short-term annual deficit targets – putting both growth and stability at risk.

Growth in the euro zone has continued to be weak and activity in Japan remains fragile. Since the last quarter of 2000 GDP has grown by around 6 per cent in the UK and the US, but by less than 1 per cent in Germany and Japan, around 2 per cent in Italy and France, the Euro area as a whole.

This weaker performance in the euro area is partly due to structural problems, evidenced by both high unemployment and sluggish labour force growth. But the role of macroeconomic frameworks in allowing monetary and fiscal policy to operate fully is also an issue. Which brings me to the Stability and Growth Pact (SGP).

Fiscal stabilization in EMU

Some have argued that the Stability Pact is not necessary. I disagree.

It is necessary for reasons of fiscal coordination so that monetary and fiscal policy can work sensibly together without putting undue upward pressure on interest rates – a challenge which is inherently more difficult when the counterpart to the monetary authority is not one sovereign state but twelve countries and where coordination between fiscal authorities is a necessary precondition for effective coordination between fiscal and monetary policy.

It is necessary for reasons of fairness and legitimacy – to prevent high debt counties from simply continuing to run high deficits and debts and spreading the risk of default across all the members of the monetary union. The question is whether it is also necessary – as we set out in the UK's Euro assessment – to have a Pact that can legitimise a degree of fiscal flexibility for individual member states.

The Stability Pact has become less mechanistic. As is has evolved to meet the new challenges, more recognition has been given in the detailed operation of the Pact to the importance of the cycle and of sustainability. But has it so far proved – at the present time and in its current form – the best possible vehicle for delivering the fiscal discipline that is necessary in a monetary union?

In the euro area, general gross debt averaged around 70 per cent of GDP in 2002; and some member states have debt levels above 100 per cent of GDP, compared to 38 per cent in the UK and 60 per cent in the US.

And, of course, the 3 per cent deficit ceiling makes it difficult to fully operationalize the automatic stabilizers and to deliver fiscal flexibility in the face of global economic shocks.

Our interest in the future evolution of the Stability and Growth Pact is not just because the success of the euro, in which the UK has a substantial national interest, depends on an effective pro-stability and pro-growth fiscal counterpart to the ECB and because the UK continues to be subject to fiscal surveillance under the Treaty.

It is also because we are committed in principle to membership of the euro – a principled commitment strengthened by our assessment. Upon joining the euro, the UK would become subject to the full implementation of the Stability and Growth Pact. So how that SGP operates in practice is of critical importance to how the UK could operate fiscal policy in EMU.

This latter issue is a complex one – set out in detail in both the five tests assessment and the supporting paper I have referred to, *Fiscal Stabilisation and EMU* (HM Treasury, 2003).

That background study – the eighteenth of the eighteen published alongside the assessment – has attracted a number of comments. It was described as 'an imaginative set of proposals' by the FT's Martin Wolf; 'extremely interesting and valuable' by Professor Wickens, 'a return to Keynes' by *The Business* newspaper. It was even described by the economics editor of the *Times* as 'a raunchy report, the economic equivalent of Jilly Cooper' which was quite a tribute to the Treasury economists who wrote it.

I cannot hope to do justice to the subtlety of all the arguments in that paper in this one chapter. But I will first summarize the proposals we have set out for consultation to amend our current fiscal regime if we were to join the euro. I will then set out how these proposals are consistent with a well-functioning – credible but flexible – Stability Pact.

The five tests assessment sets out in detail the benefits from which, based on sustainable and durable convergence, the UK could benefit as a member of the euro.

It also sets out how, once a British set interest rate is replaced by a European wide interest rate, other adjustment mechanisms in the economy become more important.

Outside the euro there are four possible ways for the economy to adjust in the fact of a shock to that country in order to sustain stability and growth: monetary policy, exchange rate adjustment, fiscal policy or flexibility in wages and prices.

Once a country joins a monetary union, the range of macroeconomic policy levers available to national authorities narrows.

First, a country necessarily loses monetary policy as a country-specific stabilizer. ECB monetary policy would still play a stabilizing role for the UK to the extent that the UK contributes to a rise or a fall in the overall Euro inflation objective, but this is clearly a much less effective tool for UK stabilization than a UK interest rate.

Second, a country loses the nominal exchange rate as a source of national real exchange rate adjustment.

So the adjustment to an economic shock must come through some combination of

- flexibility in wages, prices, quantities and capital movements;
- or a greater reliance upon fiscal policy as a tool for domestic stabilisation.

That is why the Five Tests assessment emphasizes the second flexibility test and why we have embarked on a series of reforms to the labour, product and capital markets to enhance flexibility.

But while flexibility in the economy can and must be enhanced, relying solely on greater flexibility in prices and quantities to accommodate shocks could potentially be disruptive to both stability and growth. So the question naturally arises, if the UK were to join the euro, is there a case for a larger role for UK fiscal policy as a tool for national stabilization, either through the use of the automatic stabilizers or discretionary action, in the face of UK-specific shocks or a more pronounced UK reaction to a common shock? And how could the current fiscal framework be modified to mitigate the impact of economic shocks and help smooth out the resulting gyrations in output and inflation?

It is important to strike a note of caution. The history of fiscal activism and fine-tuning in Britain has not always been a happy one. The historical discussion in the Treasury paper demonstrates that in the 1950s and 1960s, when the exchange rate was part of a fixed exchange rate system and in which fiscal policy was the main stabilization tool, the UK experienced rather unstable output. The *Fiscal Stabilisation* paper argues that this was primarily due to three factors:

- rather than taking a symmetric approach to the economic cycle, there was a bias towards loosening – it was always easier to loosen fiscal policy when the economy was weaker than to tighten it when the economy was stronger;
- the existence of long decision and implementation lags meant that, too often, what governments thought were counter-cyclical policy decisions tended to be pro-cyclical and therefore destabilising;
- and there was a lack of coordination between spending and tax decisions with spending decisions often more than offsetting adjustments on the revenue side done for demand-management reasons.

It is clear – on reflection – that these problems with fiscal stabilization in the 1950s and 1960s were exactly the problems which undermined the role of monetary policy and fiscal policy in the 1980s and early 1990s.

Yet while fiscal policy is inherently more complex and less predictable than monetary policy, there are no intrinsic reasons – theoretical or empirical – why fiscal policy cannot work effectively as a tool for stabilization. The challenge, as we set out in the background study to the euro assessment paper, is to apply the same principles that we have successfully applied to monetary policy.

That means, in addition to our two fiscal rules, the fiscal stabilization regime would also need to have:

A clear long-term policy goal:

- Symmetric – to deal with that danger of a bias towards loosening and ensure that the regime was operational in both phases of the cycle;
- And explicitly forward-looking in order to avoid pro-cyclicality – the danger of the government getting caught behind the curve and tightening or loosening too late.

Clear and transparent operating rules:

- so that fiscal policy can be used in a counter-cyclically in a predictable and orderly way without putting fiscal stability at risk

And be transparent:

- both for reasons of credibility and legitimacy to ensure that stabilization policy was, as far as possible, separated from other government policy objectives.

One option would be for the UK to stick with its current fiscal framework and simply rely on the automatic stabilizers. The automatic stabilizers are clearly symmetric, operate without policy lags and do not require an active choice to trade off with other objectives.

But while the automatic stabilizers are important – we have been looking at their effectiveness relative to other countries and whether there is a case for enhancing them – they are insufficient by themselves.

First, in the face of large shocks, as the simulations accompanying the euro assessment show, they only partly dampen the shock. And secondly, while appropriate for a demand shock, in the face of a permanent supply shock, the automatic stabilizers will tend to give a perverse outcome. In the case of a negative supply shock, actual output will tend to be higher than and lag behind the fall in potential output, leading to a positive output gap (so that if anything, a fiscal tightening would be needed). However, as the level of output falls, so falling incomes will tend to lead to a drop in tax revenues through the automatic stabilizers, which would loosen fiscal policy.

But as in domestic monetary policy, it is when governments need to turn to discretionary fiscal policy that risks to credibility start to arise. And in the euro, this would be further complicated by the risk of tension between domestic stabilization, the ECB's Europe-wide inflation objective and the demands of the Stability and Growth Pact.

So what we have looked for is a system in which discretionary fiscal policy would be the exception rather than the norm – but an exception which, as the Peter Westaway modelling of shocks and adjustment mechanisms in EMU shows, a prudent government would want the flexibility to employ if necessary (Westaway, 2003).

So how could such a flexible and legitimate national regime be designed for national fiscal policy with the euro zone?

First long-term objectives.

The objective of this fiscal stabilization rule is clear – subject to the ECB's inflation target, to minimize deviations of output and employment from the economy's trend.

This objective could be specified as a UK inflation target alongside the ECB inflation target. Ideally, these would be the same target to ensure inflation expectations were aligned correctly. But there would be a real presentational risk of confusion because there would be times when the best way to respond to a UK-specific shock would be to accommodate the shocks through a temporary period of higher inflation, in order to change relative prices between the UK and the rest of the euro zone.

Alternatively, the stabilization target could be based on an output gap target – though the output gap is notoriously harder to measure accurately and subject to revision. This would make it hard to commit to a rigid output-gap-based rule.

In any case, either rule applied at all times could well imply much greater fine-tuning and less flexibility in the face of different shocks than the national policy maker would want in fiscal policy.

What is needed is a way of identifying those shocks which were both sufficiently severe and where a fiscal response made sense.

That is how our thinking led us not to a policy rule but to an operational stabilization rule: that, subject to meeting our two existing fiscal rules, if at any point, the deviation of the economy away from a stable path was expected to be over a particular amount then the *option* – but not the requirement – of a fiscal response would be triggered.

In our stabilization paper, we proposed for consultation a rule based on an output gap trigger of 1 or 1.5 per cent. If the economy moved away from its sustainable path by more than 1 or 1.5 per cent, then a possible fiscal response would be triggered.

Setting a high value for the trigger point would mean that fiscal policy would be less active and therefore output could be more volatile than necessary (less stabilization than desirable). A low value means that fiscal stabilization policy would be used relatively frequently and/or the fiscal impulse itself would be larger.

Looking back over the past two decades, the output gap has exceeded 1.5 per cent for prolonged periods on only three occasions:

- During the deep recession of the early 1980s when the output gap was almost minus 7 per cent at its widest point.
- During the boom of the late 1980s when the output gap peaked at over 4 per cent; and
- During the bust of the early 1990s when the output gap approached minus 4 per cent.

There are clear advantages in defining the rule in this way:

First, it is clear that the trigger relates to the underlying objective – avoiding excessive instability in UK output.

Secondly, the trigger is symmetric so that if the economy is too strong the rule triggers the option of a fiscal tightening; if the economy is weak the option of a fiscal loosening is triggered.

Thirdly, while the trigger is predictable, the policy response is not automatic. In each circumstance, the obligation is on the government to justify whether or not it has decided to use fiscal policy to stabilize the economy – just as the MPC, in the current UK system, often has to explain to the markets and Parliament why it has chosen not to act in any particular month.

And fourthly, it establishes an explicit link between flexibility and sustainability across the economic cycle and the level of net debt. Because the immediate question becomes: would the use of fiscal policy to support growth put the government's other fiscal rules at risk? It is only in circumstances where the government is clearly meeting the net debt rule, and the public finances are sustainable, that the government can, in a credible way, deliver stability by triggering the stabilization rule.

Having established the rule, the next requirement is to establish a pre-commitment to institutional arrangements which ensure that the discretion to actively use fiscal policy over the cycle is being used in a way which is symmetrical and stabilizing.

I explained earlier why, in the current regime, we considered and rejected the option of attempting to mirror the Monetary Policy Committee with an independent fiscal authority. In my view complexity and parliamentary sovereignty would, if anything, be more important issues if the UK were to join the euro.

Instead, our fiscal paper proposes a different institutional device – a fiscal version of the Open Letter system in which if the output gap were forecast to be greater than, say, 1.5 per cent then the government would write a letter to Parliament explaining whether, and how, it intends to use fiscal policy to meet its stabilization and wider economic objectives.

It is, of course, a different kind of open letter from the monetary policy Open Letter system – indeed an even more significant and forward-looking one. In the case of the MPC the committee is explaining to the Chancellor how the actions it has already taken are consistent with meeting the inflation target. In the case of the fiscal Open Letter system, the fiscal open letter is signalling a new decision based on a forecast of the future. The letter would need to explain why the shock is occurring, whether it is right to act, if so, how, how long it will take for output to come back towards trend and also how that action is consistent with the government's fiscal rules, the Stability and Growth Pact, the ECB inflation target and the government's wider objectives for growth and stability.

The third requirement is transparency.

Because the communication of fiscal policy becomes critically important both to deliver stability in the economy and to explain to the public why action is or is not justified.

That is why we have proposed a regular Treasury stabilization report, produced on a quarterly or six-monthly basis, which would effectively take over from the Bank of England Inflation Report as the prime domestic document in which the government analysed economic developments, published its forecast of the output gap and alongside which a fiscal open letter would be published if necessary.

There are, of course, a large range of secondary issues that I have not been able to address – including ways of further enhancing transparency, parliamentary procedure and the potential role for different fiscal instruments. But I have highlighted that the same principles that have guided our approach to monetary and fiscal policy making up to now would, under these arrangements, guide our approach if the UK were to join the euro.

The evolution of the Stability and Growth Pact

It is clear from this discussion that the future evolution of the Stability and Growth Pact is of critical importance.

Within a modernized Stability Pact, decisive action by government to both reduce debt and tighten fiscal policy during the above-trend phase of the economic cycle could allow governments the flexibility to respond to asymmetric shocks during the below-trend phase of the cycle – better promoting stability and growth.

But the arrangements we have set out for the operation of UK fiscal policy in EMU would only work within the euro area as a whole if the times when, for individual countries, fiscal activism makes sense are predictable, exceptional and confined to low debt countries.

So the challenge is to have an SGP that is both disciplined and sufficiently accommodating to allow such symmetric stabilizing action to take place. It would require an SGP which can deliver:

- a commitment to fiscal discipline, symmetrical over the cycle for all countries, with a sharper focus on debt so that high-debt countries reduce debt at all stages of the economic cycle but particularly when the economy is above trend – thus establishing greater credibility;
- a recognition of the differences between countries, including in their fiscal rules and attitude towards investment, as well as levels of debt sustainability pressures and the state of their economic cycle and which allows flexibility for low-debt countries to use – in certain circumstances – fiscal stabilization to ensure stability and growth while keeping debt low and public finances sustainable.
- and effectively enforced fiscal coordination between national governments, as well as with the ECB, which would enhance its legitimacy.

What does this mean for the current SGP?

The current SGP has clear policy rules. But in order to build credibility and reduce national fiscal flexibility, the SGP has been based on annual rules without recognition of the importance of the economic cycle.

While the implementation of the Pact has evolved, it was perhaps understandable at the outset that dealing with so many countries, the Pact would resort to mechanistic rules, rather than guiding principles which could afford some constrained discretion. While precise dates by which countries should balance their cyclically adjusted budgets have been dropped, they have been replaced by a target annual reduction of 0.5 per cent of GDP that cannot of themselves take account of debt levels or public investment needs.

So without a clear pre-commitment to flexible operating rules, and as a consequence of the initial failure to make the cycle an issue, the result has been an asymmetric application. In particular, we do not have a mechanism to promote tightening of fiscal policy in the above-trend phase of the cycle, even for high-debt countries.

Perversely countries can end up cutting spending or raising taxes at the wrong stage of the cycle, at the expense of stability and growth, in an attempt to make up the lost ground that should have been made up when the economy was stronger.

There is also a case for saying that without a more precise inflation target and thus a clear and well-specified monetary reaction function there is less incentive for countries to agree on the difficult collective fiscal decisions.

Some have argued that the SGP should be scrapped. That would be a mistake: collective fiscal discipline and coordination is essential for a successful monetary union.

Others have suggested starting again from scratch with new – and often rather complex – fiscal rules and Treaty amendments, such as exempting Member States from the SGP based on an index of national institutional reform, tradeable deficit permits among Member States, and permanent balance rules that ensure that the net present value of future government revenues does not exceed the net present value of future expenditure.

The UK, by contrast, has consistently argued not for a root-and-branch reform, but instead for an evolutionary approach to a more sensible and credible interpretation of the Maastricht Treaty: a prudent interpretation of the Stability and Growth Pact, grounded in robust economic rationale, which takes account of the economic cycle – and is applied symmetrically throughout the cycle; – which distinguishes between high- and low-debt countries; and which allows for borrowing for public investment within prudent limits.

The issue is not fundamental overhaul or Treaty change, but evolution in its institutional design:

- focusing policy in higher-debt countries on the need for fiscal consolidation – particularly when the economy is above trend. And combining that with
- greater flexibility by allowing not only the automatic stabilizers to work fully across the economic cycle – and especially in the below-trend phase – but also allowing countries with low debt and sustainable public finances the extra flexibility – when necessary – to use discretionary fiscal policy to support stability and growth.

This is not an impossible task. Indeed, there are important and encouraging signs that the SGP is steadily evolving in the right direction. The EU Council has approved:

- a greater focus on cyclical adjustment
- a recognition publicly that the automatic stabilizers should be allowed to work
- a greater focus on long-run sustainability, including the impact of ageing populations
- a greater emphasis on debt reduction in highly indebted countries
- and a little more emphasis on the importance of the quality of public expenditure – which is a polite way of talking about the current–capital split.

But the question is whether we should now codify these principles within an institutional framework which recognises that it is for governments, collectively and intergovernmentally, to take into account:

- the stage of the economic cycle in each country
- borrowing for capital spending
- the difference between high and low debt countries

The implication of this prudent approach is that there would, occasionally, be circumstances in which a low-debt country should be allowed – with the agreement of the Council – to breach for exceptional and temporary reasons the 3 per cent reference value – either because of the impact of the automatic stabilizers or discretionary fiscal action and after adjusting for investment spending.

The challenge is to find institutional arrangements which can both enforce discipline in the above-trend phase and in high-debt countries and at the same time credibly sanction exceptional fiscal action in low-debt countries during a downturn.

It is clear that such an approach would imply not a weakening but a strengthening of the degree of fiscal coordination within the Council.

Moreover, as part of a robust institutional framework, where the Council retains responsibility and accountability for enforcing fiscal discipline while exceptionally sanctioning fiscal stabilization, there would also be a case at the EU level for strengthening the role of independent monitoring, surveillance and transparency.

Some independent surveillance and monitoring already occurs in the European context: for example, under the Excessive Deficit Procedure and through the annual Stability and Convergence programmes.

While retaining the principle of peer review of fiscal policies by Member States, one possibility would be to strengthen the independent surveillance process in the EU as part of wider reforms to the Stability and Growth Pact. For example, the EU could establish an intergovernmental 'fiscal surveillance committee', staffed by Member State and European Commission representatives, with delegated authority to conduct analysis and surveillance of national fiscal policies and advise the Council.

It is instructive to ask what would have happened if the existing proposals for a prudent interpretation of the Stability Pact and the UK fiscal open letter had been applied together since 1999. Any euro member country with an output gap deviating more than 1.5 per cent of GDP from trend, would have been required publicly to write to the Council a fiscal open letter setting out its fiscal strategy and how it was consistent with the reformed SGP. As now, it would have been for the Council to agree or reject that strategy.

Would such a regime have led fiscal policy more effectively to support monetary policy throughout the economic cycle?

Or would it have led to an outbreak of fiscal fine-tuning, over and above the automatic stabilizers, which would have put pressure on both monetary policy and fiscal sustainability?

The only European governments in 2003 or 2004 with a negative output gap in excess of 1.5 per cent on the basis of EU 2003 Autumn forecasts and the trend methodology – and which therefore would have been required to produce a fiscal open letter explaining whether or not it was taking discretionary fiscal action to support growth – would have been Germany with an output gap of 1.6 per cent in 2003 and the Netherlands and Portugal with output gaps of 1.9 per cent and 2 per cent respectively forecast for 2004. The fact that each country was only above 1.5 per cent in one year, and that both Germany and Portugal have gross debt-GDP ratios around or above 60 per cent, would clearly have influenced the content of their letters and the judgement of the Council.

In 2000, by contrast, the following countries had a positive output gap in excess of 1.5 per cent of GDP – Belgium (2.6 per cent), Spain (1.8 per cent), France (2 per cent), Ireland (6.7 per cent), Luxembourg (7.2 per cent), the Netherlands (3.9 per cent), Austria (2 per cent), Portugal (3.6 per cent) and Finland (4.2 per cent) – all of whom would have published a fiscal open letter explaining whether or not they were tightening fiscal policy. Yet only Ireland, Finland – two of the countries with the lowest debt – Austria and the Netherlands tightened fiscal policy in 2000 relative to 1999.

So far from sanctioning imprudence, such a SGP applied symmetrically over the economic cycle would have led either to fiscal tightening in a number of higher-debt countries or fiscal open letters explaining why fiscal tightening was not, in fact, necessary for the Council to consider. The result should have been more fiscal consolidation in the early years of EMU when economies were largely above trend.

And in the below-trend phase, while allowing the automatic stabilizers to work, there would not have been a rash of fiscal open letters proposing discretionary fiscal loosening.

Of course, these figures are endogenous. The very existence of the regime might have implied different outcomes. But the implication is clear – that fiscal tightening would have occurred in the above-trend phase of the economic cycle, a fiscal tightening which would have made it easier for countries to allow the automatic stabilizers to operate in more recent years. But few or no countries would have been in a situation where discretionary fiscal loosening would have been triggered by the regime.

Conclusion

In conclusion, the lesson I draw from the experience of the SGP so far is a general one applying to both monetary and fiscal policy within and outside EMU: it is possible to design policy frameworks which are both credible in their commitment to sound long-term goals and in which countries have the flexibility to deal with the ups and downs of the global economy. While rigidity does not work – in monetary and fiscal policy – constrained discretion can work. With our British model we are trying to show in our own country how to make it work. And with the right evolution of policy including transparency, it can be made to work in monetary unions too. In this way stability and growth can be advanced and sustained together.

This chapter is based heavily on the inaugural Ken Dixon Lecture which Ed Balls delivered at the Department of Economics, University of York in early 2004.

7
Macroeconomic Policy: Theory and Institutional Practice[1]

Christopher Allsopp

7.1 Introduction

This chapter is concerned with the design of macroeconomic policy, from both a theoretical and an institutional perspective. Much of the focus is on the new monetary arrangements in the UK, which mark a decisive break with the past. The adoption of the new framework in 1997 reflected both a past history of macroeconomic failure (and the lessons drawn from that) as well as important developments in the theory of monetary policy. Above all, however, the changes in the UK exemplify the purposeful design of a set of new institutions (the Monetary Policy Committee and associated procedures) intended to deliver both inflation control and macroeconomic stability. Thus far, the new framework appears to have been remarkably successful in meeting those objectives.

The emphasis in this account is on the two-way interaction between policy and academic enquiry – which is approached from the standpoint of someone engaged, for a time, in the monetary policy process. As compared with the situation a decade or so ago, there is a recognisable consensus on what macroeconomic policy should aim to achieve and (in broad terms) on how it should be conducted. Thus the interaction has been benign, with developments in theory, in empirical analysis and in policy pulling, so to speak, in the same direction. It was not always so – and, of course, there are still echoes of old disputes (some of which are touched on below) over 'rules versus discretion' or over 'Keynesian' versus 'monetarist' accounts of how the economy works. The emerging consensus meant that theoretical concerns were unusually important in the design of the new institutional arrangements in the UK.

The rest of this chapter is structured as follows. Section 7.2 is a characterization of the emerging consensus. Section 7.3 goes back to consider the wider historical and theoretical debate over macroeconomic policy rules. Whilst the consensus has it that interest-rate policy reaction functions should be 'rule-like' (Taylor, 1993; Meyer, 2002) and 'predictable' (Woodford, 2003), it is equally true that systems such as that in the UK can be described as embodying 'constrained discretion' (Bernanke and Mishkin, 1997, p. 106; King, 1997a, p. 440; Balls, 2001). Where does this leave the 'rules versus discretion' debates of the past? And how rule-bound should central banks be in practice? Section 7.4 outlines some of the features of the current UK system, which seem particularly important from the point of view of system design. Section 7.5 turns, in a highly selective way, to some of the unresolved issues. How, for example, should policy makers treat fluctuations in asset prices? What difference does the openness of the economy to impacts from overseas make? How can forecasts and policy reactions be improved in the face of various types of uncertainty? What is, or should be, the role of fiscal policy? Section 7.6 concludes.

7.2 The consensus

A rough characterization of the developing consensus on macroeconomic policy design would include the following:

1. There is no long-run trade-off between nominal developments (inflation) and the real economy. (In other words, in the long run, the Phillips curve is vertical.)
2. It is essential to establish a credible, non-accommodating, policy to control the price level and inflation.
3. The primary responsibility for the control of inflation should be assigned to monetary policy.
4. Monetary policy should be carried out by an independent central bank.
5. The principal instrument of monetary policy is the short-term interest rate.
6. The central bank's responsibilities in controlling inflation in the medium term should be carried out at minimum cost in terms of deviations of output from potential and deviations of inflation from target.

Clearly, different parts of the consensus have different status. Thus, whilst 1 and 2 may be regarded as fundamental, 3, 4 and 5 are instrumental and more contentious – alternative choices and arrangements could be made and have existed in the past. The important qualification, 6, requires welfare judgements or at least some scheme for weighting together different costs.

Recent legislation, defining mandates for central banks, reflects these complex objectives. Thus, the European Central Bank (ECB) is charged with maintaining price stability and *without prejudice to that*, to support the policies of the European Commission as laid out in Article II of the Treaty – which include growth and employment. The Bank of England Act, similarly, adopts a *hierarchical* or *lexicographic* ordering, charging the Monetary Policy Committee with maintaining price stability and, *subject to that*, with supporting the policies of the government for employment and growth. In the United States, there are multiple objectives, but given the widespread agreement on 1 and 2 above, there has, in recent years, been a hierarchical ordering there too.

In the economics literature, the monetary authority's behaviour is typically described in terms of the abstract concept of its *reaction function*, which delineates how the instruments of policy are adjusted in response to (a) its targets, and (b) its assessment of the current and future state of the economy. Assuming that the instrument of policy is the short-term nominal interest rate, the *interest rate reaction function* can thus be seen as an algorithmic rule or feedback system describing how the monetary authority attempts to 'home in' on its objectives. Simple versions of such reaction functions abound, including the Taylor Rule (where the interest rate is taken as responding to current deviations of inflation from target and output from potential) and that implicit in *inflation forecast targeting regimes* (such as that in the UK) where interest rates react to deviations of forecast inflation from target.[2] In practice, the reaction function is embedded in an institution – usually the central bank together with associated constitutional and other arrangements – and may involve a complex set of procedures and judgements. It is unlikely to be expressible as a single simple rule – at the least it would involve a set of anticipated contingent responses.[3]

The reaction function approach brings out several intertwined aspects of the current practice of monetary policy. The first might be termed the *nominal anchor* function: the assignment of responsibility for the control of the price level or inflation in the medium and longer term to the monetary authority. This function, in turn, has two dimensions. The first is the target itself – which may be explicitly quantified (as in the UK) or implicitly defined, for example as 'price stability' (as in the mandate for the ECB). The practical question of how the target should be made operational and measured is not as straightforward as sometimes appears. The second dimension is the instrument (or instruments) of policy and the feedback system, which together must be sufficiently powerful to achieve the medium-term objective for prices and inflation.

The second general aspect of current practice is the *stabilization* function, capturing the idea that the medium-term objective should ideally be achieved at minimum cost (e.g. in terms of deviations of inflation from target and output from potential). The optimum reaction function clearly depends on the characteristics of the economy, on the shocks anticipated, and on the welfare judgements made. Since, in theoretical work, the optimum reaction function is likely to be sensitive to alternative models and specifications and shocks, there is interest in simple rules which produce reasonably good results and which appear robust. The practical policy analogue is the search for a set of procedures, which delivers a sensible reaction function with desirable properties in a wide range of possible circumstances.

The monetary policy reaction function is thus an extremely important part of the way in which the economic system as a whole functions; and for the system to function well, it must have, and be perceived to have, appropriate properties. With forward-looking economic behaviour, it is the credibility of policy as embodied in the reaction function that stabilizes expectations of inflation. But there is more to it than that. Combined with a standard 'natural-rate' or 'accelerationist' view of inflationary pressure, an 'appropriate' reaction function should lead to the anticipation of longer-term economic growth at potential rates and public understanding that deviations of output from potential and inflation from target will (in some sense) be as small as possible given the shocks hitting the economy. Thus, monetary policy should stabilize not just expectations of inflation but also expectations of growth at its potential rate. This 'two-for-one' aspect of inflation target regimes has been stressed (in the context of euro area monetary policy) by, for example, Alesina *et al.* (2001). The idea that well-designed inflation-targeting regimes are also 'employment-friendly' is of the utmost importance in gaining public and political acceptance of the framework. The same general line of argument points to the importance of accountability and of transparency – on which more below.

The analysis so far has concentrated on a certain type of monetary policy regime, which combines longer-term control of inflation with activist stabilization in the short term. Such a regime may be thought of in terms of a reaction function of appropriate type (e.g. a Taylor Rule) or in terms of the monetary authorities operating within a framework of 'constrained discretion' – where the overriding, rule-like, commitment is to controlling inflation in the medium term and the 'discretion' allows for stabilization. Within such a framework, one can imagine many different institutional arrangements – many different reaction functions, some, no doubt, better than others. Like other matters of definition, it is hard to define exactly what is meant by an 'appropriate' regime, but we mostly recognise it when we see it.

From a political-economy point of view, what really matters is that an appropriate policy framework with the right general properties should be put in place – and be understood by the public to be in place. That then leads on to a second set of questions about improving or even optimizing performance. To use an analogy, a boat without a helmsman is an indeterminate system. With a helmsman in place, there is a good chance that the boat will move across the bay in the direction desired by the operator. The really big question is whether there is a purposeful helmsman in the boat or not. If there is a helmsman, then in order to predict where the boat is likely to go, two things are required. The first is knowledge of the desired destination. The second is some confidence that the helmsman has the instruments needed and enough skill in using them to achieve that overall aim. But, of course, the boat would function much better and more predictably with a skilled steersman than with a novice. The debate about monetary policy design has now moved, it may be argued, beyond the question about how to pin down the rate of inflation and provide a nominal anchor, to centre on how to become better at steering the economy – an essentially technical question.

7.3 Rules versus discretion

Where does this leave the debate over rules versus discretion in macroeconomic policy making? The debate has been going on for a very long time – but, for present purposes, a convenient starting point is Friedman's (1968) advocacy of a fixed (3–5 per cent per annum) growth rule for the money supply. Clearly, one aspect of the proposal was the advocacy of commitment to a *money supply* target as the medium-term nominal anchor of the system. The other, more negative, aspect was to eschew activist short-term stabilization (via shorter-term money supply changes). The most important reason for this second aspect of the proposal was a belief in the self-stabilizing properties of the economy, which would mean that it was hard for the authorities to improve on a policy of inactivity in the face of shocks – especially given uncertainty over lags in the system. However, there was also an argument that politicians were not to be trusted to use discretion wisely.

Monetarism

In modern (or semi-modern) dress, we would say that a policy of fixing the growth of the money supply would set up an implicit interest-rate reaction function against price and output disturbances – the interest-rate responses being endogenous and depending on the demand-for-money function. But would it be a good reaction function in the sense described above? There are a number of reasons, with long historical pedigrees, why it might not be, even if the paradigm of the money supply as the policy instrument were accepted. As is well known, Keynes, in the *General Theory*, argued that the 'self-regulating' mechanism of price flexibility may work badly, and may even be unstable if all that policy does to anchor the system is to fix the money supply. If price rises trigger increases in inflation expectations, real interest rates could even fall in the short run, a perverse response.[4] There is thus a danger that money supply rules would fail to meet the 'Taylor principle': that is, expressed in the form of interest-rate reaction functions of the type studied empirically by Clarida, Galí, and Gertler (1998), the monetary policy arrangements should have the property that *real* interest rates rise with any increase in inflation.[5] If we think, somewhat more realistically, of the monetary base rather than the money supply as the control instrument, potential instabilities could be magnified by pro-cyclical movements in the velocity of circulation of money or of the supply of commercial bank deposits.[6] There is a clear danger too that the nominal anchor function of the money supply rule would be compromised if the demand-for-money function was unstable over time – which, in practice, turned out to be the case for the principal aggregates targeted.

The Friedman paradigm was influential in the widespread adoption of monetary targets in the 1970s. One reason was that the central bank practice of operating on and stabilizing nominal interest rates risked producing falls in real interest rates in the face of upward price shocks (such as occurred in the early 1970s), a perverse and destabilizing response. Switching to a fixed money supply rule would, it was claimed, lead to real interest rate rises in such circumstances – a better (though not necessarily optimal) response.

In fact, the money supply is not, in practice, the instrument of policy. There is really no dispute – nor was there in the early 1970s – that the central bank's control over money in developed financial systems is indirect, via the short-term interest rate. So the adoption of monetary targets involved using the short-term interest rate (and using it actively) to try to meet the intermediate target of the money supply rule.[7]

With the interest rate taken as the policy instrument, the reaction-function approach gives a coherent account of how monetary targeting works in practice. The reaction function involves the monetary authorities using the interest rate to meet a target for the quantity of money (the term 'money supply' is best avoided). If the chosen aggregate really were related causally to the price level, this would provide an appropriate nominal anchor. But it is not necessary for there to be a causal link. Even if money is endogenously supplied (given the interest rate) by the private banking sector, the policy could work so long as the chosen aggregate were a good indicator of the state of the economy and so long as, in the longer term, the quantity of 'money' was closely related to the final objective (the price level, for example) – that is, so long as there were a reasonably stable money demand function. The system could even work if the monetary target were completely meaningless causally in determining prices (e.g., if the chosen target were notes and coins in the hands of the public, which are supplied on demand). The interest-rate reaction function would be doing the work, with the monetary aggregate performing the role of *indicator*.

The abandonment of monetary targeting in most countries reflected the bitter experience that monetary aggregates turned out to be a very poor basis for a monetary policy reaction function designed to provide a nominal anchor and to stabilize the economy. For the UK, Nigel Lawson, in his autobiography, noting that the chosen target aggregate (Sterling M3) proved 'treacherous', sounds an appropriate note of regret: 'We did not abandon the monetarist guiding light. It was the light that abandoned us' (Lawson, 1992, p. 987). Other (interest rate) reaction functions, such as those based on targeting the exchange rate, also failed, sometimes spectacularly as with the ejection of the pound sterling from the European Monetary System in 1992.

Cecchetti (2000), amongst many others, is sceptical, even scathing, about monetary targets. He finds no use for them, preferring instead a policy of targeting inflation itself (though this does not, of course, rule out the possible statistical usefulness of various monetary aggregates as part of the overall process of assessing likely future developments in inflation). In fact, the abandonment of monetary targeting did not lead, as Lawson had feared, to a wholesale return to government discretion and judgement, but progressively to the adoption of inflation target-type regimes based on interest-rate reaction functions and 'constrained discretion' of the general type discussed above. This does not represent the abandonment of the objectives of monetary rules. On the contrary, the recognition of the need for a medium-term nominal anchor has, if anything, been strengthened. The automatic function of 'money' as nominal anchor has had to give way, however, to policy targets for inflation itself and the instrument of policy is seen as the short-term interest rate rather than the money supply. Automatic responses to shocks have been replaced by a policy-determined feedback system. Finally, with the reintroduction of Keynesian stabilization concerns, there is recognition that the reaction function needs to be designed to provide the medium-term nominal anchor at minimum cost in terms of output-gap and price fluctuations.

Credibility and commitment

The other main strand of the rules literature arises from a seminal article, by Kydland and Prescott (1977), which demonstrated that the government's commitment to control inflation could suffer from the problem of 'time inconsistency'. The problem, which applies equally to a strict monetary target and to inflation or price-level targets supported by reaction functions, is that such policies might not be 'credible' – that is, they might not be believed by the public. In practice, there are many reasons other than time-inconsistency why this might be so – including perceptions of lack of competence or lack of instruments. The huge literature on time-inconsistency focuses, however, on one particular problem: the possibility that if the inflation target were achieved, the policy maker would face a temptation to 'cheat', leading, in simple models, to an 'inflation-bias'. The policy maker's discretion means that inflation in equilibrium has to be high enough to reduce to zero the incentive for the policy maker to produce an unexpected rise in inflation.[8] But the resulting inflation produces no benefit in terms of output or unemployment. What this demonstrates is that, because the economic behaviour of the private sector depends on anticipations of future policy, a better outcome can be achieved if the policy maker can *commit* to certain kinds of future policy as well. (In the simple example of an 'inflation-bias', a commitment to maintain the low inflation policy produces the better outcome.)

Commitment to what?

This strand of the literature was widely interpreted, in policy terms, as reviving the case for rules as opposed to discretion. It certainly does demonstrate the potential advantages of 'tying one's hands' when the public's anticipations of future policy affect the way the economy functions. But there is no reason to suppose that it justifies simple 'rules' like fixing the 'money supply'. To be sure, a commitment to a 'nominal anchor', such as the money supply, may be better than no commitment at all. But it might be a very bad rule – for the reasons (such as an unstable or varying relationship with inflation) outlined above. It might not even work – e.g. if the implicit reaction function failed to satisfy the 'Taylor principle'. What is needed is commitment to an 'appropriate' monetary policy reaction function and, ideally of course, to an optimal one.[9] Thus, in practice, the requirement is for commitment to a possibly complex set of principles and procedures, which are well-designed and (crucially) well-understood by the public. (Woodford (2003) has suggested that the monetary authority might be thought of as operating in a way analogous to a judge operating within a known framework of law.)

How can policy makers commit?

The other big issue raised by this literature is the question of how policy makers and politicians can commit themselves (and their successors) to future behaviour, which leads to better outcomes. How can they tie their hands? This is, of course, a general issue, which goes far beyond the question of how to arrange monetary policy institutions.

An influential story, due to Rogoff (1985), is to delegate monetary policy to a 'conservative' central banker who is much more concerned about inflation than about output or unemployment (relatively more concerned than society as a whole). This reduces the inflation bias. There are two parts to this. The first, by assumption, is that the central banker's incentives are compatible with lower equilibrium inflation. The second is that commitment can be achieved by such delegation. The second is not obvious: if the authorities can delegate in this way, then they could also reverse or override the arrangement, reintroducing the problem that the commitment to low inflation would not be 'credible'. The usual argument is that there would be heavy political costs in so doing, strengthening commitment to the institutional arrangement. There is an obvious problem, however, with this story, limiting its political relevance, which is that the financially 'conservative' central banker really is 'conservative' – so society would be delegating monetary policy to an 'inflation nutter'. This is fine as far as the nominal anchor function of monetary policy is concerned; it is not at all appropriate as far as the 'stabilization' function is concerned. Society wants the commitment to low inflation in the medium term, but *also* wants an appropriate degree of stabilization of output and unemployment (see item 6 in the listing of aspects of the consensus above). As a solution, Walsh (1995) suggests that optimal contracts for central bankers can be designed to align incentives – so as to remove the inflation bias whilst not compromising an appropriate degree of stabilization.

Another approach to the commitment problem is via *reputation* in repeated interactions (games) between the authorities and the private sector (see, especially, Barro and Gordon, 1983b, Barro, 1986). In the simplest approaches, there is uncertainty about the authority's 'type' – say 'hard' (with a very large weight given to inflation compared to output or unemployment) or 'soft'. It may then be beneficial to the authorities to develop a reputation for being 'hard', even if they are not. At the practical level, it is clear that the idea that the monetary authorities need to develop their 'credibility' by developing a reputation for being 'hard' on inflation has considerable political power. It needs to be stressed, however, that the desirable commitment is to an appropriately designed reaction function, a potentially complex set of behaviours. There is much more to 'credibility' than a reputation for being tough on inflation – though that is part of it.

Institutions

The natural political approach to the requirement for commitment to a complex set of objectives and procedures is via institutional design. Such an institution needs to have clearly specified responsibilities and objectives embodying the commitment to fulfil the nominal anchor function but must also allow for sufficient flexibility to respond appropriately to different shocks and situations. The hierarchical ordering of objectives in the mandates of the ECB and of the Monetary Policy Committee of the Bank of England captures the notion of commitment with flexibility pretty well. So does the idea of 'constrained discretion'. Delegation of responsibilities away from the political process is likely to be important for a number of reasons – further discussed below, in the context of the UK. Above all, the 'reaction function approach', discussed above, suggests that the behaviour of the institution needs to be 'rule-like' (Taylor (1993)) and 'predictable' (Woodford, 2003), since one of the main insights of the theoretical literature is that much of the effect of monetary policy works via private sector anticipations of future policy responses. This points to the key importance of 'transparency', not just about procedures but also about the underlying values and beliefs about the economy (the 'models' for short) that condition the behaviour of the institution.

7.4 The system in the UK

UK postwar history is littered with attempts to design a macroeconomic framework to provide a nominal anchor against inflation combined with a reasonable amount of stabilization. Most ended in failure, usually with serious conflict between internal and external objectives. Inflation targeting was introduced in 1992 after Sterling was ejected from the ERM. The present regime, with monetary policy delegated to the Monetary Policy Committee at the Bank of England, was instituted in May 1997.

UK policy clearly owes much to the 'demonstration effect' from the perceived reaction function of the independent Federal Reserve in the US. US experience could not, however, be simply transplanted. The Federal Reserve is both goal-independent and instrument-independent and, in formal terms, the reaction function is hardly pinned down at all. One of its objectives is 'price stability', but the nearest anyone has come to defining what is meant by price stability is Greenspan's (2002a, p. 6) famous remark that 'price stability is best thought of as an environment in which inflation is so low and stable over time that it does not materially enter into the decisions of households and firms.' Instead, the perceived interest rate reaction function in the US is reputational – deduced from historical behaviour since the early/mid 1980s. (The original Taylor Rule was put forward as descriptive of Federal Reserve behaviour, though Taylor himself has argued (e.g. 1999, 2000) that it has desirable properties across a wide variety of possible models of the economy.)

In the UK, the reputational route to the establishment of a credible reaction function was not really available in 1997. Not only was there a new government, but also there was a history of monetary failure, reflected in financial market expectations and risk premia, despite the relatively good inflation performance from 1992–93 onward. What was needed was the establishment of a credible monetary policy – a credible and appropriate reaction function – via institutional design.

This is not the place for a lengthy account of the UK system, the broad characteristics of which are well known.[10] But it may be useful to emphasize a few points, which seem especially important from the point of view of system design.

7.4.1 The target

The general commitment to price stability (and, subject to that, to supporting the government's policies for growth and employment) is defined in the Bank of England Act 1998, where it is also laid down that it is the Chancellor of the Exchequer's responsibility to set the target for inflation. A well-known feature is that the target is set as a single number (not a range), and that it is set in a forward-looking but effectively time-independent manner. The target was initially set at 2.5 per cent for the annual rate of change of the retail price index excluding mortgage interest payments (RPIX) and was maintained unchanged each year until it was replaced by a 2 per cent target rate for the CPI on 10 December 2003. An oft-cited reason for retaining governmental responsibility for setting and defining the target is that it is the government that is democratically accountable to the public. It also means that the delegation of responsibility for meeting the target to the MPC is particularly clear-cut.

With a point target which defines an aspiration in a timeless way, it is obvious to all that it will not be exactly met, so that ideas of shocks, uncertainty, and constrained discretion are, arguably, built-in from the start. The *symmetry* of the objective, whereby shortfalls in inflation are treated as of equal importance to overshoots, is appropriate to a reaction-function type of feedback system and, as already noted, has proved extremely important in gaining public acceptance of the inflation target regime.[11]

7.4.2 Central bank independence and delegation

Thus the Bank of England is instrument-independent not goal-independent. It has long been recognised in the UK that the principal instrument of monetary policy is the short-term interest rate,[12] so the task of the MPC is, in principle, very straightforward: to use its control of the short-term interest rate to meet, as far as possible, the externally-given objective. But what is the reason for delegation?

It is tempting to see the answer in terms of the academic literature on time-inconsistency and the inflation bias, in particular the argument made famous by Rogoff (1985) that the bias would be reduced by delegation to a 'conservative' central banker. I would not want to deny that this literature was, in general terms, influential, but it does not really ring true as the reason for the institutional change. If there were an inflation bias, it could still apply to the target-setters – the government – though the institutional change can be seen as a form of self-imposed commitment, with considerable political costs involved in opportunistically changing or abolishing the target. But, as far as the monetary authority itself is concerned, it is widely argued that the time-inconsistency problem is not an issue, not least because MPC members are statutorily responsible and accountable for their decisions (as expressed in their votes). In an influential paper, Bean (1998a) simply removes the temptation to 'cheat' or 'renege' from the central bank's objective function,[13] a procedure which can be seen as supported by statements by Blinder (1998), who, writing about the US, sees no temptation to generate surprise inflation, and, more recently, by Meyer (2002), who also down-plays any importance of time-inconsistency issues.[14] Vickers (1998), writing as the Bank of England's chief economist and a member of the MPC, suggested further that no Walsh (1995)-type incentives are neces-sary, as there is no incentive to want to generate inflationary surprises or to run the economy at anything other than at its natural rate of out-put/unemployment. He states that, 'Quite apart from our statutory duty, we have the strongest professional and reputational incentives, which in my opinion are incapable of being enhanced by financial incentives, to get as close as we can to the inflation target.'

This means that the main point of delegation is not to employ con-servative financiers, nor to set up a system of compensating incentives, but simply to hand over responsibility for the 'reaction function' to a technically-competent authority charged with doing the job as well as possible. Credibility is important, but credibility here has little to do with the meaning derived from the inflation bias literature, and a great deal to do with clearly specified objectives and with competence and trust that the job will be done as well as possible. This means that expla-nation of procedures, transparency and accountability are key aspects of the system.

The split UK system, with the target set by the government, and the MPC statutorily responsible for meeting it, is interesting. In principle, as noted above, the time-inconsistency problem could continue to apply due to the government's control over the target, or, more generally, the government could renege and be seen to be likely to renege, by altering or abandoning the system itself. It was argued, above, that such behaviour is constrained, and can be seen to be constrained, by the reputational and political losses involved in opportunistically changing the target or weakening the system. This, however, is subject to the major caveat that such costs must actually be present. Arguably, they will be present and highly constraining, if the system is publicly understood and commands general political support – and not otherwise. The practical point here is that a constituency of general support for non-accommodating policies and inflation control is necessary for the system to work as intended. If that support is present, then the institution itself may be durable and hard to change. It is notable that, in the UK, all three main political par-ties have in broad terms, publicly endorsed the MPC system.

7.4.3 The operation of the MPC

The system in the UK is as transparent and accountable as any in the world. The nine members of the MPC (five 'internal' and four 'external') are individually accountable under the Act for their votes: interest-rate decisions are by simple majority: the votes of each member are published within the Minutes, which appear after two weeks. Moreover, the MPC is severally responsible for the quarterly *Inflation Reports*, and the assessments and two-year-ahead forecasts for GDP growth and inflation published therein. (The forecasts are published as fan-charts, with probability ranges, to emphasize the inevitable uncertainty.) There are other checks and balances, such as appearances before Parliament's Treasury Select Committee and supervision of procedures by the Court of Directors of the Bank of England.

As far as the operation of policy is concerned, the process can be described as an inflation forecast target regime – a process which, along with the institution of the *Inflation Report*, was taken over from the system in place in 1992–97. The usual justifications for the focus on future inflation (e.g. Svensson, 1997, 2002) are lags in the transmission mechanism, and the need to take account of a potentially large number of influences on the inflation process. Decisions are taken at relatively high frequency on a monthly timetable, with procedures in place for additional meetings if necessary.[15] The forecasts are quarterly. Pragmatically, it is sometimes useful to see the process as being divided into two: the assessment of the current and future state of the economy on the one hand; and the response or reaction to that assessment on the other. Given the structure of the MPC, there are, in principle, nine different assessments, nine potentially different reaction functions, and a majority voting procedure that translates all that into an interest-rate decision. Despite the underlying complexity, the broad characteristics of the overall reaction function (using the term rather generally) are discernible and relatively predictable.

A feature of the UK system with individual accountability and transparency is that it leads to publicly expressed disagreements and dissent as well as public knowledge of closely split votes. Early concerns that both of these would work against credibility and be destabilizing now appear unfounded. If, as argued, the relevant meaning of 'credibility' is a reputation for competence and trust in the system, then this should not be surprising. Given large uncertainty, it is presumably reassuring rather than otherwise that disagreements and differing assessments occur, are discussed and are resolved, as far as policy is concerned, by the decision-making procedures.

The discernibility and predictability of monetary policy in the UK were, I would argue, greatly enhanced during the early years of operation of the new system. I would stress two aspects. The first is the consequence of the successful offsetting response to the Asia crisis and the Russian Default (the latter occurred in late August 1998). Interest rates were substantially cut in stages against the developing consensus perception that a quite serious recession was more or less inevitable in 1999. In the event, that incipient recession was headed off: the reaction function worked. Perhaps even more importantly, it led to public understanding that the reaction function really was intended to operate symmetrically – and that inflation targeting also involved offsetting action against recessions. The second point is that in innumerable speeches, presentations and discussions by members of the MPC, it has been the practice to stress the conditionality of policy. Thus, it is well understood that lower growth, should it eventuate, would (other things being equal) trigger a monetary easing. It is well understood that, should inflationary pressure arise, whether for demand-side or for supply-side reasons, monetary tightening would ensue – and if that proved insufficient, there would be further interest rises until it *was* sufficient. It is also understood that, should fiscal policy change, there would be compensating interest-rate reactions to maintain consistency with the inflation target. (Thus, doubts about the monetary response to a fiscal tightening, which have been expressed, for example, about the system in place in the euro area, do not seem to be problem in the UK context.) All this means that the broad features of the reaction function in place in the UK increasingly seem to be publicly-understood and built into expectations. The reaction function could not easily be expressed as a simple policy rule – but appears 'rule-like' in the sense of Taylor (1993), with the caveat that the rule-like behaviour involves contingent responses.

7.4.4   Did it work?

On the face of it, in terms of outcomes for inflation and growth, the UK system has worked well – though it is usual to qualify such remarks with the observation that it is too soon to tell. Figure 7.1 displays the record on annual RPIX inflation. It suggests that there has been a remarkable improvement in inflation since inflation targets were adopted in 1992 and a moderate undershoot in the last few years. If anything, the figure suggests that it was the adoption of an inflation-targeting regime that was important rather than the radically new arrangements introduced in 1997.

Figure 7.2, taken from HM Treasury (2002), shows much more clearly the effect of the new arrangements. There was a marked effect on inflation expectations at the time of the announcement of the new regime, suggesting that institutional change had indeed had a substantial effect

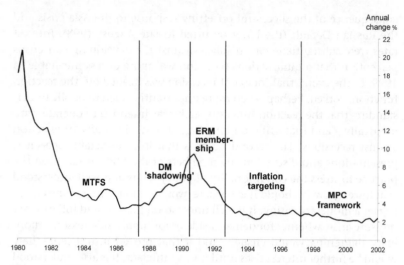

Figure 7.1 UK inflation performance under different monetary regimes
Source: HM Treasury, *Budget 2002*.

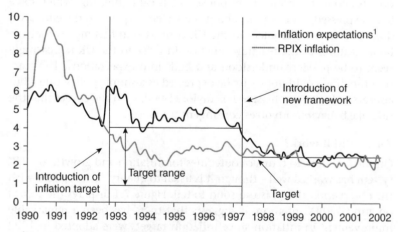

Figure 7.2 Inflation performance and expectations
Source: HM Treasury, *Budget 2002*.

on the credibility of macroeconomic policy. Other evidence, not detailed here, confirms a slower but highly favourable effect on public expectations and anticipations. And, as noted above, the more qualitative impression is that the reaction function in the UK has come to be increasingly well understood and that the regime change commands a high degree of public support.

All this suggests that the UK system can be seen as a monetary policy regime of the right sort, embodying a reaction function (using the term generally) of the right type. To revert to an earlier analogy, the boat has a helmsman and the objectives are clear. This is a very big change. But a caveat is again necessary. Most previous attempts at redesigning UK macroeconomic policy were also put forward as solutions to the problem of combining inflation control with economic stability – and failed. Why should the new system fare differently? The answer, I believe, is that the system is better-designed, since it incorporates not only some of the major lessons from history, but also the major insights that have come from theoretical and empirical research on monetary policy and monetary policy rules.

7.5 Some issues

Thus, arguably, the system in the UK is well designed, both institutionally and in terms of some of the main lessons from the policy rules literature. It may not have been fully 'tested in adversity' – though it has survived some pretty major shocks since its inception. That said, there are a number of issues of continuing concern, which illustrate the processes involved in the refinement and adaptation of institutional procedures. The following is a selective account of some of them.

7.5.1 Asset prices: the stock market and house prices

What might be described as the prevailing central bank consensus on this issue is well set out by Vickers (1999). He argues that (a) asset prices should not be part of the definition of the target for inflation or of the loss function of the monetary authorities; (b) that asset prices contain considerable information relevant to forecasting the future state of the economy; and (c) that in an inflation forecast targeting regime, 'it is neither necessary nor desirable for monetary policy to respond to changes in asset prices, *except to the extent that they help to forecast inflationary or deflationary pressures*' (Bernanke and Gertler, 1999, p. 115: emphasis added by Vickers).

This baseline view, which the late Rudi Dornbusch labelled 'the received wisdom' (Dornbusch, 1999, p. 129), has been challenged by Cecchetti *et al.* (2000, 2002), who argue that it is consistent with inflation-forecast targeting for monetary policy to react to contain bubbles or other departures from the 'fundamentals'. These authors are also reasonably optimistic that such departures can be identified in practice – they suggest that the problem is probably no worse than the problem of identifying the natural rate (or NAIRU). Clearly, the question of whether boom/bust cycles in asset prices should be headed off by monetary policy became highly topical from around the turn of the twenty-first century – focussing, obviously, on the behaviour of the stock market in the US and, to a lesser extent, on the house price boom in the UK. Moreover, there have been spectacular episodes in the past where boom/bust cycles have been associated with major instability and economic problems – notably, as far as stock-market prices are concerned, the Great Crash in the US in the interwar years and, more recently, the asset price bubble in Japan in the late 1980s with its deflationary aftermath which is still continuing (see, for example, Borio and Lowe, 2002). And as far as house prices are concerned, the UK boom of the late 1980s and subsequent bust is still regarded as an exemplar of bad macroeconomic policy.[16] There is no doubt that asset-price movements of the boom/bust type are perceived as a problem by policy makers and, unfortunately, there is no particular reason to believe that the potential problems would simply go away just because a successful inflation-targeting regime had been established. There is an issue, however, as to whether the monetary authorities should alter their behaviour as a result.

Suppose the problem is thought of, in stripped-down terms, as involving the anticipation of a large positive shock followed by a large negative shock with the negative shock (roughly) balancing the positive shock – so that the negative shock is larger, the larger the preceding positive shock. (Such a pattern could result, for example, from some stock/flow adjustment processes.) The baseline position is that the consequences would be taken into account in the forward-looking procedures of the monetary authority and that the consequences for output and price instability would then be minimized in terms of some loss function. That is the end of the story as far as interest rates are concerned.

Clearly, however, if there were some other policy instrument capable of lowering the magnitude of the first shock (and by construction therefore the second shock as well), it would be desirable that that policy should be used.[17] The task of the monetary authorities would be eased and, of course, short of completely successful offsets by the monetary authorities, the instability of the economy would be reduced and welfare would be increased. The first-best response – which may of course be unrealistic or costly for other reasons – is that sources of instability should be tackled at source, removing or lowering the magnitude of the negatively correlated shocks themselves. As a practical example, consider the house price boom in the UK. If the rising house prices are regarded as a problem because they are likely to reverse and pose problems in the future, there are many who would argue that a first-best solution is that the factors behind such destabilizing behaviour in the housing market should be tackled directly rather than by interest rates.[18]

From the inflation-targeting perspective, the interesting question is what should be done in the absence of alternative policies. As 'second best', should interest-rate policy be diverted from its normal role, not to target an asset price, but to check some cumulative process early on – in effect, to lower the magnitude of the correlated shocks under discussion? The argument for so doing would be that the variances of inflation and output would be thereby reduced – which is perfectly consistent with standard interpretations of the loss function.[19] But there is a trade-off involved (Bordo and Jeanne, 2002). The reduction in the shocks likely to hit the economy, if it can be achieved (it is quite a big if), takes the monetary authorities closer to their objective. But the diversion of the instrument from its normal role takes them further away (effectively imposing additional variability on the economy). The first needs to be bigger than the second for the policy to be desirable.

One can see why much of the discussion in favour of central banks using interest rates in this way is conducted in terms of heading off bubble-type phenomena. The presumption is that the longer a bubble path goes on, the bigger the bust when it comes. There is an easy-to-make assumption that a timely upward move in interest rates, even though not justified in terms of the inflation target and the normal reaction function, would 'prick' the bubble, lowering both the upward and downward aspects of the shock. Typically, it is further assumed that the upward movement of the interest rate is not too large and that it is short-lived (so the costs from this aspect of the policy are small) and the benefit in terms of shock reduction is large. Such arguments are usually helped by 20/20 hindsight. In practice, the difficulties in reliably identifying bubbles or other persistent departures from the 'fundamentals' are acute and the risks involved in such a strategy may be considerable (Greenspan, 2002b).

The most persuasive argument against using interest rates to moderate destabilizing processes (even if they can be identified) is one of credibility and transparency. It is hard enough to establish a credible reaction function based on clear objectives with the interest rate being used to meet the inflation target and, consistent with that, to offset shocks – including shocks from the endogenous processes of the economy itself – as far as possible. If the interest rate has another role as well, being used to moderate the shock structure (e.g. by heading off bubbles from time to time), the reaction function becomes less rule-like and predictable, and the system is likely to be less transparent and accountable. There may be cases where interest rates would, in effect, have to be used to reverse some cumulative process. But the potential costs to credibility and transparency weigh heavily against.

7.5.2 Open economy issues and the exchange rate

The exchange rate can be treated as an asset price – so much of the above can be thought to apply to exchange-rate misalignments as well (Cecchetti *et al.*, 2002). However, the UK context over the past decade illustrates the difficulties regarding 'misalignments' and 'fundamentals' rather well. In a nutshell, it is very hard to be at all sure what the equilibrium rate for Sterling actually is, especially, it may be added, when the dollar versus the European currencies – since 1999, the euro – are swinging about as well. Figure 7.3 shows the Sterling real effective exchange rate (unit labour cost basis). Sterling declined substantially on exit from the ERM in 1992, which was widely seen as a reversion towards fundamental value. The hypothesis that this was a move towards 'fundamental value' seemed to work well until about 1996, after which the real exchange rate rose very substantially – in fact to levels well *above* those pertaining to the ERM period – and, by and large, has stayed there since.

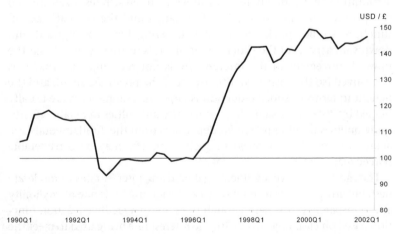

Figure 7.3   Sterling real effective exchange rate (unit labour cost based)
Source: *International Financial Statistics.*

Views about the 'equilibrium' have changed (perhaps as a lagged response to movements – or, perhaps more accurately, non-movements – in the actual exchange rate), but there is very little in the way of good explanation of the changes that have occurred, and the changes were not generally predicted *ex ante*. What is more, predictions of reversion proved false – at least up to the end of 2004. What should policy makers do, given that one of the chief transmission mechanisms from monetary policy to the economy is (according, for example, to the Bank of England's macroeconomic forecasting model) through the exchange rate?

In fact, forecasts and assessments are based on 'technical assumptions' about the exchange rate. For a start, some of the noise in exchange-rate movements is removed by basing the starting point of forecasts on the average during a 15-day window.[20] Second, forecasts are now made using a simple average of the path predicted by Uncovered Interest Parity (UIP) – which can be taken as the market expectation – and a no-change assumption (the random walk hypothesis). The possibility of reversion – modelled as a probability each period of a step change downwards in the exchange rate – has, however, frequently been a feature of the risks and skews presented in the fan-charts published in some *Inflation Reports*: taken by itself, this factor introduces an upward skew to the inflation forecast. All in all, this illustrates the practical point that interest-rate policy would be a great deal easier if better models of the exchange rate were available and policy makers had a better handle on the elusive concept of its longer-term equilibrium value.

The question of how interest-rate policy should react to the anticipation that there might be a downward 'correction' of the exchange rate is not simple. Suppose that interest rates are judged to be appropriate on the assumption that the exchange rate remains (over the forecast horizon) where it is. Now impose an upward skew on anticipated inflation due the anticipation that the exchange rate might fall. This suggests that interest rates should be raised. But this risks prolonging the assumed overvaluation. A 'bubble-pricking' strategy would lean against the wind in the opposite direction, lowering interest rates in the short term against the anticipation that they would have to be raised when and if this caused the exchange rate to fall. All this raises the credibility issues referred to above – and suggests that a strategy of reacting to large exchange-rate movements only when they occur has considerable attractions.

Turning to the question of how policy should react to an exchange-rate change when it does occur, the answer should depend, conventionally, on why it occurred and on the model adopted (as well as, of course, on whether the change is expected to permanent or transitory). That is not terribly helpful and not very transparent. And yet contingent policies are important in perceptions of the reaction function. The underlying question also relates to the rules literature in terms of whether the rule should include a term in the exchange rate (e.g. Ball, 1999) and in terms of what particular inflation index should be targeted. (Thus, Clarida, Galí, and Gertler, 2001, for example, suggest targeting domestic-goods price inflation, thereby excluding the import price component from the CPI, whereas Engel, 2002, suggests targeting the exchange rate.)

A natural way of approaching the issue is in terms of the procedures followed by the MPC. In broad terms, it is clear that an exchange-rate depreciation (assumed persistent) would feed through the Bank's forecasting procedures to import prices and, thence directly onto RPI inflation. The pass-through to import prices would lead (ignoring the dynamics) to a step-change upward in the price level. There would be further effects on aggregate demand – negatively in the short run because of the effect on real incomes and positively from expenditure-switching effects. There would also be potential wage and price pressure as real wage falls were resisted and from effects on inflation expectations. Thus, the prediction that an exchange rate fall would lead (other things being equal) to a compensating rise in real interest rates appears pretty safe on the basis of the target inflation rate set by the Chancellor and the known procedures of the MPC – including the characteristics of the Bank's forecasting model, which is published.

I have argued before (Allsopp, 2001) that, in the face of a real impact, such as the one described, the ideal strategy for controlling inflation is to 'accept' the price-level effect, whilst not accommodating the second-round effects via wage price pressure and via effects on inflation expectations. (See also Balls, 2001, and Meyer, 2002, who take a similar line for the UK and US respectively.) This is on the grounds that the 'level effect' is not really 'inflation'. Such a view is in line with Meltzer (1977, p. 183), who argues: 'a one-time change in tastes, the degree of monopoly, or other real variables changes the price level ... [W]e require a theory that distinguishes between once-and-for-all price changes and maintained rates of price change.' It is also in line with those who argue, on New Keynesian grounds (with the assumption that price stickiness applies to domestically produced goods), that monetary policy should not attempt to insulate the CPI from short-run fluctuations arising from terms-of-trade movements (Clarida, Galí, and Gertler, 2001). It needs to be recognised, however, that a policy of allowing level effects, whilst curtailing second-round effects, would be practically difficult and would require a considerable degree of explanation and transparency if credibility were to be maintained.

But are the effects as assumed? Kara and Nelson (2002) demonstrate that the stylized facts for the UK are that, although there is considerable evidence of exchange-rate pass-through to import prices, there is no correlation of exchange rate changes with RPIX inflation. If this is the case, then it throws doubt on whether there would be a large effect on inflation from an exchange rate fall, were it to occur.

These questions of pass-through and of the appropriate design of policy in the face of exchange-rate changes are of immense practical importance and are under continual discussion. They illustrate well the fact that monetary policy operates against a background of considerable uncertainty about key relationships. They also illustrate the ongoing interaction between academic enquiry – what Taylor (2001, p. 263) has termed the 'new normative economic research' – and the institutional processes of policy formation.

7.5.3 Forecasting

Clearly, forecasts – interpreted generally to include the procedures and techniques that lie behind forward-looking assessments of the economy – are a key part of an inflation-targeting regime. Here, I concentrate on two aspects of a very large subject. The first concerns the consequences of non-stationarity – especially about the consequences of possible 'structural shifts' in key parameters. A number of authors in discussing policy rules have pointed to the large uncertainty about key parameters and data moments, such as trend productivity, potential GDP growth (or, in the labour market, the natural rate or NAIRU), and the neutral rate of interest. (See, for example, Kohn, 1999.) Moreover, there is an influential and developing literature which uses policy rules to illuminate the consequences of (real time) errors of assessment in explaining past policy mistakes (including notably Orphanides, 2000, on the US, and Nelson and Nikolov, 2001, on the UK). The second is about procedure – how forecasting models and forecasts enter into the policy making process.

Hendry and his co-authors have made the point (for example, in Hendry and Mizon, 2000) that if the economy were stationary in a statistical sense, one would not observe *systematic* forecast errors (though poor models would, of course, generate inefficient forecasts). They trace systematic forecast errors, which are, in fact, frequently observed, to 'deterministic shifts' – i.e. shifts in the unconditional means of key variables not accounted for by the existing forecasting model. Putting the point more simply, systematic errors arise from 'structural changes' in the economy. They make a number of points of practical policy importance. The first is that these kinds of non-stationarities may justify *ad hoc* and informal forecasting techniques, as well as practical procedures such as intercept adjustments and over-differencing, which are certainly a major feature of real-world forecasting and assessment exercises. A second is that the forecasting performance of a model may be a poor and misleading criterion for selecting a policy model – and vice versa: that good models for policy analysis may not be good forecasting models.

Any practical forecaster knows the potential importance of 'deterministic shifts'. In an important sense, there is little that can be done about them – since they are unforecastable from within the model. If they do occur, forecasts will go wrong. There is, however, an extremely important question about how quickly they are detected and how quickly they are taken into account. In the MPC process, for example, a large proportion of the time is typically spent on the question of whether new data should be treated as 'noise' or 'news' and, if the latter, what should be done about it. The response might be an intercept adjustment, or, it might lead, over a longer time period, to the re-estimation of important relationships, or even to the adoption of a new model as a forecasting/policy tool. This means that when it comes to understanding the practice of monetary policy, one is not concerned just with the process of forecasting and policy formation at a moment in time but also with the 'meta' reaction function which describes how the institution adapts and changes as information accrues, as mistakes are made, and as learning occurs – including the embodiment of the results of new research as they accrue (Allsopp and Vines, 2000).[21] As with other aspects of the 'reaction function', it is important that this aspect be transparent, and, as far as possible, publicly understood, as well.

Forecasting errors have been an important reason for major policy mistakes in the past – for example, in the UK in the late 1980s.[22] There is also a developing debate as to whether over-optimistic or, for that matter, over-pessimistic assessments of productivity performance have been a feature of US experience since the mid-1990s. An important question, however, is whether a well-functioning system should operate to moderate the effects of possible systematic forecasting errors. In principle it should.

The basic point is that, with a high frequency policy-making process, targeted on future inflation, forecasting errors should reveal themselves, triggering appropriate reactions. In the ordinary course of events this means that policy errors, due to poor data or forecast mistakes, should not cumulate. A mistake made one month should not be repeated the next – and, arguably, so long as the error is not great, does not matter very much. With systematic errors, the process is more complicated. But once the problem has been detected, it should trigger responses, such as intercept adjustments and reassessments of model properties, which should work to curtail and eliminate the systematic error. The crucial point is that the forecasting system itself needs to react quickly and appropriately to the signals provided by the economy. The authorities are committed to an objective for inflation, not to a particular forecasting model or set of procedures (Svensson, 2002).[23]

A potential difficulty is that the economy may not give good signals. It has been suggested, on these grounds, that with successful policies of low inflation – leading to rather flat Phillips curve responses – policy needs to react to other indicators, for example to prospects for demand or unemployment (Begg *et al.*, 2002). A low-inflation environment with high inertia may also increase the likelihood of bubbles in asset prices and other cumulative phenomena because, with the authorities focussed on inflation, interest-rate responses appear unlikely to market participants.

It is clear that forecasting needs to be seen as a process and as one that adapts through time. The role of forecasts in the policy process varies greatly between different systems. In the US, a staff forecast and assessment is available to members of the FOMC and is one input into the decision-making process.[24] In the UK, however, the MPC is responsible for the *Inflation Report* and the forecasts. The process is iterative – or back and forth (Vickers, 1998) – between Bank of England staff and the MPC. It is well recognised that nine MPC members are unlikely to agree on prospects for inflation, yet alone on the details, and they are intended to represent the centre of gravity of individual views.[25] The iterative and interactive process is widely regarded as an extremely important part of the formation of policy in the UK. Clearly, though, it raises intricate issues about the exact status of forecasts as well as other difficulties – issues detailed in a report by Don Kohn of the Federal Reserve (now a member of the FOMC) (Kohn, 2000).

With an interactive process such as that in the UK the choice of models and procedures is particularly important. (There is an ongoing programme of model development. A new model with a radically improved theoretical structure was introduced in 2003 (Bank of England, 2005).) But how should models be chosen and what kinds of models should be used? In practical terms, there may be a tension between theoretical sophistication and the needs of the interactive process of forecasting and assessment – which can be seen as mirroring the point made above that the best forecasting model may not be the best policy model – and vice versa.

7.5.4   Interaction with other policies

The establishment of a monetary policy reaction function clearly does not mean that other aspects of policy are unimportant in inflation control and in stabilization: it remains the overall framework and stance of macroeconomic policy that matters. Here I touch on some aspects of the interaction with fiscal policy.

There is, as for monetary policy, a developing consensus over some aspects of fiscal policy. First, it is widely agreed that there needs to be some fiscal closure rule or feedback device to rule out explosive debt/GDP trajectories in the longer term – though the form that commitment should take is highly contentious, as is illustrated by the debates over the Stability and Growth Pact in the EU (for example, Allsopp, 2002; Buiter and Grafe, 2002). The Governor of the Bank of Canada argues, for example, that their new monetary arrangements only started to work as intended with major changes in the fiscal framework (Dodge, 2002). Second, there is agreement, in practical terms, that fiscal policy should have a stabilization role in the short term, usually involving the pragmatic compromise of allowing the 'automatic stabilizers' to operate 'over the cycle'. Thus, the 'fiscal policy reaction function', like the monetary policy reaction function, can be seen as combining a longer-term commitment (here to sustainable debt and deficits) with a role in stabilization.

In the UK fiscal policy is constrained by the 'Code for Fiscal Stability', formalized in the Finance Act 1988 and by two (self-imposed) rules introduced in the 1997 election manifesto and confirmed in subsequent budgets (Balls and O'Donnell, eds, 2002, chapter 9). The 'Golden Rule', which states that 'over the economic cycle, the Government will borrow only to invest and not to fund current spending' is a 'balanced budget' rule for current spending: the 'Sustainable Investment Rule' that 'over the economic cycle, public debt as a proportion of GDP will be held at a stable and prudent level' is designed to ensure sustainability. In practice, the stable and prudent level for the debt ratio has been defined as not more than 40 per cent of GDP.

The Treasury argues that, given the framework, coordination problems between monetary and fiscal policy should not arise (Balls and

O'Donnell, 2002, chapter 6). Bean (1998b) has suggested that, in a system such as that in the United Kingdom, the fiscal authorities are effectively in the position of a Stackelberg leader, free to set fiscal policy but constrained by the monetary policy reaction function – which operates at high frequency. Formal coordination is not necessary so long as the interest rate reaction function is predictable. Moreover the monetary arrangements mean that fiscal policy cannot generate 'surprise inflation', which deals with a potential time-inconsistency problem. It is notable, however, that, in such a system, it is the fiscal authority which is responsible for monetary/fiscal mix – which may, for example, affect interest rates in the medium term and the exchange rate.

In fact, given the *assignment* of the 'nominal anchor' function of policy to the Monetary Policy Committee and, subject to that, of 'stabilization' as well, it can be argued that the details of fiscal policy are of secondary importance (so long as the commitment to fiscal sustainability is credible). The interest rate reaction function would take account of the fiscal arrangements. For example, if the automatic stabilizers are allowed to operate over the cycle, and these help to offset demand shocks, less stabilization needs to be provided by the monetary authorities.

Perhaps reflecting this assignment of roles and responsibilities, the formal analysis of fiscal policy rules is relatively underdeveloped compared with monetary policy rules. This assignment is, for the UK, relatively new. Under the Bretton Woods system, with monetary policy outside the United States assigned to meeting exchange rate commitments, stabilization was typically assigned to fiscal policy. Fiscal fine-tuning, however, fell into disrepute, partly because the evidence suggested, in the United Kingdom at least, that it was frequently destabilizing (Dow, 1964) and partly because the system failed to provide a nominal anchor against rising inflation. The design of fiscal policy rules and procedures is likely, however, to become a matter of increasing concern within countries that are members of EMU – since national monetary policies cannot be used to offset country-specific shocks.

It is interesting in this respect that a Swedish report by a group of experts (Committee on Stabilisation Policy, 2002), studying the implications of possible EMU entry, recommends giving a substantial public role regarding stabilization decisions to a fiscal policy council.[26] The arguments used draw heavily on the monetary policy rules literature. In principle, fiscal instruments could be used to support a non-accommodating policy against inflation as well. The issues have been discussed in the UK (in the similar context of the 2003 Euro deliberations and the '5 tests assessment'). Again, the problems are being looked at in terms of the establishment of a 'fiscal policy reaction function' drawing on the lessons that can be drawn from successful monetary policy institutions (see, especially, the discussion paper 'Fiscal Policy in EMU', HM Treasury 2003).

7.6   Concluding remarks

I have argued that monetary policy in the UK has succeeded in setting up a reaction function, which is recognisably of the appropriate type. I have also suggested that the new system should be reasonably robust, largely because its design reflects both the lessons of history and some of the main insights from the policy rules literature.

Performance so far has been good – indeed, remarkable by historical standards. However, though the system has survived some considerable shocks, there remains an important sense in which it has not been tested in adversity. So far, the accent has been on stabilization. The MPC has not yet been called on to react to a major increase in inflationary pressure, threatening the nominal anchor objective, which would involve decisive and, presumably, unpopular action. Yet the perception that such action would be taken, if necessary, is a crucial part of the system. The hope, of course, is that the commitment to take such action if necessary makes it less likely that it will be necessary.

I have noted that, in normal times, the perceived reaction function should stabilize expectations of both inflation and of growth. The confidence that policy will work in a particular way alters the way the economy works (including perceptions of risk). To an extent, 'thinking makes it so', and the private sector does much of the work via the effect of the policy framework on expectations.

The system requires a high degree of credibility or trust – which could be threatened from several directions. Clearly, credibility would be threatened if the policy makers were seen to be likely to cheat. Equally, however, it would be threatened if policy makers were perceived to be incompetent, or to lack appropriate instruments. (This latter worry is one of the reasons why the possibility of deflation with nominal interest rates reaching their lower bound, as in Japan, is worrying.) The better the system functions and the more public understanding of how it is supposed to function, the more credible it is likely to become.

I have discussed a number of issues of current concern. One of these is asset prices. I have subscribed to the 'received wisdom' that generally it is neither necessary nor desirable for interest rates to respond to asset prices except to the extent that they contribute to inflationary or deflationary pressures, but with the recognition that there could be cases where diverting the interest-rate instrument to reducing particular kinds of shocks could be justified on second-best cost benefit grounds if destabilizing shocks can thereby be reduced. Considerations of credibility – hard enough to establish anyway – weigh heavily against such policies. A far better strategy would be to tackle the destabilizing dynamic processes, e.g. those involved in bubble-type phenomena, more directly with other policies.

There is a worry, however, that the perception that economic policy will *not* react to phenomena such as asset-price bubbles or exchange-rate misalignments might encourage the phenomena themselves. This is most likely to be the case if there is a perceived 'disconnect' between the phenomena and prospects for growth and inflation – since then the interest rate consequences implicit in the normal reaction function are, in effect, shorted out, making destabilizing cumulative processes the more likely. There are historical instances, for example, where 'benign neglect' of the exchange rate (with the concentration of policy on the domestic economy) has appeared to lead to exchange-rate misalignments and instability. This is not to argue for giving a special role to exchange rates of asset prices in inflation targeting, still less should it be seen as an argument for altering the target. It should serve, however, to reinforce the point that the successful establishment of an inflation-targeting regime does not mean that all macroeconomic policy problems are dealt with. On the contrary, it is likely to highlight other aspects of the overall policy regime.

This is particularly true with regard to fiscal policy. There is consensus that a credible monetary policy requires a credible fiscal framework to go with it. So far, however, research on fiscal policy reaction functions seems relatively underdeveloped.

Finally, if I were asked what would make the most difference to the procedures of practical monetary policy making, it would be better and more reliable data and better understanding of key economic relationships. Given the uncertainties, the process of assessment and forecasting is bound to be judgemental – and in that sense, not rule-like. But if the goals are clear and the process is open and transparent, the resulting policy is, to a large extent predictable, which is what matters for the stabilization of expectations.

Notes

1　This chapter is an edited and updated version of a speech presented at a conference on 'Policy Rules – the Next Steps' in Cambridge, September 2002 (Allsopp, 2002) when the author was a member of the Monetary Policy Committee. The views expressed are personal and obviously should not be interpreted as those of the Bank of England, then or now, or of other members of the MPC. The author is very grateful to Amit Kara and Ed Nelson for intellectual and practical assistance during the preparation of the original paper and would also like to thank Jagjit Chadha and Richard Mash for extremely useful comments and discussions.

2　See Svensson (1997) for pioneering academic work on inflation forecast targeting, and Batini and Haldane (1999) for a discussion of incorporating inflation forecasts into policy rules with emphasis on the UK.

3　In the simplest approaches involving demand shocks and price shocks (often described misleadingly as 'supply shocks'), policy involves offsetting demand shocks completely whilst price-level or Phillips curve shocks involve a trade-off between the variability of the output gap and inflation.

4　Keynes (1936, chapter 19) was more concerned with the problem of real interest rates rising during price deflation – a pathology now familiar in Japan.

5　The idea that non-inflationary stability can be achieved by fixing the money supply is still extraordinarily influential. Hicks wrote in 1967: 'We still have a Currency School, seeking in vain – but one sees why – for a monetary system that shall be automatic' (Hicks, 1967, p. viii). This is much less true now, largely reflecting the experience with monetary targeting.

6　Patinkin (1969) argues that the interwar Chicago tradition (as represented, for example, by Henry Simons) favoured counter-cyclical monetary policy for these reasons. Friedman (1967) and King (1997b, p. 85) also discuss Simons' views on monetary policy. It should be noted that Simons specifically rejected a monetary policy framework based on targeting future inflation. He advocated targeting current values of a cyclically-sensitive price index: 'The index must be highly sensitive; otherwise, the administrative authority would be compelled to postpone its actions unduly after significant disturbances or (Heaven forbid!) obliged to use discretion in anticipating changes' (Simons, 1948, p. 329).

7　It is ironic that the adoption of supposedly non-activist money supply targets involved monetary activism via (discretionary) changes in the short-term interest rate.

8　There are a number of different accounts of why the policy maker would want to produce surprise inflation. The most usual one is that, due to distortions in the economy, the natural rate of unemployment is sub-optimally high. Another is that unexpected inflation produces effectively lump-sum revenues for the government (which are not available from general taxation which is distortionary). In both these cases, the policy maker is benign and is acting in the interests of society. Of course, the policy maker might not be 'benign' – which raises rather different issues.

9　With the caveat, as usual, that estimates of the 'optimal reaction function' may be model and shock specific – so that, in practice, the reaction function needs to be robust to different contingencies and to model uncertainty.

10 There are many accounts of the operation of the Monetary Policy Committee in the UK. See especially King (1997a, 2002), Balls (2001), Balls and O'Donnell (2001), and Bean and Jenkinson (2001).

11 An 'open letter' system operates, also symmetrically, if the divergence from target in any given month exceeds one percentage point, and should be regarded more as an 'enabling device' in the event of major shocks (such as oil crises) than as a sanction in the event of divergence from target. Surprisingly, given historical experience in the UK, no open letter has been triggered since the inception of the new system. Even more surprisingly, the nearest it has come to being triggered was on the *downside* in July 2002 when annual RPIX inflation for June came in at 1.5 per cent.

12 There was a brief flurry of debate in the UK over monetary base control in the early 1980s, which fizzled out. Monetary targeting in the UK was of the 'indicator' variety, with interest rates used to try to meet the intermediate objective. From this point of view, the chosen aggregate was unfortunate in that broad money was not easily controllable by the instrument (since it was interest-bearing), and the relationship between the monetary aggregate and the final objectives was weak, unreliable, and changing over time.

13 This practice does not preclude the possibility that the steady-state value of potential GDP is inefficiently low from society's point of view, due to, for example, monopolistic distortions, but effectively delegates responsibility for eliminating the effects of these inefficiencies to microeconomic policy (as advocated by, for example, Meade, 1951, and Rotemberg and Woodford, 1997).

14 See also Posen (1993), McCallum (1995), King (1996, 1997b), and Taylor (1997) for related discussions.

15 This has happened once since inception – after the terrorist attacks of 11 September 2001.

16 Similar experiences took place in several Scandinavian countries.

17 It is perhaps notable, that, in his newspaper column, Krugman (2002), criticizing Chairman Greenspan for having allowed the US stock market boom to develop to the point where a destabilizing bust was likely, suggested that margin requirements to discourage speculation should have been introduced early on in the boom. He did not suggest that the interest-rate instrument should have been used.

18 Housing market issues were the subject of two independent reviews instituted in 2003 – the Barker Review (Barker, 2004) and the Miles Review (Miles, 2004), the latter concentrating on the UK's mortgage market.

19 Vickers (1999, p. 434) notes that, since the variance matters, 'expected inflation somewhat under target with moderate inflation uncertainty might be better than expected inflation on target with high inflation uncertainty'.

20 From time to time a different 'window', such as five days, has been used if the 15-day window is judged misleading.

21 Though formal analysis of such learning processes is difficult, it is not really that much more difficult conceptually than the process by which people learn to drive unfamiliar vehicles. But see Sargent (1999) on US monetary policy and inflation.

22 Hendry and Mizon (2000) ascribe this to a 'deterministic shift' applying to the models of the consumption function then current. Of course, recognition of the problems may lead on to better models which 'explain' the

deterministic shifts – e.g. in terms of previously omitted variables. Over-optimistic assessments of the productivity trend were another reason for policy error (Nelson and Nikolov, 2001).

23   Svensson goes on to argue, more contentiously, that inflation-targeting frameworks entail (or should entail) publicly-specified objective functions with explicit announcements of the functional form and numerical weights in the functions.

24   One disadvantage of staff forecasts is that it is, in bureaucratic terms, difficult to make them public since the policy makers might be seen to be disagreeing with their own staff. In the US, the full forecasts are published after five years.

25   The explanation at the beginning of the *Inflation Report* reads: 'Although not every member will agree with every assumption on which are projections are based, the fan charts represent the MPC's best collective judgement about the most likely paths for inflation and output, and the uncertainties surrounding those central projections.'

26   For the UK, Wren-Lewis (2000) has suggested that policy could be improved in the UK if control over some fiscal variables was assigned to the MPC.

8
The Untied Kingdom[1] as Monetary and Fiscal Union

Mark H. Robson[2]

The ghost of referenda yet to come

It is May 2008, in the small hours of Friday. Counting is well underway of the referendum votes on the question 'Do you want to have the euro instead of the pound as your currency?' As the piles of bundles mount, it becomes clear that the startling exit poll results were broadly correct. In England and Wales a clear majority have said 'no'. In Scotland a large majority have said 'yes'. In Northern Ireland, while the results are predictably split by polling district along familiar sectarian lines, a clear majority here too have said 'yes', following the recent years of *de facto* dual currency.

You are a middle-ranking policy official in the Treasury, with responsibility for economics of the regions and liaison with the Department for Constitutional Affairs. The minister's private secretary there has just telephoned (yes, at 2 in the morning as they sometimes do) in the certain knowledge that you will be at home absorbed in the television coverage. The minister is in a panic. An announcement must be made at the 10.30 press conference. Is it conceivable, feasible, expedient (never mind 'wise') that Scotland and/or Northern Ireland might be able to join the euro without England and Wales? The minister must have a brief for 9.30, with an agreed Treasury line.

No problem, you assure your interlocutor, hang up your bedside phone and settle back to sleep. Because, as the conscientious public servant that you are, you have already prepared the brief for just this, and for each alternative outcome, of the previous day's events.

An everyday story of Whitehall folk. But an intriguing scenario, and one that I have found generates surprisingly confused responses when posed across the dinner table.

Since the devolution programme began in earnest, I have often had occasion to wonder about the technical aspects of possible monetary and/or greater fiscal independence for different parts of the Untied (as I consistently mistyped) Kingdom. In many respects the technical aspects are perhaps rather more interesting than the politics, which certainly dominate. It has been the policy of the Scottish National Party since 2003 that Scotland should immediately join the euro if political independence from the remainder of the UK were achieved.

This chapter therefore explores some of the technical aspects – *could* it be done? – without worrying too much about the economic and political *shoulds* of potential euro membership, which have already been, and will surely continue to be, very widely discussed – on more or less informed bases.

Monetary disunion

The United Kingdom is a monetary and fiscal union of three territories with distinct legal systems: England and Wales; Scotland; and Northern Ireland. Wales is, at the time of writing, inconceivably independent, with an extremely limited role for the Assembly other than as a discussion forum. Scotland is evidently a nation with considerable independence already. Northern Ireland is a province, only intermittently self-governing at all, comprising six of the 32 counties that formed the nation and island of Ireland until partition. The Republic of Ireland ceased to be in fiscal union with the UK at that point, with the first Finance Act of its own in 1922. However, it remained in monetary union with the UK, through a transition period that led to the Irish punt retaining fixed parity with the pound sterling until 1979. What happened at that time may provide interesting pointers as to what monetary disunion for Scotland or Northern Ireland might lead.

There are, of course, currently no instances of EU Member Sub-States adopting the euro on their own. There are, indeed, no parts of any Member State in monetary disunion from other parts of that same Member State. But the position of the United Kingdom and the Republic of Ireland is the closest. These two remain in a very special relationship, not just because of their common (and at the same time, uncommon) history and sole common land border. There have always been reciprocal residence, voting and tax-relieving rights since partition, long pre-dating the more general arrangements that apply within the EU. The two economies are obviously closely interdependent. So we can usefully start by looking briefly at the abandonment of United Kingdom/Republic of

Ireland fixed parity in 1979, as a potentially informative case study. Two interesting papers document the Irish experience through the 1980s and 1990s (Lane, 1999; Thom and Walsh, 2002).[3]

Until 1979, Ireland had first been politically and, *inter alia*, monetarily integrated with Great Britain since 1801 and then, after partition in 1922, had maintained a strictly fixed parity with the pound Sterling, initially by means of a Currency Commission. A Central Bank of Ireland was created in 1943.

Inflationary experience in Ireland averaging 13.9 per cent per year was regarded as highly unsatisfactory in the 1970s, following the break-up of the Bretton Woods system of internationally fixed exchange rates based on the gold standard that prevailed from 1944 to 1971.[4] The German experience averaging 5.2 per cent per year was viewed with envy. The UK had been widely expected to join the European Monetary System at its launch on 13 March 1979, but as a result of sudden strengthening of the pound, was in the event the only one of the then nine EU Member States not to join. Irish parity was therefore broken on 30 March, in a comparatively rare economic policy swap of one nominal anchor for another.

The new managed exchange rate system was hardly an unequivocal success. There were 11 EMS realignments by 1987; as early as 1981 the punt had fallen as low as 0.73 pounds Sterling (see Figure 8.1). The Irish

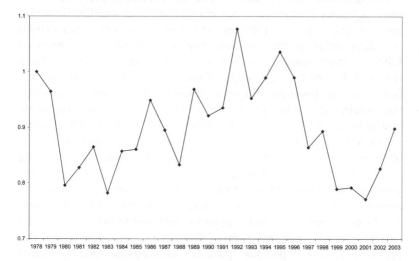

Figure 8.1   Irish punt to UK pound Sterling exchange

Source: Year-end official exchange rates, from IMF, *International Finance Statistics*.

punt's three devaluations within the ERM, however (in 1983, 1986 and 1993), each occurred as a result of Sterling's relative weakness – following its strength in the 1979–81 early Thatcher period – and in an attempt to maintain Irish competitiveness.[5]

In 1979 Ireland had a budget deficit of around 8 per cent of GDP. At the same time the government debt to GDP ratio stood at 65 per cent; it grew steadily through a series of minor political crises until 1986, when the debt/GDP ratio was at 116 per cent and the cost of debt servicing had reached 6.7 per cent of GDP. Towards the end of this period, however, a combination of expenditure cuts and increasing taxes on labour and consumption had stabilized the fiscal position – but at considerable costs. With no attempt to coordinate bargaining, wage growth kept pace with inflation and unemployment rose from 7 per cent in 1980 to 17 per cent in 1986. Real wages grew slowly and take-home pay was cut by the substantial increase in labour taxes.

In 1986, immediately before a general election, inflation had fallen below 5 per cent. But the nominal 'anchor' of the EMS failed for a second time, with an 8 per cent devaluation against the deutschmark (DEM), as the centrepiece of the European monetary policy. Investor confidence was low, with major capital outflows arising from political fears. The incoming Fianna Fail government, however, imposed even tougher fiscal measures. Public expenditure was cut further rather than reducing the tax burden, with a new social partnership that traded wage moderation for a reduction in labour taxes and price stability, through a more credible link to the DEM. In fact this held until 1993, with a 10 per cent devaluation required to reduce the high real interests experienced following the inglorious exit in the previous September of Sterling from the ERM, having finally joined in October 1990. But over the decade from 1987, the Irish economy enjoyed spectacular success, with average inflation of only 2.4 per cent (better even than 2.6 per cent in Germany, and as against 4.3 per cent in the UK) and sustained high GDP growth.

In a very different inflationary climate, does this economic adventure offer any obvious lessons for Scotland or Northern Ireland in leaving Sterling for the euro, via at least two years in ERM II (institutional arrangements which are discussed below)? The motivation would not apparently be a switch to a better nominal anchor, unless something wholly extraordinary should happen to relative inflation in the UK and euroland in the next few years. Although euro membership would provide access to deep capital markets and improved trade conditions through elimination of euro exchange rate risk – undoubtedly attractive to EU-inward investors – the Irish experience seems to indicate that maintaining competitiveness with the economy (or economies) of greatest integration may be of dominating importance for a small country. The nominal anchor expected to be provided by the EMS proved opportunistic and later largely irrelevant, as independent counter-inflationary strategies were developed. It is rather difficult to see how euro membership would be particularly useful – from a macroeconomic perspective – for Scotland or Northern Ireland, although in the latter case it would facilitate greater, exchange-rate-risk-free, integration with its neighbour. This is certainly a significant microeconomic benefit. Indeed it is no exaggeration to note that, for a country with sufficient confidence that its monetary policy will continue to deliver low and stable price inflation indefinitely, the advantages of monetary union can only be microeconomic. The macroeconomic impact can only be disadvantageous because of the loss of flexibility involved in sacrificing independence. We return to this point, which does not seem to be well understood in public debate, in considering the theory of optimal currency areas below.

But the key lesson drawn from the Irish experience for our present purpose is that there is no technical or practical obstacle to a small country leaving a long-standing monetary union and joining a loose association (i.e. now ERM II) and improving its economic structure – given the political will to do so.

Independence for Slovakia

The Irish Republic left the pound in 1979 in order to join the newly forming EU Exchange Rate Mechanism. It is much more unusual to find modern cases of monetary disunion that do not arise from the intention of one party to form a monetary union with a larger economy. But there is one recent case: the division in January 1993 – the so-called 'Velvet Divorce' – of the former Czechoslovakia into two republics, with simultaneous monetary and fiscal disunion. For some commentators, such a division demonstrates the possibility of Scotland – with a population of the same order as that of Slovakia – divorcing England and Wales.[6] However, although the political history of the Czech and Slovak case is certainly interesting, a parallel for the UK is not so obvious. The United Kingdom is already a member of the EU. For Slovaks, the prize was, with patience, to enter the OECD and shortly after the EU as an independent republic.

The division of Czechoslovakia was driven by fundamental differences between political parties. In brief, the Communist Party had dropped its claims to a leading political role at the end of 1989. The pre-Communist Federal Assembly was reconstructed, and central planning abandoned. A serious Czech/Slovak conflict emerged when the Assembly discussed a proposal to drop the attribute 'socialist' from the name of the country. Many Slovak deputies then demanded that the country return to its original name Czecho-Slovakia, adopted by the Treaty of Versailles in 1918 (the hyphen was dropped in 1923). After unexpectedly fierce discussions, the country was renamed as the Czech and Slovak Federal Republic in April 1990. At the same time, the Slovak National Party was founded and the first free elections for 40 years were held in June.

Serious jurisdictional disputes soon emerged between Federal and Slovak governments. Economic conditions under early liberalization were tough: demand for Czechoslovak goods in the Soviet Union and other Eastern European countries had collapsed and domestic macro-economic policies led to a collapse of domestic demand as well. Real wages fell by 27 per cent in the first half of 1991 and personal consumption dropped by 37 per cent; falling industrial production led to unemployment, virtually non-existent before 1990, in excess of 12 per cent in Slovakia.

The results of the elections of June 1992 reflected the growing split between the two lands. The following month, Slovakia declared itself a sovereign state, meaning that its laws took precedence over those of the federal government. In November the federal parliament voted to dissolve the country officially on 31 December, despite polls indicating that the majority of citizens opposed the split. So in January 1993 the Czech and Slovak Federal Republic was replaced by two independent states, becoming IMF members simultaneously. The process of privatization slowed noticeably in Slovakia, which had been enjoying higher growth but still a lower level of GDP per head than its Czech neighbours for some years. Within three years, the Czech Republic had been admitted to the OECD, although the Slovaks had to wait for a further five years, until the end of 2000. Both then became EU members, with another eight accession countries, in May 2004.

As might be expected, the smaller, less economically developed and more cautiously liberalizing country's currency depreciated significantly relative to its neighbour (see Figure 8.2).

With the benefit of hindsight, however, the disunion does not appear to have harmed the Slovak economy at all. It delayed OECD membership because of the slower liberalization, but it did not impede EU accession. The devaluation afforded improved competitiveness

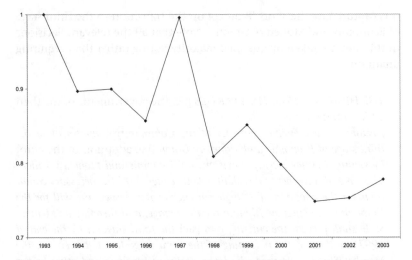

Figure 8.2 Czech korunas per Slovak koruna exchange rate
Source: Year-end official exchange rates, from IMF, *International Finance Statistics*.

with its neighbour while, as in the Irish case, not apparently affecting trade volumes adversely simply by introducing exchange rate variability. At the technical level, central bank fission in 1993 proved unproblematic.

'Ins' and 'outs': the third stage of EMU

All EU members are officially expected to adopt the euro; or, at least, required to be keen to adopt it at the earliest appropriate opportunity. This surprising, perhaps provocative, statement will be justified by reference to the official position of the ECB and other European institutions, as explained below. Choosing to opt out when you could be in is simply not seen as playing the European game.

The European legislation providing for the establishment of the ECB is the 'Protocol on the Statute of the European System of Central Banks and of the European Central Bank'. The Statute was provided for by Article 4a of the (Maastricht) Treaty establishing the European Community, as published in the *Official Journal* on 29 July 1992. The UK, in common with all the other members (but not, of course, Austria, Finland or Sweden, who joined only in 1995) was a signatory. It is a long and detailed document, but the essence of what was going on politically was captured by the short 'Protocol on the transition to the third stage of Economic and Monetary Union'. (Note that all the relevant decisions in this area are taken by qualified majority voting rather than requiring unanimity.)

> *THE HIGH CONTRACTING PARTIES* [i.e. the governments of the then 12 Member States],
> *Declare the irreversible character of the Community's movement to the third stage of Economic and Monetary Union* [i.e. adoption of the euro] *by signing the new Treaty Provisions on Economic and Monetary Union. Therefore all Member States shall, whether they fulfil the necessary conditions for the adoption of a single currency or not, respect the will for the Community to enter swiftly into the third stage, and therefore no Member State shall prevent the entering into* [sic] *the third stage. If by the end of 1997 the date of the beginning of the third stage has not been set, the Member States concerned, the Community institutions and other bodies involved shall expedite all preparatory work during 1998, in order to enable the Community to enter the third stage irrevocably on 1 January 1999 and to enable the ECB and the ESCB to start their full functioning from this date.*
> *This protocol shall be annexed to the Treaty establishing the European Community.*

The terms applicable to the current three 'opting-out' countries – the UK, Denmark and Sweden – were individually negotiated. The first was obviously needed for the UK, as a signatory to the Maastricht Treaty, and is couched in rather different terms than 'fulfilling the necessary conditions' as above. The four specific criteria referred to in Article 109j are

- achievement of a high degree of price stability (rate of inflation close to that of the best performing Member States);
- sustainability of the government financial position (budgetary position without an excessive deficit);
- observation of the normal fluctuation margins provided by the Exchange Rate Mechanism for at least two years without devaluing against the currency of any other Member State (apparently including the 'outs'); and
- durability of convergence achieved and participation in the ERM being reflected in long-term interest rate levels.

The Protocol on certain provisions relation to the United Kingdom of Great Britain and Northern Ireland begins as follows:

THE HIGH CONTRACTING PARTIES,
RECOGNIZING that the United Kingdom shall not be obliged or commit-
ted to move to the third stage of Economic and Monetary Union without a
separate decision to do so by its government and Parliament,
NOTING the practice of the government of the United Kingdom to fund its
borrowing requirement by the sale of debt to the private sector,
HAVE AGREED the following provisions, which shall be annexed to the
Treaty establishing the European Community:
1. The United Kingdom shall notify the Council [of Ministers] *whether*
it intends to move to the third stage before the Council makes its assess-
ment under Article 109j(2) of this Treaty [i.e. of whether the convergence criteria are met].
Unless the United Kingdom notifies the Council that it intends to move
to the third stage, it shall be under no obligation to do so.

In the paragraphs 2 to 11 that follow, if the UK notified the Council that it did not intend to move to the third stage – as indeed it did – then it was to retain its monetary policy powers, with no participation in voting for the members of the Executive Board of the ECB, the Bank of England not subscribing share capital of the ECB on the same basis as the 'ins', and continuing to provide a borrowing (known as 'Ways and Means') facility to the government as long as remaining an 'out'.

But paragraph 10 is particularly interesting for the present discussion:

10. If the United Kingdom does not move to the third stage, it may change
its notification at any time after the beginning of that stage. In that event:
(a) The United Kingdom shall have the right to move to the third stage
provided only that it satisfies the necessary conditions. The Council, acting
at the request of the United Kingdom and under the conditions and in
accordance with the procedure laid down in Article 109k(2) of this Treaty,
shall decide whether it fulfils the necessary conditions.
(b) The Bank of England shall pay up its subscribed capital, transfer to
the ECB foreign reserve assets and contribute to its reserves on the same
basis as the national central bank of a Member State whose derogation has
been abrogated.
(c) The Council, acting under the conditions and in accordance with the
procedure laid down in Article 109l(5) of this Treaty, shall take all other nec-
essary decisions to enable the United Kingdom to move to the third stage.
If the United Kingdom moves to the third stage pursuant to the provisions
of this protocol, paragraphs 3 to 9 shall cease to have effect.

It is therefore not difficult for the UK to enter, as a latecomer to the party, although the terms – and in particular the extent to which the same convergence criteria as applied to the 12 original members could and would be applied to the UK as an original 'out' – remain unclear. But some idea can surely be gleaned, notwithstanding that they are all smaller than the UK, from the terms offered to the 10 accession countries, considered below. And, of course, Scotland and Northern Ireland are of comparable size to several of these territories. So if the Commission and the ECB and the Council of Ministers (bearing in mind that only QMV, not unanimity, is required) and the European Parliament, decided that this subnational territories would be welcome, subject to a new Protocol, then there would not appear to be major technical obstacles.

Denmark, as well as the UK, also originally had a special Protocol referring to the need for a referendum under its constitution. Having in fact decided not to participate in the first wave, it has been granted an indefinite exemption, similar in effect to a formal derogation; but its formal position is less 'out' than the UK. Indeed, until the addition of three of the accession countries in July 2004, it was the only Member State in ERM II. At least in theory, the EU institutions could opt a Member State with a derogation into the euro unless its government took steps to sabotage its convergence. The *realpolitik* might, one would imagine, be a little different and indeed the case of Sweden bears this out. On accession to the EU together with Austria and Finland in 1995, Sweden was not granted an exemption similar to that afforded to Denmark and the UK. In principle, therefore, it cannot stay out indefinitely even though, unlike Greece, in the initial round of assessment it did meet the convergence criteria. The Swedish position, of a derogation that is being treated as a unilateral opt-out, has been justified by the government on the basis of a statement made when the accession negotiations opened in February 1993 – 'A final Swedish position relating to the transition from the second stage to the third stage will be taken in the light of further developments and in accordance with the provision in the Treaty' – and that public opinion, strongly euro-sceptic, is more important than legal niceties.[7] This is perhaps a little problematic for the EU institutions in relation to the accession countries, which we now turn to consider.

The position of the May 2004 accession countries

Although there is little merit in examining the precise circumstances of all of the 10 accession countries individually, the terms and expectations under which they have joined are certainly of interest, because several of them are comparable in size of population and economy to Scotland and Northern Ireland.

Formally, these countries are in the same position in relation to the third stage of EMU as Sweden: they all joined the EU with a derogation but are expected to adopt the euro at the earliest possible opportunity. The ECB's view of their position in the meantime, expressed as a series of illuminating FAQs on its website, is highly recommended reading. Certainly, most of these countries' governments appear publicly keen to join. Given the way in which the convergence criteria are framed, two years' membership of the ERM are required. The earliest time at which the eurozone could be enlarged by some or all of these accession countries is therefore mid-2006 (it is possible than Denmark, but only Denmark, could enlarge it before then).

In practice, as in the case of Sweden, if popular opinion or the government of the day should look unfavourably on the prospect then it is difficult to see how sanctions could be imposed. Expulsion from the EU looks rather implausible. Since the countries are all relatively small, they cannot do anything other than perhaps a little political harm by choosing to stay out. And a wish to stay out, whether politically or economically motivated, could formally be satisfied by simply contriving not to meet one or more of the convergence criteria – most straightforwardly, probably, a token devaluation against the currency of another Member State – including any of the other 12 'out' countries.

We take Estonia as an example of interest. Notwithstanding its success in maintaining a currency board peg to the deutschmark and then the euro since 1992, Estonia as an EU Member State is still being required to spend the minimum two years in ERM II as one of the convergence criteria for the third stage. The standard fluctuation band remains $+/-15$ per cent. On 27 June 2004, together with Lithuania and Slovenia, Estonia joined Denmark, making four ERM II members, maintaining its existing currency board structure and exchange rate policy. But Estonia's policy of pegging to the euro is only regarded by the ECB as a unilateral commitment, imposing no obligations on euro members until the margins of the fluctuation band are reached (and even then the eurozone countries have a possible opt out, in the interest of maintaining price stability).[8]

In its press release the ECB rather portentously announced:

The agreement on participation of the kroon in ERM II is based on a firm commitment by the Estonian authorities to continue with sound fiscal policies, which are essential for preserving macroeconomic stability, for supporting an orderly and substantial reduction of the current account deficit, and for ensuring the sustainability of the convergence process. The authorities will closely monitor macroeconomic developments together with the responsible EU bodies, and they will strengthen the fiscal stance if warranted. To help reduce the external imbalance and contain it at a sustainable level, they will take the necessary measures to contain domestic credit growth and ensure effective financial supervision, and they will promote wage moderation. Structural reforms aimed at further enhancing the economy's flexibility and adaptability will be implemented in a timely fashion so as to strengthen domestic adjustment mechanisms and maintain the overall competitiveness of the economy.

The population of Estonia has been falling, to only 1.34 million at the beginning of 2004, although it is larger in area than Denmark or Switzerland. What lessons might be learned from such a small less developed country, with a very different political background and rapidly growing GDP, for Scotland and Northern Ireland?

The most technically difficult factor is evidently the requirement to spend two years in ERM II before being permitted to join the euro. In the case of Estonia and Lithuania (but not Slovenia, nor, of course, Denmark) the currency board and full backing supports a fixed exchange rate. If Scotland and Northern Ireland were able to join using Sterling as their currency, then intervention would be expected to occur close to the 15 per cent (or whatever limit should be fixed from time to time) margins around the central rate. But at some point a fixed rate against the euro would need to be established. Because there have not as yet been any second round joiners, no one can be entirely sure as to how that will work in the case of any country which has not already sought to peg its rate. And there is no plan, at least publicly, to narrow the band like a funnel back towards the 2.25 per cent limit that applied before the ERM crisis. Indeed, it is not straightforward to see how ERM II can help countries joining at different times with free-floating exchange rates, when the minimum waiting time is fixed at two years, if the bands are the same for all. The rules were designed for countries joining at the same time, as indeed they did in the first wave. A true funnel to aid exchange rate convergence would set different and narrowing band widths for different currencies as an explicit function of their expected waiting time remaining.

Non-Sterling currencies within the UK

The requirement to spend two years in ERM II with at best only a unilateral commitment to an exchange rate peg raises the interesting question of whether there could (indeed, would need to) be Scottish and Northern Irish pounds, floating off from sterling at the point of joining ERM II or some later date, much as did the Irish punt in 1979.

Three Scottish and four Northern Irish commercial banks do issue their own banknotes; but since these are required to be backed wholly by Bank of England notes,[9] they are really only like advertising wrappers. The Bank of England has been able to achieve a monopoly on note issue in England and Wales since the Bank Charter Act of 1844, even though it remained privately owned until 1946. The last private bank notes in England and Wales issued under the 1844 transitional arrangements were by the Somerset bank, Fox, Fowler and Co in 1921.

There is a distinct possibility, however, that – rather than the costly exercise of issuing its own notes in entirely new designs – a new central bank of Scotland and/or Northern Ireland could instead simply provide the backing of the Bank of England for the existing distinctive notes – which would float off from sterling. So we now turn naturally to consider a partial precedent for such a new central bank.

Would a separate central bank be required for Scotland and/or Northern Ireland?

The formal answer to this question is yes but, in practice, not really as we know it; just as the new Central Bank of Ireland had only rather limited functions in 1943. One small Member State, Luxembourg (with a population of around half a million), has enjoyed monetary union in its modern, formal sense with Belgium since 1922, when parity of their respective francs was established, followed by a general monetary agreement in 1935, when Belgian coins and banknotes became legal tender in Luxembourg.

The earlier monetary history was convoluted. The 'franc germinal' had been introduced by the Emperor Napoleon in 1803; in 1842 Luxembourg become a member of the celebrated German customs union or *Zollverein* and the thaler was introduced as currency. In 1848 the franc was introduced for administrative and official documents and then in 1856 the privately owned Banque Internationale à Luxembourg (BIL) was founded and obtained the authorization to issue banknotes. From 1873 to 1881 there was a proto-central bank, the Banque Nationale du Grand-Duché de Luxembourg, issuing banknotes in Thalers and in francs originally, later in marks. But then the BIL reverted to being the sole issuer of banknotes, which were adopted as the legal currency in 1914; in 1918 a grand-ducal decree first used the expression 'Luxembourg franc'.

Monetary policy after 1935 was, in effect, handled entirely by the Belgian National Bank, with a branch in Luxembourg, which had never had a national central bank in the customary sense. Rather, Article 1.2 of the 1979 Protocol on the ECB specifically provided that 'The Institut monétaire luxembourgeois will be the central bank of Luxembourg'. This institute was only created in 1983, specifically with a view to ensuring that the third stage criteria could be demonstrably met. It was the subject of a European Parliament study[10] because of concerns that the letter of the statutes might not be able to be complied with. An objective observer might be forgiven for wondering whether there is not something more than a little surreal about interfering in the institutional arrangements of a perfectly satisfactory, long-standing monetary union for sake of a much riskier experiment? But to be fair, the irrevocable nature of the euro union imposes all sorts of non-monetary requirements, and the fiscal systems and positions of Belgium and Luxembourg are very different.

National central banks are required to fulfil several obligations to the ECB, including on a delegated basis most of the monetary policy and external operations of the eurosystem, provision of payment and securities settlement facilities, management of the euro banknote issue, analysis and research and collection of statistical data.[11] What they do not perform, of course, other than through their Governors acting independently and in a personal capacity, are the usual policy functions of a central bank.

The Banque centrale de Luxembourg was created on 1 June 1998 at the same time as the ECB. Of course, it had to be separately capitalized and provided with reserves in order to contribute to funding and governance of the ECB in exactly the same way as every other national central bank. The Institut, as its predecessor, was primarily responsible for financial sector supervision – carried out in the UK by the Financial Services Authority – and managing the issue of currency. So it is perfectly feasible for a small country to have a 'central bank light' regime – while in monetary union with a larger country or group of countries.

Within the UK, however, there is a further and unusual complication. The Bank of England, primarily as a result of its odd history as a privately owned (until 1946) national bank with monopoly rights to note issue, does not own the national foreign exchange reserves, which are the property of the government, nor can it benefit from its note-issuing activities, since all the profits must be remitted directly to the Treasury. An agency fee is paid to the Bank for managing the reserves, and the note issue is ring-fenced in the accounts as the Issue Department.

Not for these reasons but others, the Bank of England could not join the eurosystem as presently constituted under the Bank of England Act 1998, which provided for independence of monetary policy from government control. The basis of accounting would need to change to the common ESCB format, with the accounting date moving from 28 February to 31 December, and the collection of statistical data; and evidently the role of the Monetary Policy Committee would change dramatically to one of advising the governor in a non-binding way, if indeed it continued to exist. The main operational changes would be to the means of conducting monetary policy operations, with all credit institutions required to hold minimum reserves, and to the payments systems infrastructure.[12] A new Act of Parliament would, in any event, be required – as, of course, it would to establish a regional central bank and put it in funds to enable it to become a member of the eurosystem.

Every member of the ESCB, whether 'in' or 'out', contributes capital to the ECB in proportion to a 'capital key' calculated using data on GDP and population which is adjusted every five years and on a change in membership. The 'outs' only pay up 7 per cent (until 1 May 2004, 5 per cent) of their share in subscribed capital – i.e. what they would contribute if they were 'in' – as a contribution to the operating costs of the ECB. Not being involved in the common monetary policy they do not contribute reserves, nor do they share in 'monetary income' (the ECB expression for seigniorage, the revenues arising from the fact that banknotes do not bear interest). The capital keys and subscriptions as of 1 May 2004 are as shown in Table 8.1.

If Scotland and/or Northern Ireland were to 'break in' to the eurozone then they would move from the bottom to the top part of the table. Their central banks would have to contribute 100 per cent instead of the 7 per cent of subscription, and be put in funds to provide reserves to back the additional issue of euro notes, replacing the Scottish or Northern Irish notes previously in issue and backed by a part of reserves held in the Issue Department of the Bank of England.

Legislative independence

Domestic laws are not usually passed by Westminster for Scotland and Northern Ireland at the same time as they are for England and Wales. There are some exceptions. Tax legislation, in Finance and consolidation Acts, applies uniformly throughout the United Kingdom and the consequences of that are explored below. Some recent legislation is, unusually, structured so as to address the different legal positions of the

Table 8.1 Capital keys and paid-up capital of the ECB as at 1 May 2004

NCB	Capital key (%)	Paid-up capital (€)
Euro area NCBs		
Nationale Bank van België /	2.5502	141,910,195
Banque Nationale de Belgique		
Deutsche Bundesbank	21.1364	1,176,170,750
Bank of Greece	1.8974	105,584,034
Banco de España	7.7758	432,697,551
Banque de France	14.8712	827,533,093
Central Bank and Financial	0.9219	51,300,685
Services Authority of Ireland		
Banca d'Italia	13.0516	726,278,371
Banque Centrale du Luxembourg	0.1568	8,725,401
De Nederlandsche Bank	3.9955	222,336,359
Oesterreichische Nationalbank	2.0800	115,745,120
Banco de Portugal	1.7653	98,233,106
Suomen Pankki – Finlands Bank	1.2887	71,711,892
Total	**71.4908**	**3,978,226,562**
Non-euro area NCBs		
Danmarks Nationalbank	1.5663	6,101,159
Sveriges Riksbank	2.4133	9,400,451
Bank of England	14.3822	56,022,530
Subtotal initial non-euro area NCBs	**18.3618**	**71,524,140**
Česká národní banka	1.4584	5,680,859
Eesti Pank	0.1784	694,915
Central Bank of Cyprus	0.1300	506,384
Latvijas Banka	0.2978	1,160,010
Lietuvos bankas	0.4425	1,723,656
Magyar Nemzeti Bank	1.3884	5,408,190
Central Bank of Malta	0.0647	252,023
Narodowy Bank Polski	5.1380	20,013,889
Banka Slovenije	0.3345	1,302,967
Národná banka Slovenska	0.7147	2,783,948
Subtotal new non-euro area NCBs	**10.1474**	**39,526,847**
Total	**28.5092**	**111,050,987**

component parts of the UK in a single Act of the Westminster Parliament. The Civil Partnership Act 2004, for example, has an introductory Part 1, Part 2 applicable to England and Wales, Part 3 applicable to Scotland, Part 4 applicable to Northern Ireland and Part 5, applicable to partnerships created outside the UK, includes separate references to jurisdiction and construction in England and Wales, Scotland and Northern Ireland as necessary. Explicit consent of the Scottish Parliament was felt necessary, and was obtained, to the inclusion of Scottish provisions in a Westminster Bill.

It is a complicated structure, but the juxtaposition has the merit of exposing very clearly the fundamental differences in legal structures, and the commencement machinery of section 263 demonstrates the constitutionally delicate processes involved in making national legislation in the Untied Kingdom. The Secretary of State [for Trade and Industry!] will make the order for Part 2 on his initiative alone, and for Parts 1 and 5, after consulting both the Scottish Ministers and the [Northern Ireland] Department of Finance and Personnel. But he is only consulted on Parts 3 and 4, the orders for which will be made respectively by the Scottish Ministers and by the Department of Finance and Personnel (the concept of a department of the civil service making an order by statutory instrument is itself pretty odd, in constitutional terms). Further powers (section 259) may be exercised by any Minister of the Crown; or by the Scottish Ministers, in relation to a relevant Scottish provision; or by a Northern Ireland department, in relation to a provision which deals with a transferred matter; or even by 'the National Assembly for Wales, in relation to a provision which ... deals with matters with respect to which functions are exercisable by the Assembly'.

From this brief consideration we can conclude that, although rather tortuous, there is certainly enough flexibility in the modern legislative apparatus in the UK to allow for an Act introducing a separate central bank for either Scotland (with the consent of the Scottish Parliament) or Northern Ireland. Powers could be delegated to regional ministers or departments outright or to be exercised in consultation with a Whitehall minister, or regional consultation required before a Whitehall minister could act.

The irrelevance of the theory of Optimum Currency Areas

The theory of Optimum Currency Areas was proposed by Robert Mundell[13] in and for a macroeconomic world of the 1950s and 1960s that is unrecognisable today. Wages and prices were assumed to be sticky and – crucially – international capital mobility, with widespread exchange control and poorly developed capital markets, assumed to be too low to be able to influence functioning of domestic policies. The nominal exchange rate therefore determined the real exchange rate and, in turn, the current account balance, and so could be used to maintain external balance, leaving monetary and fiscal policies to maintain internal balance. The key to resolving the constraints imposed by the assumed rigidities in the face of a relative change in demand from the goods of one country to that of a second was perfect labour mobility. But Mundell himself went on to note that this criterion 'hardly appeals to common sense', in the face of which Kenen, explaining the limitations of this model very clearly, suggests that without perfect labour market clearing 'we would have to treat every pocket of unemployment due to imperfect labor mobility as an optimum currency area'.[14] This goes to the very heart of euro-economics. Why would any large and successful country, unless as a prelude to full-blown political federal union, wish to surrender not so much its autonomy *per se* to Frankfurt, but rather its flexibility to adjust, for macroeconomic purposes, monetary policy to optimize national growth and employment when inflation risks are irrelevant? In 2005 the advantages of inter-country monetary union are all microeconomic, taking out exchange rate risk and the need to convert physical currencies.

From a macroeconomic perspective it seems clear from the theory that Optimum Currency Areas should be as small as practicable, although from a microeconomic perspective 'the optimum currency area is the world'. Somehow these opposing considerations need to be traded off in setting policy, for which the theory is really not very helpful: particularly in a world in which foreign exchange controls on the mobility of capital have almost disappeared, but immigration controls on the mobility of labour have become almost universal.[15]

A series of empirical studies by Rose and colleagues on the effects of monetary integration is often cited.[16] The strongest result found is that pairs of countries having the same currency trade three times as much as pairs of countries having different currencies. But this is an ahistorical conclusion that abstracts from particular circumstances. It is hardly plausible that the volume of trade between Ireland and the UK, or between Czech and Slovak republics, should have fallen by as much as two-thirds when their currency unions were broken; nor is such a result plausible within the UK. Incidents of monetary disunion are too unusual to admit of generalization; conversely, in the case of the euro, one can only guess what alternative managed exchange rate arrangements might have emerged within the EU in the absence of monetary union in 1999.

Fiscal flexibility without monetary disunion

The Taxes Acts of the United Kingdom apply uniformly to the whole of the United Kingdom. That is to say, all the national taxes apply to

England and Wales, Scotland and Northern Ireland without the need for separate legislation to be passed in Westminster and/or the Welsh Assembly, the Scottish Parliament and the Northern Ireland Legislative Assembly (whenever that body is in fact sitting). Most Acts of the Westminster Parliament apply either to England and Wales or to Scotland; Northern Ireland tends to lag behind legislatively and, indeed, judicially.

Sometimes the uniformity of the tax system can appear rather artificial. In 1972 there was intense concern in Westminster and Whitehall about the situation in Northern Ireland. Relieving the tax burden was one way of helping to support the business community. Ministers were advised that it was not possible simply to legislate as exempt an entire class of taxpayers located in a particular part of the United Kingdom. But regional aid was certainly permissible, if objectively justifiable (the UK was just joining the European Communities, and there was evidently less concern than in later years about the anti-State Aid provisions in the Treaty of Rome). So a Corporation Tax Grant was devised, to enable all companies in Northern Ireland, on a claim, exactly to meet their corporation tax liability.

There are other, more subtle differences in the underlying law that can confer *de facto* favourable tax treatment. In one of the most famous cases concerning tax avoidance in the 1970s,[17] the student may be surprised to discover that the Vestey family, having substantial interests in the Argentinean beef industry, also had strong family connections to Northern Ireland, including trusts located there. In fact, Northern Ireland was chosen as the location for the trusts used to avoid tax simply because the so-called Thellusson Act,[18] which limited the length of the period during which income could be accumulated by trustees, and hence rolled up at a lower rate of tax, had never been extended to Northern Ireland.

Whether one views these historic regional variations as curious, quaint or merely anachronistic, it would be hard to disagree with the proposition that a greater degree of fiscal subsidiarity, decentralization or what is normally referred to, perhaps politically insensitively in a still unitary state, as 'federalism' in the UK is highly desirable. This was certainly the conclusion of the 'balance of funding' review group[19] examining the financing arrangements for English local authorities, and holds whether one prefers a model of central collection with allocation or assignment of revenues to regions, regional collection following national policy, or a measure of local autonomy over policy itself.

Fiscal federalism has been much written about, both positively and normatively, with discussion of fiscal policy usually being much more complicated than monetary policy because of the wider variety of available instruments. Central bank independence over monetary policy implementation is generally held to have no equivalent for fiscal policy, since decisions on how to raise a given level of tax revenue are explicitly political. But for precisely that reason, fiscal issues need not detain us too long for the present purpose.

In an excellent introduction to fiscal federalism, the OECD (Joumard and Kongsrud, 2003)[20] notes, *inter alia*, that in 2001, across all OECD countries the UK was more centralized in its tax levying and gathering than all except Mexico, Greece, Ireland, the Netherlands and Slovakia. The measure of total tax revenue attributed to the sub-national level stood in the UK at 4.1 per cent (down from 10.2 per cent in 1985, before the uniform business rate) compared to the average of 17.8 per cent.

In a thoughtful – in respect of fiscal policy – recent paper (MacDonald and Hallwood, 2004) (which nevertheless unfortunately glosses far too quickly and superficially over the monetary policy question), MacDonald and Hallwood summarize effectively the case for greater regional fiscal autonomy in Scotland. As of 2005, the only tax-imposing powers available to the Scottish Parliament are still the possibility of varying personal income taxes by up to +/− three pence in the pound, and setting non-domestic rates, uniform across Scottish local authorities but independent of the rate set by Westminster for England and Wales.

The authors advocate three components to a more devolved system: expenditures and local revenues better matched, whether through assignment, devolution or sharing of some taxes; intergovernmental transfers, for equity considerations; and the possibility of regional borrowing – which has effectively been banned for local authorities in the UK for over thirty years.

The UK is bound, as are all the EU Member States whether in or out of the euro, by the fiscal discipline – originally a strict discipline – imposed by the Stability and Growth Pact.[21] Highly fiscally decentralized countries need internal versions of the SGP, horizontally and vertically; indeed, one can regard the original SGP itself as having being modelled in these terms horizontally, as though the eurozone was a federal nation. To the very public dismay of EU central bankers, ECOFIN proposed, under the guise of 'strengthening and clarifying the implementation' of the Pact, in March 2005 to water down to the point of meaninglessness the absolute 3 per cent debt to 1 per cent 'on a cyclically adjusted basis, net of one off and short term measures' for constraint for 'low debt/high potential growth' euro and ERM II members.[22]

Wherever there is much freedom of policy on tax design, it is important to avoid the Tiebout effect.[23] This states simply that devolved taxes levied on mobile factors will be unstable. If regions can compete by lowering expenditures and matching income taxes on residents, high-income households will migrate to the lower tax jurisdiction, expanding its tax base and allowing rates to be lowered further as the high-income households require or demand lower average public expenditure. Conversely, low-income households preferring higher public expenditure will migrate to the high-tax, high-spend jurisdiction but, as average income falls, marginal tax rates will increase. The same result applies to sales and profits taxes.

The only way to achieve stability is either to harmonize rates across localities – the reason why business rates were made uniform in England and Wales – or to devolve only taxes on immobile factors, land in particular. The most successful division of the tax base in this way is perhaps to be found in Switzerland, where the confederation collects income taxes and the cantons rely heavily on land taxes (including capital gains on housing) and location-specific rents where available (local tax rates are highest in Zurich and lowest in its mountainous tax haven neighbour, Zug).

Under the present UK regional arrangements, with almost all revenue collected centrally, the Barnett[24] formula simply 'sends money down a tube'. Alternative fiscal arrangements can, of course, be put in place while the UK remains a monetary union. But if one or more regions were to adopt the euro, in order to achieve and demonstrate *regional* compliance with the Stability and Growth Pact criteria, or any successor arrangements, would flexible equalization arrangements within the UK be required, in the absence of complete territorial independence? Since the SGP imposes a limit primarily on the budget deficit, if Scottish taxes fell significantly short of Scottish expenditure[25] but the gap was funded by a Barnett-type transfer from England and Wales, that would appear to be acceptable so long as the 3 per cent rule was being met at both the regional and national (ie. Scottish and UK) levels. What would be problematic, in the absence of such a transfer, would be Scottish borrowing to finance a deficit that would formerly have been funded by a Whitehall transfer. But provided that is not the position – which is to say that England and Wales would be prepared to continue to subsidize a Scotland (or Northern Ireland) no longer in monetary union; for otherwise it is difficult to see what sort of union remains at all – then the intra-UK fiscal framework should not be relevant. However, having said that, there remains the independent possibility of attempts by the

Commission to harmonize further both tax bases and rates across the EU, in the name of enhancing the single market.

If the UK as a whole were to join the euro, then without the ability of monetary policy to respond to shocks, the stabilization role for fiscal policy would clearly need to be enhanced, as the Treasury's assessment noted (HM Treasury, 2003). In fact there have been 'regulator' powers to change indirect tax rates for demand management purposes without prior authority of Parliament since 1961,[26] but they fell out of fashion at the end of the 1970s when monetary policy assumed the primary stabilization role – while retaining a few staunch advocates (Vines, Maciejowski and Meade, 1983). Assuming that only part of the UK was to join the euro, with increased fiscal devolution short of independence, then it would seem highly advisable for some component of demand management by taxes to be exercisable independently. This need mean no more than that the VAT regulator could be exercisable in the devolved territory independently, so that VAT and/or excise rates in Scotland could be varied as well as income tax rates. There is then a cross-border tax shopping issue, but only one that is already a very familiar experience from the intra-EU Republic/Northern Ireland and England/France borders. As the Treasury document and Vines *et al.* discuss, because the impact of the VAT regulator is primarily to deter or advance planned spending, its effect is intended to be short-term in any case; easy cross-border shopping due to tax differentials displaces spending regionally rather than over time, but the immediate and local effects are not so dissimilar. Long-term, substantial differentials in expenditure or income taxes are more problematic, taking us back to Tiebout problems.

Conclusion

The idea that only a part of the Untied Kingdom might join the euro may seem at first to be perverse, but there are in fact many aspects of the Union that could facilitate such a development, including separate legal systems and banknotes. A new and separate central bank would be required, and more flexible fiscal arrangements, desirable in their own right; but there are satisfactory precedents elsewhere for those. Whitehall and Westminster have experimented in Scotland before, with both the Community Charge and the police and criminal evidence regimes in Mrs Thatcher's time. While the prospect of part of an 'out' Member State coming 'in' to the euro would raise several intriguing technical challenges, it would be an attractive political prize for the ECB and other EU institutions, which would therefore be likely to do everything to assist.

Notes

1 In the early days of discussion about devolution, my unconscious repeatedly prompted me to mistype 'United', without the benefit of spell-checking detection. It now seems legitimately appropriate.
2 Treasurer and Official Fellow, Lady Margaret Hall, University of Oxford. Economic Adviser to the Board of Inland Revenue 1985–90, Principal Administrator in the Fiscal Affairs Division of the OECD 1993–95, Senior Manager at the Bank of England 1995–2003, and a member of the IMF Panel of Fiscal Experts.
3 Some earlier analyses by distinguished authors, such as Dornbusch (1989), appear premature in stopping short of the most interesting part of the cycle, before the 1987 turnaround.
4 For a commentary see, for example, Bordo and Eichengreen, 1993.
5 The troubled history of the first Exchange Rate Mechanism of the European Monetary System is objectively and concisely summarized by Klein, 1998; broader context is provided by Bordo and Jonung, 1999, and the experience of the early years is analysed in more detail by Giavazzi and Giovannini, 1989.
6 See, for example, McLean, 2001b.
7 The history and issues are well explained in European University Institution, 2000, 22–5.
8 The *Conventions and Procedures for the Exchange Rate Mechanism II* are announced by ECB press release from time to time; the current version of 28 June 2004 immediately preceded the joining of the three accession countries.
9 Beyond a small issue authorized in nominal terms by legislation, following the 1844 Act, which effectively permitted limited competition in note issue to continue outside England and Wales. Special £1 million and, from 2005, £100 million Bank of England internal notes are used to provide this backing. £26.5 million worth of Northern Bank notes were stolen from its head office in Belfast on 20 December 2004. The Bank's only possible response was to announce that all of the current note issue would be withdrawn quickly in favour of a new design; all legitimate holders would be able to exchange within a fairly short time limit. Criminally acquired notes are normally laundered in small quantities over a long period of time.
10 *L'association monétaire belgo-luxembourgeoise: les effets de l'UEM sur l'Institut Monétaire Luxembourgeois*, Briefing 25 for the Task Force on Economic and Monetary Union of the European Parliament, 17 January 1997.
11 A comprehensive account of the relationship between the ECB and the NCBs, developed largely pragmatically, as well as details of the statutory framework can be found in Keller, 2004.
12 Details were sketched in Part III.B Annex A of the May 2002 issue of the Bank of England's series *Practical issues arising from the euro*.

13 Originally in Mundell, 1961.
14 See Kenen, 2002, p. 82, or Kenen's very similar December 2002 contribution to the UK Treasury assessment paper *Submissions on EMU from Leading Academics*. Coincidentally, exactly the same point was made by Peter Jay in discussion: why not use the flexibility afforded by highly localized free-floating currencies to overcome industry- or even factory-specific wage and price stickiness and hence unemployment?
15 Even without formal controls, labour mobility within the EU is much lower than in the US, as noted by Eichengreen, 1993.
16 Rose, 2000; Rose and Engel, 2000; and Rose and Glick, 2002.
17 *Vestey* v. *Inland Revenue Commissioners (Nos 1 and 2)*, House of Lords [1980] AC 1148, [1979] 3 WLR 915, 54 Official Tax Cases 503.
18 The Accumulations Act 1800, introduced following the case of *Thellusson* v. *Woodford*, 4 Ves.Jr. 227, 31 Eng. Rep. 117 (Ch. 1798). In fact the Law Commission proposed to abolish these provisions in its March 1988 report (Law Commission, 1988), on which the Department for Constitutional Affairs consulted in September 2002.
19 Office of the Deputy Prime Minister, 2004.
20 One of the present editors has provided two informative recent case studies: McLean, 2002, 2003.
21 The main commitment of Member States under the Stability and Growth Pact is that their fiscal policies should result in medium-term (ie. automatic stabilizers can operate in the short-term) budgetary positions 'close to balance or in surplus'. There are 'reference values' of 3 per cent for budget deficits and 60 per cent for debt to GDP. The current, revised detailed provisions are to be found in the document COM (2002) 668 final, *Communication from the Commission to Council and the European Parliament: Strengthening the Co-ordination of Budgetary Policies*.
22 *Improving the Implementation of the Stability and Growth Pact*, Report from Council (ECOFIN) to European Council, 22–3 March 2005, UEM 97/ECOFIN 104.
23 After Charles Tiebout (Tiebout, 1956).
24 For a succinct description of how and why this operates and what an alternative might look like, see McLean and McMillan, 2003.
25 Measurement of regional expenditure is highly inadequate at present, but Chris Allsopp's *Review of Statistics for Economic Policymaking*, HM Treasury, December 2003 and March 2004, has addressed those issues.
26 Introduced as section 9 of the Finance Act 1961, for excise duties and purchase tax with a 10 per cent, variation, it was used in the 1960s. VAT was given a separate regulator power when introduced to replace purchase tax in 1972, originally of 20 per cent. This is now to be found in section 2(2) of the Value Added Tax Act 1994, although it has never been used: '*The Treasury may by order increase or decrease the rate of VAT for the time being in force by such percentage thereof not exceeding 25 per cent as may be specified in the order, but any such order shall cease to be in force at the expiration of a period of one year from the date on which it takes effect, unless continued in force by a further order under this subsection.*'

9
Using and Abusing Economic Theory*

Paul Klemperer

9.1 Introduction

For half a century or more after the publication of his *Principles* (1890), it was routinely asserted of economic ideas that 'they're all in (Alfred) Marshall'. Of course, that is no longer true of the theory itself. But Marshall was also very concerned with applying economics, and when we think about how to use the theory, the example that Marshall set still remains a valuable guide. In this chapter, therefore, I want to use some of Marshall's views, and my own experience in auction design, to discuss the use (and abuse) of economic theory.[1]

Although the most elegant mathematical theory is often the most influential, it may not be the most useful when dealing with practical problems. Marshall (1906) famously stated that 'a good mathematical theorem dealing with economic hypotheses [is] very unlikely to be good economics', and continued by asserting the rules '(1) translate [mathematics] into English; (2) then illustrate by examples that are important in real life; (3) burn the mathematics; (4) if you can't succeed in 2, burn 1'! Certainly this view now seems extreme, but it is salutary to be reminded that good mathematics need not necessarily be good economics. To slightly update Marshall's rules, if we can't (1) offer credible intuition and (2) supply empirical (or perhaps case-study or experimental) evidence, we should (4) be cautious about applying the theory in practice.[2]

Furthermore, when economics is applied to policy, proposals need to be robust to the political context in which they are intended to operate. Too many economists excuse their practical failure by saying 'the politicians (or bureaucrats) didn't do exactly what I recommended'. Just as medical practitioners must allow for the fact that their patients may not take all the pills they prescribe, or follow all the advice they are given, so economics practitioners need to foresee political and administrative pressures and make their plans robust to changes that politicians, bureaucrats, and lobbyists are likely to impose. And in framing proposals, economists must recognise that policies that seem identical, or almost identical, to them may seem very different to politicians, and vice versa.

Some academics also need to widen the scope of their analyses beyond the confines of their models which, while elegant, are often short on real-world detail. Marshall always emphasized the importance of a deep 'historical knowledge of any area being investigated and referred again and again to the complexity of economic problems and the naivety of simple hypotheses.'[3] Employing 'know it all' consultants with narrowly-focused theories instead of experienced people with a good knowledge of the wider context can sometimes lead to disaster.

One might think these lessons scarcely needed stating – and Marshall certainly understood them very well – but the sorry history of 'expert' advice in some recent auctions shows that they bear repetition. So although the lessons are general ones, I will illustrate them using auctions and auction theory: auction theory is often held up as a triumph of the application of economic theory to economic practice, but it has not, in truth, been an unalloyed success. For example, while the European and Asian 3G spectrum auctions famously raised over 100 billion euros in total revenues, Hong Kong's, Austria's, the Netherlands', and Switzerland's auctions, among others, were catastrophically badly run, yielding only a quarter or less of the per capita revenues earned elsewhere – and economic theorists deserve some of the blame.[4,5] Hong Kong's auction, for example, was superficially well-designed, but not robust to relatively slight political interference that should perhaps have been anticipated. Several countries' academic advisors failed to recognise the importance of the interaction between different countries' auction processes, and bidders advised by experts in auction theory who ignored (or were ignorant of) their clients' histories pursued strategies that cost them billions of euros. Many of these failures could have been avoided if the lessons had been learnt to: pay more attention to elementary theory, to the wider context of the auctions, and to political pressures – and pay less attention to sophisticated mathematical theory.[6]

Of course, mathematical theory, even when it has no direct practical application, is not merely beautiful. It can clarify the central features of a problem, provide useful benchmarks and starting points for analysis and – especially – show the deep relationships between problems that are superficially unconnected. Thus, for example, the sophisticated tools of auction theory that have sometimes been abused in practical contexts turn out to have valuable applications to problems that, at first blush, do not look like auctions.

Section 9.2 briefly discusses what is often taken to be the 'standard auction theory', before discussing its real relevance. Sections 9.3–9.5 illustrate its abuse using examples from the Asian and European 3G auctions, and discuss the broader lessons that can be drawn from these misapplications. Section 9.3 is in large part based on Klemperer (2000b, 2002a–d) where many additional details can be found – and this section may be skipped by readers familiar with that material – but the other sections make different points using additional examples. Section 9.6 illustrates how the same concepts that are abused can have surprisingly valuable uses in different contexts. Section 9.7 concludes.

9.2 The Received Auction Theory

The core result that everyone who studies auction theory learns is the remarkable *Revenue Equivalence Theorem* (RET).[7] This tells us, subject to some reasonable-sounding conditions, that all the standard (and many non-standard) auction mechanisms are equally profitable for the seller, and that buyers are also indifferent between all these mechanisms.

If that were all there was to it, auction design would be of no interest. But of course the RET rests on a number of assumptions. Probably the most influential piece of auction theory apart from those associated with the RET is Milgrom and Weber's (1982) remarkable paper – it is surely no coincidence that this is also perhaps the most elegant piece of auction theory apart from the RET. Milgrom and Weber's seminal analysis relaxes the assumption that bidders have independent private information about the value of the object for sale, and instead assumes bidders' private information is *affiliated*. This is similar to assuming positive correlation,[8] and under this assumption they show that ordinary ascending auctions are more profitable than standard (first-price) sealed-bid auctions, in expectation.

Milgrom and Weber's beautiful work is undoubtedly an important piece of economic theory and it has been enormously influential.[9] As a result, many economists leave graduate school 'knowing' two things about auctions. First, that if bidders' information is independent then all auctions are equally good, and second, that if information is affiliated (which is generally the plausible case) then the ascending auction maximises the seller's revenue.[10]

But is this correct?

9.2.1   Relevance of the Received Theory

Marshall's (updated) tests are a good place to start. The value of empirical evidence needs no defence, while examining the plausibility of an intuition helps check whether an economic model provides a useful caricature of the real world, or misleads us by absurdly exaggerating particular features of it.[11]

The intuition behind the exact RET result cannot, to my knowledge, be explained in words that are both accurate and comprehensible to lay people. Anyone with the technical skill to understand any verbal explanation would probably do so by translating the words back into the mathematical argument. But it is easier to defend the weaker claim that it is ambiguous which of the two most common auction forms is superior: it *is* easy to explain that participants in a sealed-bid auction shade their bids below their values (unlike in an ascending auction), but that the winner determines the price (unlike in an ascending auction), so it is not hard to be convincing that there is no clear reason why either auction should be more profitable than the other. This is not quite the same as arguing that the standard auction forms are approximately similarly profitable, but the approximate validity of the RET (under its key assumptions) in fact seems consistent with the available evidence. (Some would say that the mere fact that both the ascending auction and the sealed-bid auction are commonly observed in practice is evidence that neither is always superior.) So the 'approximate RET' seems a reasonable claim in practice, and it then follows that issues assumed away by the RET's assumptions should be looked at to choose between the standard auction forms. These issues should include not just those made explicitly in the statement of the theorem, for example bidders are symmetric and risk-neutral; but also those that are implicit, for example bidders share common priors and play non-cooperative Nash equilibrium; or semi-implicit, for example the number and types of bidders are independent of the auction form.

However, as already noted, much attention has focused on just one of the RET's assumptions, namely independence of the bidders' information, and the theoretical result that if information is non-independent (affiliated) then ascending auctions are more profitable than first-price sealed-bid auctions. There is no very compelling intuition for this result. The verbal explanations that are given are unconvincing and/or misleading, or worse. The most commonly given 'explanation' is that ascending auctions allow bidders to be more aggressive, because their 'winner's curses' are reduced,[12] but this argument is plain wrong: the winner's curse is only a feature of common-value auctions, but common values are neither necessary nor sufficient for the result.[13]

A better explanation of the theoretical result is that bidders' profits derive from their private information, and the auctioneer can profit by reducing that private information.[14] An ascending auction reveals the information of bidders who drop out early, so partially reveals the winner's information (if bidders' information is correlated), and uses that information to set the price (through the runner-up's bid), whereas the price paid in a sealed-bid auction cannot use that information. Since the ascending and sealed-bid auctions are revenue-equivalent absent any correlation (that is, with independent signals), and provided the runner-up's bid responds to the additional information that an ascending auction reveals in the appropriate way (which it does when information is affiliated), this effect makes the ascending auction the more profitable. Of course, this argument is obviously still incomplete,[15,16] and even if it were fully convincing, it would depend on the *exact* RET applying – which seems a very strong claim.

Furthermore, before relying on any theory mattering in practice, we need to ask: what is the likely order of magnitude of the effect? In fact, numerical analysis suggests the effects of affiliation are often tiny, even when bidders who exactly fit the assumptions of the theory compute their bids exactly using the theory. Riley and Li (1997) analyse equilibrium in a natural class of examples and show that the revenue difference between ascending and first-price auctions is very small unless the information is very strongly affiliated: when bidders' values are jointly normally distributed, bidders' expected rents are about 10 per cent (20 per cent) higher in a sealed-bid auction than in an ascending auction even for correlation coefficients as high as 0.3 (0.5). So these results suggest affiliation could explain why a 3G spectrum auction earned, for example 640 rather than 650 euros per capita when bidders' valuations were 700 euros per capita. But the actual range was from just 20 (*twenty*) to 650 euros per capita! Riley and Li also find that even with very strong affiliation, other effects, such as those of asymmetry, are more important and often reverse the effects of affiliation, even taking the numbers of bidders, non-cooperative behaviour, common priors, and so on, as given.[17] This kind of quantitative analysis surely deserves more attention than economists often give it.

Finally, all the previous discussion is in the context of single-unit auctions. Perry and Reny (1999) show that the result about affiliation does not hold – even in theory – in multi-unit auctions.[18]

Given all this, it is unsurprising that there is no empirical evidence (that I am aware of) that argues the affiliation effect is important.[19,20]

So there seems to be no strong argument to expect affiliation to matter much in most practical applications; independence is not the assumption of the RET that most needs relaxing.

The theory that really matters most for auction design is just the very elementary undergraduate economics of relaxing the implicit and semi-implicit assumptions of the RET about (fixed) entry and (lack of) collusion.[21] The intuitions are (as Marshall says they should be) easy to explain – we will see that it is clear that bidders are likely to understand and therefore to follow the undergraduate theory. By contrast, the intuition for affiliation gives no sense of how bidders should compute their bids, and the calculations required to do so optimally require considerable mathematical sophistication and are sensitive to the precise assumptions bidders make about the 'prior' distributions from which their and others' private information is drawn. Of course, this does not mean agents cannot intuitively make approximately optimal decisions (Machlup, 1946; Friedman, 1953), and individual agents need not understand the intuitions behind equilibrium group outcomes. But we can be more confident in predicting that agents will make decisions whose logic is very clear, especially in one-off events such as many auctions are.

Not surprisingly, practical examples of the undergraduate theory are easy to give (as Marshall also insists). But there is no elegant theory applying to the specific context of auctions; such theory is unnecessary since the basic point is that the main concerns in auctions are just the same as in other economic markets, so much of the same theory applies (see below). Furthermore, some of the key concerns are especially prominent when the assumption of symmetry is dropped, and models with asymmetries are often inelegant.

So graduate students are taught the elegant mathematics of affiliation and whenever, and wherever, I give a seminar about auctions in practice,[22] I am asked a question along the lines of 'Haven't Milgrom and Weber shown that ascending auctions raise most revenue, so why consider other alternatives?'. This is true of seminars to academics. It is even more true of seminars to policy makers. Thus, although a little knowledge of economic theory is a good thing, too much knowledge can sometimes be a dangerous thing. Moreover, the extraordinary influence of the concept of affiliation is only the most important example of this. I give a further illustration, involving over-attention to some of my own work, in the next subsection. In short, a little graduate education in auction theory can often distract attention from the straightforward 'undergraduate' issues that really matter.[23]

9.3 The elementary economic theory that matters

What really matters in practical auction design is robustness against collusion and attractiveness to entry – just as in ordinary industrial markets.[24] Since I have repeatedly argued this, much of the material of this section is drawn from Klemperer (2000b, 2002a, 2002b) and any reader familiar with these papers may wish to skip to Section 9.4.

9.3.1 Entry

The received theory described above takes the number of bidders as given. But the profitability of an auction depends crucially on the number of bidders who participate, and different auctions vary enormously in their attractiveness to entry; participating in an auction can be a costly exercise that bidders will only undertake if they feel they have realistic chances of winning. In an ascending auction a stronger bidder can always top any bid that a weaker bidder makes, and knowing this the weaker bidder may not enter the auction in the first place – which may then allow the stronger bidder to win at a very low price. In a first-price sealed-bid auction, by contrast, a weaker bidder may win at a price that the stronger bidder could have beaten, but didn't because the stronger bidder may risk trying to win at a lower price and can't change his bid later. So more bidders may enter a first-price sealed-bid auction.[25]

The intuition is very clear, and there is little need for sophisticated theory. Perhaps because of this, or because the argument depends on asymmetries between bidders so any theory is likely to be inelegant, theory has largely ignored the point. Vickrey's (1961) classic paper contains an example (relegated to an Appendix, and often overlooked) which illustrates the basic point that the player who actually has the lower value may win a first-price sealed-bid auction in Nash equilibrium, but that this cannot happen in an ascending auction (with private values). But little has been said since.

In fact, some of what has been written about the issue of attracting entry provides a further illustration of the potentially perverse impact of sophisticated theory. Although the point that weaker bidders are unlikely to win ascending auctions, and may therefore not enter them, is very general, some work – including Klemperer, 1998[26] – has emphasized that the argument is especially compelling for 'almost-common-value' auctions, and this work may have had the unintended side-effect of linking the entry concern to common values in some people's minds;[27] I have heard economists who know the latter work all too well say that because an auction does not involve common values, therefore there is no entry problem![28] To the extent that the almost-common values theory (which is both of more limited application, and also assumes quite sophisticated reasoning by bidders) has distracted attention from the more general point, this is another example of excessive focus on sophisticated theory at the expense of more elementary, but more crucial, theory.

There is an additional important reason why a first-price sealed-bid auction may be more attractive to entrants: bidders in a sealed-bid auction may be much less certain about opponents' strategies, and the advantage of stronger players may therefore be less pronounced, than standard equilibrium theory predicts. The reason is that in practice, players are not likely to share common priors about distributions of valuations and, even if they do, they may not play Nash equilibrium strategies (that is, a sealed-bid auction induces 'strategic uncertainty'). So even if players were in fact ex-ante symmetric (that is, their private information is drawn from identical distributions) the lower-value player might win a first-price sealed-bid auction, but would never win an ascending auction (in which bidders' strategies are very straightforward and predictable). When players are not symmetric, Nash equilibrium theory predicts that a weaker player will sometimes beat a stronger player in a sealed-bid auction, but I conjecture strategic uncertainty and the absence of common priors make this outcome even more likely than Nash equilibrium predicts. Since this point is very hard for standard economic theory to capture, it has largely been passed over. But it reinforces the point that a sealed-bid auction is in many circumstances more likely than an ascending auction to attract entry, and this will often have a substantial effect on the relative profitabilities of the auctions.

The 3G auctions provide good examples of oversensitivity to the significance of information revelation and affiliation at the expense of insensitivity to the more important issue of entry. For example, the Netherlands sold five 3G licences in a context in which there were also exactly five incumbent mobile-phone operators who were the natural winners, leaving no room for any entrant. (For competition-policy reasons, bidders were permitted to win no more than one licence each.) The problem of attracting enough entry to have a competitive auction should therefore have been uppermost in planners' minds. But the planners seem instead to have been seduced by the fact that ascending auctions raise (a little) extra revenue because of affiliation and also increase the likelihood of an efficient allocation to those with the highest valuations.[29] The planners were probably also influenced by the fact that previous spectrum auctions in the US and UK had used ascending designs,[30] even though they had usually done so in contexts in which entry was less of a concern, and even though some US auctions did suffer from entry problems. The result of the Netherlands auction was both predictable, and predicted (see, for example, Maasland, 2000 and Klemperer, 2000b quoted in the Dutch press prior to the auction). There was no serious entrant.[31] Revenue was less than a third of what had been predicted and barely a quarter of the per capita amounts raised in the immediately preceding and immediately subsequent 3G auctions (in the UK and Germany respectively). The resulting furore in the press led to a Parliamentary Inquiry.

By contrast, when Denmark faced a very similar situation in its 3G auctions in late 2001 – four licences for sale and four incumbents – its primary concern was to encourage entry.[32] (The designers had both observed the Netherlands fiasco, and also read Klemperer 2000b.) It chose a sealed-bid design (a '4th price' auction) and had a resounding success. A serious entrant bid, and revenue far exceeded expectations and was more than twice the levels achieved by any of the other three European 3G auctions (Switzerland, Belgium and Greece) that took place since late 2000.

The academics who designed the UK sale (which was held prior to the Netherlands and Danish auctions) also thought much harder about entry into their 3G auction.[33] The UK had four incumbent operators, and when design work began it was unclear how many licenses it would be possible to offer given the technological constraints. We realized that if there were just four licenses available it would be hard to persuade a non-incumbent to enter, so we planned in that case to use a design including a sealed-bid component (an 'Anglo-Dutch' design) to encourage entry. In the event, five licenses were available so, given the UK context, we switched to an ascending auction, since there was considerable uncertainty about who the fifth strongest bidder would be (we ran the world's first 3G auction in part to ensure this – see section 9.5).[34] 13 bidders entered, ensuring a highly competitive auction which resulted in the highest per capita revenue among all the European and Asian 3G auctions.

9.3.2 Collusion

The received auction theory also assumes bidders play non-cooperatively in Nash equilibrium. We have already discussed how Nash equilibrium may be a poor prediction because of 'strategic uncertainty' and the failure of the common priors assumption, but a more fundamental problem is that players may behave collusively rather than non-cooperatively. In particular, a standard ascending auction – especially a multi-unit ascending auction – often satisfies *all* the conditions that elementary economic theory tells us are important for facilitating collusion, even without any possibility of interaction or discussion among bidders beyond the information communicated in their bids.

For example, Waterson's (1984) standard industrial organization textbook lists five questions that must be answered affirmatively for firms to be able to support collusion in an ordinary industrial market: (1) can firms easily identify efficient divisions of the market? (2) can firms easily agree on a division? (3) can firms easily detect defection from any agreement? (4) can firms credibly punish any observed defection? (5) can firms deter non-participants in the agreement from entering the industry? In a multi-unit ascending auction: (1) the objects for sale are well-defined, so firms can see how to share the collusive 'pie' among them (by contrast with the problem of sharing an industrial market whose definition may not be obvious), (2) bids can be used to signal proposals about how the division should be made and to signal agreement, (3) firms' pricing (that is, bidding) is immediately and perfectly observable, so defection from any collusive agreement is immediately detected, (4) the threat of punishment for defection from the agreement is highly credible, since punishment is quick and easy and often costless to the punisher in a multi-object auction in which a player has the ability to raise the price only on objects that the defector will win,[35] and (5) we have already argued that entry in an ascending auction may be hard.

So collusion in an ascending auction seems much easier to sustain than in an 'ordinary' industrial market, and it should therefore be no surprise that ascending auctions provide some particularly clear examples of collusion, as we illustrate below.

By contrast, a first-price sealed-bid auction is usually much more robust to collusion: bidders cannot 'exchange views' through their bids, or observe opponents' bids until after the auction is over, or punish defection from any agreement during the course of the auction, or easily deter entry. But, perhaps because auction theorists have little that is new or exciting to say about collusion, too little attention has been given to this elementary issue in practical applications.

In the Austrian 3G auction, for example, 12 identical blocks of spectrum were sold to six bidders in a simultaneous ascending auction (bidders were allowed to win multiple blocks each). No one was in the least surprised when the bidding stopped just above the low reserve price with each bidder winning two blocks, at perhaps one-third the price that bidders valued them at.[36] Clearly the effect of 'collusion' (whether explicit and illegal, or tacit and possibly legal) on revenues is first-order.

Another elegant example of bidders' ability to 'collude' is provided by the 1999 German DCS-1800 auction in which ten blocks of spectrum were sold by ascending auction, with the rule that any new bid on a block had to exceed the previous high bid by at least 10 per cent.[37] There were just two credible bidders, the two largest German mobile-phone companies T-Mobil and Mannesman, and Mannesman's first bids were 18.18 million deutschmarks per megahertz on blocks 1–5 and 20 million deutschmarks per MHz on blocks 6–10. T-Mobil – who bid even less in the first round – later said 'There were no agreements with Mannesman. But [we] interpreted Mannesman's first bid as an offer (Stuewe, 1999, p. 13). The point is that 18.18 plus a 10 per cent raise equals 20.00. It seems T-Mobil understood that if it bid 20 million deutschmarks per MHz on blocks 1–5, but did not bid again on blocks 6–10, the two companies would then live and let live with neither company challenging the other on the other's half. Exactly that happened. So the auction closed after just two rounds with each of the bidders acquiring half the blocks for the same low price, which was a small fraction of the valuations that the bidders actually placed on the blocks.[38]

This example makes another important point. The elementary theory that tells us that 'collusion' is easy in this context is important. The reader may think it obvious that bidders can 'collude' in the setting described, but that is because the reader has been exposed to elementary undergraduate economic theory. This point was beautifully illustrated by the behaviour of the subjects in an experiment that was specifically designed to advise one of the bidders in this auction by mimicking its setting and rules: the experimental subjects completely failed to achieve the low-price 'collusive' outcome that was achieved in practice. Instead 'in [all] the [experimental] sessions the bidding was very competitive. Subjects went for all ten units in the beginning, and typically reduced their bidding rights only when the budget limit forced them to do so' (Abbink *et al.*, 2002). So the elementary economic theory of collusion which makes it plain, by contrast, that the 'collusive' outcome that actually arose was to be expected from more sophisticated players does matter – and I feel confident that the very distinguished economists who ran the experiments advised their bidder more on the basis of the elementary theory than on the basis of the experiments.[39]

Both the UK's and Denmark's academic advisors gave considerable thought to preventing collusion. Denmark, for example, not only ran a sealed-bid auction, but also allowed bidders to submit multiple bids at multiple locations with the rule that only the highest bid made by any bidder would count, and also arranged for phoney bids to be submitted – the idea was that bidders could not (illegally) agree to observe each other's bids without fear that their partners in collusion would double-cross them, and nor could bidders observe who had made bids, or how many had been made.[40]

9.4   Robustness to political pressures

To be effective, economic advice must also be sensitive to the organizational and political context; it is important to be realistic about how advice will be acted on. Economic advisors commonly explain a policy failure with the excuse that 'it would have been okay if they had followed our advice'. But medical practitioners are expected to take account of the fact that patients will not follow their every instruction.[41] Why should economic practitioners be different? Maybe it should be regarded as economic malpractice to give advice that will actually make matters worse if it is not followed exactly.

For example, the economic theorists advising the Swiss government on its 3G auction favoured a multi-unit ascending auction, apparently arguing along the standard received-auction-theory lines that this was best for both efficiency and revenue. But they recognised the dangers of such an auction encouraging 'collusive' behaviour and deterring entry, and the advisors therefore also proposed setting a high reserve price. This would not only directly limit the potential revenue losses from collusion and/or inadequate entry but, importantly, it would also reduce the likelihood of collusion. (With a high reserve price, bidders are relatively more likely to prefer to raise the price to attempt to drive their rivals out altogether, than to collude with them at the reserve price – see Klemperer, 2002b; and Brusco and Lopomo, 2002b.)

But serious reserve prices are often unpopular with politicians and bureaucrats who – even if they have the information to set them sensibly – are often reluctant to run even a tiny risk of not selling the objects, which outcome they fear would be seen as 'a failure'.

The upshot was that no serious reserve was set. Through exit, joint-venture, and possibly – it was rumoured – collusion,[42] the number of bidders shrank to equal the number of licences available, so the remaining bidders had to pay only the trivial reserve price that had been fixed.

(Firms were allowed to win just a single licence each.) The outcome was met with jubilation by the bidders and their shareholders; per capita revenues were easily the lowest of any of the nine Western European 3G auctions, and less than one-thirtieth of what the government had been hoping for.[43] Perhaps an ascending auction together with a carefully chosen reserve price was a reasonable choice. But an ascending auction with only a trivial reserve price was a disaster, and the economic-theorist advisors should have been more realistic that this was a likely outcome of their advice.[44]

9.4.1 Economic similarity ≠ political similarity

Hong Kong's auction was another case where designers should perhaps have anticipated the political response to their advice. The Hong Kong auction's designers, like Denmark's, had observed the Netherlands fiasco (and had also read Klemperer, 2000b). So they were keen to use a sealed-bid design, given Hong Kong's situation.[45] Specifically, they favoured a 'fourth-price' sealed-bid design so that all four winners (there were four licences and firms could win at most one licence each) would pay the same fourth-highest bid – charging winners different amounts for identical properties might both be awkward and lead to cautious bidding by managements who did not want to risk the embarrassment of paying more than their rivals.[46]

However, the designers were also afraid that if the public could observe the top three bids after the auction, then if these were very different from the price that the firms actually paid (the fourth highest bid), the government would be criticized for selling the licences for less than the firms had shown themselves willing to pay. Of course, such criticism would be ill-informed, but it could still be damaging, because even well-intentioned commentators find it hard to explain to the general public that requiring firms to pay their own bids would result in firms bidding differently. Thus far, nothing was different from the situation in Denmark. However, whereas the Danish government simply followed the advice it was given to keep all the bids secret and reveal only the price paid, the Hong Kong government felt it could not do this.

Openness and transparency of government was a major political issue in the wake of Hong Kong's return to Chinese rule, and it was feared that secrecy would be impossible to maintain. The advisors therefore proposed to run an auction that was *strategically equivalent* (that is, has an identical game-theoretic structure and therefore should induce identical behaviour) to a fourth-price auction, but that did not reveal the three high bids to *anyone*.[47] To achieve this, an ascending auction would be run for the four identical licences, but dropouts would be kept secret and the price would continue to rise until the point at which the number of players remaining dropped from four to *three*. At this point the last four (including the firm that had just 'dropped out') would pay the last price at which four players remained in the bidding. Since nothing was revealed to any player until the auction was over, no player had any decision to make except to choose a single dropout price, in the knowledge that if its price was among the top four then it would pay the fourth-highest dropout price; that is, the situation was identical from the firm's viewpoint to choosing a single bid in a fourth-price sealed-bid auction. But, unlike in Denmark, no one would ever see the 'bids' planned by the top three winners (and since these bids would never even have been placed, very little credibility would have attached to reports of them).

However, although the proposed auction was mathematically (that is, strategically) equivalent to a sealed-bid auction, its verbal description was very different. The stronger incumbents lobbied vigorously for a 'small change' to the design – that the price be determined when the numbers dropped from five to four, rather than from four to three.

This is the 'standard' way of running an ascending auction, and it recreates the standard problem that entry is deterred because strong players can bid aggressively in the knowledge that the winners will only pay a loser's bid (the fifth bid) and not have to pay one of the winners' bids.

Revealingly, one of the strong players that, it is said, lobbied so strongly for changing the proposal was at the same time a weaker player (a potential entrant) in the Danish market and, it is said, professed itself entirely happy with the fourth-price sealed-bid rules for *that* market.

The lobbyists' arguments that their suggested change was 'small' and made the auction more 'standard', and also that it was 'unfair' to have the bidders continue to 'bid against themselves' when there were just four left, were politically salient points, even though they are irrelevant or meaningless from a strictly game-theoretic viewpoint.[48] Since the academic consultants who proposed the original design had very little influence at the higher political levels at which the final decision was taken, and since perhaps not all the ultimate decision makers understood – or wanted to understand – the full significance of the change, the government gave way and made it.[49]

The result? Just the four strongest bidders entered and paid the reserve price – a major disappointment for the government, and yielding perhaps one third to one half the revenue that had been anticipated (allowing for market conditions). Whether other potential bidders gave up altogether, or whether they made collusive agreements with stronger bidders not to enter (as was rumoured in the press), is unknown. But what is certain is that the design finally chosen made entry much harder and collusion much easier.

It is not clear what the economic theorists advising should have recommended. Perhaps they should have stuck to a (fourth-price) sealed-bid auction run in the standard way, but used computer technology that could determine the price to be paid while making it impossible for anyone other than the bidders to know the other bids made.

The moral, however, is clear. Auction designs that seem similar to economic theorists may seem very different to politicians, bureaucrats and the public, and vice versa. And political and lobbying pressures need to be predicted and planned for in advance.

When the designers of the UK 3G auction proposed a design – the Anglo-Dutch – that was very unattractive to the incumbent operators, it probably helped that two alternative versions of the design were initially offered. Whilst the incumbent operators hated the overall design and lobbied furiously against it,[50] they also had strong preferences between its two versions, and much of their lobbying efforts therefore focused on the choice between them. When the government selected the version the operators preferred (the designers actually preferred this version too) the operators felt they had got a part of what they had asked for, and it proved politically possible for the government to stick to the Anglo-Dutch design until the circumstances changed radically.[51]

Another notorious 'political failure' was the design of the 1998 Netherlands 2G spectrum auction. The EU Commission objected to the Netherlands government's rules for the auction shortly before the (EU-imposed) deadline for the allocation of the licences. The rules were therefore quickly rewritten by a high-ranking civil servant on a Friday afternoon. The result was an auction that sold similar properties at prices that differed by a factor of about two, and almost certainly allocated the licences inefficiently.[52]

Economists are now waking up to the importance of these issues: Wilson (2002) addresses political constraints in the design of auction markets for electricity, and Roth (2002) also discusses political aspects of market design. But the politics of design remains understudied by economic theorists, and underappreciated by them in their role as practitioners.

9.5   Understanding the wider context

Any consultant new to a situation must beware of overlooking issues that are well understood by those with more experience of the environment.

The danger is perhaps particularly acute for economic theorists who are used to seeing the world through models that, while very elegant, are often lacking in real-world detail and context.

The German 3G auction illustrates the importance of the wider context. As we described in section 9.3.2, in Germany's 1999 DCS-1800 auction Mannesman used its bids to signal to T-Mobil how the two firms should divide the blocks between them and end the auction at a comparatively low price. T-Mobil then cut back its demand in exactly the way Mannesman suggested, and Mannesman followed through with its half of the 'bargain' by also cutting back its demand, so the auction ended with the two firms winning similar amounts of spectrum very cheaply.

It seems that Mannesman used the same advisors in the 3G auction that it had used in the GSM auction. Although the rules for the 3G auction were not identical, it was another simultaneous ascending auction in which individual bidders were permitted to win multiple blocks. After the number of bidders had fallen to six competing for a total of 12 blocks, and when it was clear that the other four bidders would be content with two blocks each, Mannesman apparently signalled to T-Mobil to cut back its demand to just two blocks.[53] If T-Mobil and Mannesman had both done this the auction would have ended at modest prices. Instead T-Mobil seemingly ignored Mannesman's signals, and drove up the total price 15 billion euros before cutting back demand. Once T-Mobil did cut back its demand, Mannesman followed, so the auction ended with the allocation that Mannesman had originally signalled but with each of the six firms paying an additional 2.5 billion euros!

It seems that Mannesman's advisors saw the GSM auction as a template for the 3G auction; they took the view that, following previous practice, Mannesman would signal when to reduce demand, T-Mobil would acquiesce, and Mannesman would then follow through on its half of the bargain.[54] The bargain would be enforced by firms not wishing to jeopardize their future cooperation in subsequent auctions (including 3G auctions in other countries) and in negotiating with regulators, and so on. (And the short-run advantage that could be gained by failing to cooperate was anyway probably small, see Klemperer, 2002c.) But given their expectation that T-Mobil would cut back demand first, Mannesman's advisors were unwilling to reduce demand when T-Mobil did not.

Clearly, T-Mobil's advisors saw things differently. It seems that their main advisors had not been involved in the GSM auction and the example of the previous auction was certainly not in the forefront of their minds. Instead they mistrusted Mannesman's intentions, and were very unwilling to cut back demand without proof that Mannesman had already done so. True the 3G auction was a much more complicated game than the GSM auction because of the other parties involved, and Klemperer (2002c) discusses other factors that may have contributed to the firms' failure to reduce demand.[55] But T-Mobil's refusal to cut back demand very likely stemmed partly from viewing the 3G auction in a different, and narrower, context than Mannesman did.

Just as previous auctions within any country might have been an important part of the wider context, auctions in other countries are also relevant parts of the broader environment: the sequencing of the 3G auctions across countries was crucial. Countries that auctioned earlier had more entrants for three main reasons: weaker bidders had not yet worked out that they were weaker and quit the auctions; stronger bidders had not yet worked out how and with whom to do joint ventures; and complementarities between the values of licences in different countries reinforced these effects – the number of entrants in the nine Western European auctions were (in order) 13, 6, 7, 6, 6, 4, 3, 3, and 5 respectively.[56] Countries that auctioned earlier also suffered less from 'collusive' behaviour, because bidders had had less practice in learning how best to play the game. For example, when the Austrian 3G auction followed the German 3G auction that we have just described, using almost the same design, all the bidders very quickly saw the mutual advantage of coordinating a demand reduction (see section 9.3.2).[57]

The UK government's advisers anticipated this pattern of declining competition, and chose to run its auction first; indeed, we persisted in the policy of running the first auction even when others were advising us to delay (see Binmore and Klemperer, 2002). Yet in more than one country auction theorists advising on 3G auction design seemed either unaware of (!), or at least unaffected in their thinking by, the fact that there was to be a sequence of auctions across Europe. Clearly these designers had far too narrow a view of the problem.[58]

Of course, other auctions are only the most obvious aspects of the wider context that auction designers need to consider. There are many other ways in which designers showed themselves very poor at thinking about the wider game. For example, many of the 3G auction designers had a very limited understanding of how the auction process affected, and was affected by, the series of telecom mergers and alliances that the advent of 3G engendered – in the UK alone, there were no fewer than *five* mergers involving the four incumbent 2G operators, in less than a year around the auction.[59]

9.6   Using economic theory

I have argued that while a good understanding of elementary under-graduate economic theory is essential to successful auction design, advanced graduate auction theory is often less important. It is important to emphasize, therefore, the crucially important role that advanced formal theory plays in developing our economic understanding. In particular, advanced theory often develops deeper connections between apparently distinct economic questions than are superficially apparent.

For example, Klemperer (2003a) demonstrates that auction-theoretic tools provide useful arguments in a broad range of mainstream economic contexts. As a further illustration, I will discuss how a part of the received auction theory – the effect of affiliation – that was, I have argued, not central to the auctions of 3G licences, can develop useful insights about the economics of the 'M-Commerce' industry that 3G will create.[60]

9.6.1   Do e-commerce and M-commerce raise consumer prices?

Some commentators and regulators have expressed concern that e-commerce and M-commerce ('mobile commerce' in which people purchase through their mobile phones, and which is predicted to expand rapidly as a result of 3G technology) allow firms to easily identify and collect information about their customers which they can use to 'rip them off'.[61]

A simple analysis realizes that each consumer is analogous to an auctioneer, while firms are bidders competing to sell to that consumer. As we discussed in section 9.2, bidders' expected profits derive from their private information, and the auctioneer generally gains by reducing the amount of bidders' private information. So if all firms learn the same piece of information about a given consumer, this (weakly) reduces the private information that any bidder has relative to the other bidders, and so often benefits the auctioneer, that is, lowers the consumer's expected transaction price.

Although this result is a good start, it is neither very novel,[62] nor does it address the bigger concern that e- and M-commerce allow different firms to learn different information about any given consumer. However, Bulow and Klemperer (forthcoming) show how to use the mathematics of affiliation to address this issue too; in our model, even if firms learn different information about the consumers, this makes the market more competitive. In other words, a quick application of Milgrom and Weber's (1982) analysis suggests that the 'loss of privacy' caused by 3G and the internet is actually *good* for consumers.

Of course, having been cautious about the practical significance of affiliation in auction design, we should also be cautious about asserting that Bulow and Klemperer's argument shows that 3G is not as valuable to firms as some people once thought.[63] However, our model suggests a possibility which needs further study – including considering any empirical evidence and the plausibility of the intuitions – to confirm or disconfirm. Moreover, it certainly demonstrates that just because firms learn more about consumers, it does not follow that they can exploit them better – just as the RET refutes any simple presumption that one form of auction is always the most profitable. Our analysis therefore shows that firms' learning has other effects in addition to the very obvious one that firms can price-discriminate more effectively, and it helps us to see what these effects are[64] – we can then consider further whether these effects are plausibly significant. It also provides a structure which suggests what other factors not in the simplest model might in fact be important, and might perhaps yield the originally-hypothesized result.[65] And it very quickly and efficiently yields results that provide a good starting point for such further analysis.

Bulow and Klemperer pursue these issues in the context of this specific application. Klemperer (2003a) considers a range of other applications, including some that at first glance seem quite distant from auctions. The moral is that the 'received auction theory' *is* of great value in developing our understanding of practical issues. But it needs to be used in conjunction with developing intuition and gathering empirical evidence to check its applicability to specific situations.

9.7 Conclusion

This chapter is *not* attacking the value of economic theory. I have argued that elementary economic theory is essential to successful economic policy. Furthermore, the methods of thinking that undergraduate economics teaches are very valuable, for example, in understanding the important distinction between Hong Kong's two superficially similar auction designs (the one proposed and the one actually implemented). I have focused on examples from auctions, but the more I have been involved in public policy (for example, as a UK Competition Commissioner), the more I have been impressed by the importance of elementary undergraduate economics.

Nor is this chapter intended as an attack on modern, or sophisticated, or graduate economics. True, the emphasis of some graduate courses is misleading, and the relative importance of different parts of the theory is not always well-understood, but almost all of it is useful when appropriately applied; it is *not* true that all economic problems can be tackled using undergraduate economics alone.[66]

Policy errors are also less likely when expertise is not too narrowly focused in one subdiscipline – for example, auction designers should remember their industrial economics and political economy (at least) in addition to pure auction theory.

While advanced theory can be misapplied, the correct answer is not to shy away from it, but rather to develop it further to bring in the important issues that have been omitted. It may sometimes be true that 'a little bit too much economics is a dangerous thing', but it is surely also true that a great deal of economic knowledge is best of all. Moreover auction theory also illustrates that when a subdiscipline of economics becomes more widely used in practical policy making, its development becomes more heavily influenced by the practical problems that really matter. Like a rapidly growing bush, theory may sometimes sprout and develop in unhelpful directions, but when pruned with the shears of practical experience it will quickly bear fruit!

Furthermore, advanced economic theory is of practical importance in developing our economic understanding of the world, even when it cannot be directly applied to an immediate practical problem. To recapitulate only the incomplete list of its merits that was illustrated by our example in section 9.6, it refutes over-simple arguments, makes precise and quantifies other arguments, allows us to see the relationship between superficially unconnected problems, organizes our ideas, brings out the important features of problems, shows possibilities, and quickly develops general results which, even when they are not final answers, provide good starting points for further analysis.

Nevertheless, the main lesson of this chapter is that the blinkered use of economic theory can be dangerous. Policy advisers need to learn from Marshall's example to beware of the wider context, anticipate political pressures and, above all, remember that the most sophisticated theory may not be the most relevant.

Notes

* I advised the UK government on the design of its '3G' mobile-phone auction, and I am a member of the UK Competition Commission, but the views expressed in this paper are mine alone. I do not intend to suggest that any of the behaviour discussed below violates any applicable rules or laws.

This chapter was originally published in the *Journal of the European Economic Association*, 2003, 1(2–3), 272–300, and is reproduced here with the kind permission of the European Economic Association and the MIT Press. It was improved by an enormous number of helpful comments from Tony Atkinson, Sushil Bikhchandani, Erik Eyster, Nils-Henrik von der Fehr, Tim Harford, Michael Landsberger, Kristen Mertz, Meg Meyer, Paul Milgrom, David Myatt, Marco Pagnozzi, Rob Porter, Kevin Roberts, Mike Rothschild, Peter Temin, Chris Wallace, Mike Waterson and many others.

1 This chapter was the text of the 2002 Alfred Marshall Lecture of the European Economic Association, given at its Annual Congress, in Venice.

I gave a similar lecture at the 2002 Colin Clark Lecture of the Econometric Society, presented to its Annual Australasian Meeting. Like Marshall, Clark was very involved in practical economic policy making. He stressed the importance of quantification of empirical facts which, I argue below, is often underemphasised by modern economic theorists.

Similar material also formed the core of the biennial 2002 Lim Tay Boh Lecture in Singapore. Lim was another very distinguished economist (and Vice-Chancellor of the National University of Singapore), who also made significant contributions to policy, as an advisor to the Singapore government.

Finally, some of these ideas were presented in the Keynote Addresss to the 2002 Portuguese Economic Association's 2002 meetings.

I am very grateful to all those audiences for helpful comments.

2 I *mean* cautious about the theory. Not dismissive of it. And (3) seems a self-evident mistake, if only because of the need for efficient communication among, and education of, economists, let alone the possibilities for further useful development of the mathematics.

3 Sills (1968, p. 28). An attractively written appreciation of Marshall and his work is in Keynes (1933).

4 We take the governments' desire for high revenue as given, and ask how well the auctions met this objective. While an efficient allocation of licences was most governments' first priority, there is no clear evidence of any differences between the efficiencies of different countries' allocations, so revenues were seen as the measure of success. (Binmore and Klemperer, 2002, section 2 argues governments were correct to make revenue a priority because of the substantial deadweight losses of raising government funds by alternative means, and because the revenues were one-time sunk costs for firms so should be expected to have only limited effects on firms' subsequent investment and pricing behaviour.)

5 The six European auctions in year 2000 yielded 100 (Austria), 615 (Germany), 240 (Italy), 170 (Netherlands), 20 (Switzerland), and 650 (UK) euros per capita for very similar properties. True, valuations fell during the year as the stock-markets also fell, but Klemperer (2002a) details a variety of evidence that valuations ranged from 300–700 euros per capita in all of these auctions. Klemperer (2002a) gives a full description of all nine west European 3G auctions.

6 Another topical example of overemphasis on sophisticated theory at the expense of elementary theory is European merger policy's heavy focus on the 'coordinated' effects that may be facilitated by a merger (and about which we have learnt from repeated game theory) and, at the time of writing, relative lack of concern about the more straightforward 'unilateral' effects of mergers (which can be understood using much simpler static game theory). (As a UK Competition Commissioner, I stress that this criticism does not apply to UK policy!)

7   The RET is due in an early form to Vickrey (1961), and in its full glory to Myerson (1981), Riley and Samuelson (1981), and others. A typical statement is '*Assume each of a given number of risk-neutral potential buyers has a privately-known signal about the value of an object, independently drawn from a common, strictly increasing, atomless distribution. Then any auction mechanism in which (i) the object always goes to the buyer with the highest signal, and (ii) any bidder with the lowest feasible signal expects zero surplus, yields the same expected revenue (and results in each bidder making the same expected payment as a function of her signal).*'

   Klemperer (1999a) gives an elementary introduction to auction theory, including a simple exposition, and further discussion, of the RET. See also Klemperer (2003b).

8   Affiliation is actually a stronger assumption, but it is probably typically approximately satisfied.

9   Not only is the concept of affiliation important in applications well beyond auction theory (see section 9.6), but this paper was also critical to the development of auction theory, in that it introduced and analysed a general model including both private and common value components.

10 Or, to take just one very typical example from a current academic article, 'The one useful thing that our single unit auction theory can tell us is that when bidders' [signals] are affiliated ... the English [that is, ascending] auction should be expected to raise the most revenue'.

11 Whether the intuition need be non-mathematical, or even comprehensible to lay people, depends on the context, but we can surely have greater confidence in predicting agents' actions when the agents concerned understand the logic behind them, especially when there are few opportunities for learning.

12 The 'winner's curse' reflects the fact that winning an auction suggests one's opponents have pessimistic views about the value of the prize, and bidders must take this into account by bidding more conservatively than otherwise.

13 The result applies with affiliated private values, in which bidders' values are unaffected by others' information, so there is no winner's curse, and the result does not apply to independent-signal common-value auctions which do suffer from the winner's curse. (Where there is a winner's curse, the 'theory' behind the argument is that bidders' private information can be inferred from the points at which they drop out of an ascending auction, so less 'bad news' is discovered at the moment of winning than is discovered in winning a sealed-bid auction, so bidders can bid more aggressively in an ascending auction. But this assumes that bidders' more aggressive bidding more than compensates for the reduced winner's curse in an ascending auction – in independent-signal common-value auctions it exactly compensates, which is why there is no net effect, as the RET proves.)

   In fact, many experimental and empirical studies suggest bidders fail to fully account for winner's curse effects, so these effects may in practice make sealed-bid auctions more profitable than ascending auctions!

14 Absent private information, the auctioneer would sell to the bidder with the highest expected valuation at that expected valuation, and bidders would earn no rents. The more general result that, on average, the selling price is increased by having it depend on as much information as possible about the

value of the good, is Milgrom and Weber's (1982, 2000) Linkage Principle. However, in more recent work, Perry and Reny (1999) show that the Principle applies less generally (even in theory) than was thought.

15 Revealing more information clearly need not necessarily reduce bidders' profits (if bidders' information is negatively correlated, the contrary is typically true), the conditions that make the ascending price respond correctly to the additional information revealed are quite subtle, and nor does the argument say anything about how affiliation affects sealed bids. Indeed there are simple and not unnatural examples with the 'wrong kind' of *positive* correlation in which the ranking of auctions' revenues is reversed (see Bulow and Klemperer, forthcoming), and Perry and Reny (1999) also show the trickiness of the argument by demonstrating that the result only holds for single-unit auctions. A more complete verbal argument for the theoretical result is given in Klemperer (1999a, Appendix C), but it is very hard (certainly for the layman).

16 Another loose intuition is that in an ascending auction each bidder acts as if he is competing against an opponent with the same valuation. But in a sealed-bid auction a bidder must outbid those with lower valuations. With independent valuations, the RET applies. But if valuations are affiliated, a lower valuation bidder has a more conservative estimate of his opponent's valuation and therefore bids more conservatively. So a bidder in a sealed-bid auction attempting to outbid lower-valuation bidders will bid more conservatively as well. But this argument also rests on the RET applying exactly, and even so several steps are either far from compelling (for example, the optimal bid against a more conservative opponent is not always to be more conservative), or very non-transparent.

17 An easier numerical example than Riley and Li's assumes bidder i's value is $v_i = \theta + t_i$, in which θ and the t_i's are independent and uniform on $[0,1]$, and i knows only v_i. With two bidders, expected revenue is 14/18 in a first-price sealed-bid auction and 15/18 in an ascending auction, so bidder rents are 7/18 and 6/18 respectively (though with n bidders of whom $n/2$ each win a single object, as $n \to \infty$ bidder rents are 42 per cent higher in the sealed-bid auction).

With very extreme affiliation, an auctioneer's profits may be more sensitive to the auction form. Modifying the previous example so that there are two bidders who have completely diffuse priors for θ, bidder rents are 50 per cent higher in a first-price sealed-bid auction than in an ascending auction (see Klemperer, 1999a, Appendix D), and Riley and Li's example yields a similar result for correlation coefficients around 0.9 (when bidder rents are anyway small). These examples assume private-values. Auctioneers' profits may also be more sensitive to auction form with common-values and, in the previous extreme-affiliation model with diffuse priors on θ, if bidders' signals are v_i and the true common value is θ, bidders' rents are twice as high in the sealed-bid auction as in the ascending auction. But, with common values, small asymmetries between bidders are *very* much more important than affiliation (see Klemperer, 1998; Bulow and Klemperer, 2002). Moreover, we will see that other effects also seem to have been quantitatively much more important in practice than affiliation is even in any of these theoretical examples.

18   The RET, also, only generalizes to a limited extent to multi-unit auctions.

19   For example, empirical evidence about timber sales suggests rough revenue equivalence, or even that the sealed-bid auction raises more revenue given the number of bidders (Hansen, 1986; Mead and Schneipp, 1989; Paarsch, 1991; Rothkopf and Engelbrecht-Wiggans, 1993; Haile, 1996), though information is probably affiliated. The experimental evidence (see Kagel and Roth, 1995; and Levin, Kagel, and Richard, 1996) is also inconclusive about whether affiliation causes any difference between the revenues from ascending and sealed-bid auctions.

20   Like Marshall, Colin Clark (1939) emphasized the importance of quantification and real-world facts (see note 1), writing 'I have ... left my former colleagues in the English universities ... with dismay at their continued preference for the theoretical ... approach to economic problems. Not one in a hundred ... seems to understand [the need for] the testing of conclusions against ... observed facts ...' '... The result is a vast output of literature of which, it is safe to say, scarcely a syllable will be read in fifty years' time.' I think he would be pleased that an academic from an English university is quoting his words well over fifty years after he wrote them.

21   See Klemperer, 2002b. Risk-aversion and asymmetries (even absent entry issues) also arguably matter more than affiliation (and usually have the opposite effect). It is striking that Maskin and Riley's (1984, 2000) important papers on these topics (see also Matthews, 1983, and so on) failed to have the same broad impact as Milgrom and Weber's work on affiliation.

22   I have done this in over twenty countries on five different continents.

23   True, the generally accepted notion of the 'received auction theory' is changing and so is the auction theory that is emphasised in graduate programmes. And recent auctions research has been heavily influenced by practical problems. But it will probably remain true that the elegance of a theory will remain an important determinant of its practical influence.

24   Of course, auction theorists have not altogether ignored these issues – but the emphasis on them has been far less. The literature on collusion includes Robinson (1985), Cramton, Gibbons, and Klemperer (1987), Graham and Marshall (1987), Milgrom (1987), Hendricks and Porter (1989), Graham, Marshall, and Richard (1990), Mailath and Zemsky (1991), McAfee and McMillan (1992), Menezes (1996), Weber (1997), Engelbrecht-Wiggans and Kahn (1998), Ausubel and Schwartz (1999), Brusco and Lopomo (2002a), Hendricks, Porter, and Tan (1999) and Cramton and Schwartz (2000). That on entry includes Matthews (1984), Engelbrecht-Wiggans (1987), McAfee and McMillan (1987), McAfee and McMillan (1988), Harstad (1990), Engelbrecht-Wiggans (1993), Levin and Smith (1994), Bulow and Klemperer (1996), Menezes and Monteiro (1997), Persico (1997), Klemperer (1998) and Gilbert and Klemperer (2000). See also Klemperer (1999a, 2000a, 2003b).

25   This point is similar to the industrial-organization point that because a Bertrand market is more competitive than a Cournot market for any given number of firms, the Bertrand market may attract less entry, so the Cournot market may be more competitive if the number of firms is endogenous.

26   See also Bikhchandani (1988), Bulow, Huang and Klemperer (1999), Bulow and Klemperer (2002), and Klemperer and Pagnozzi (2003).

27 In spite of the fact that I have made the point that the argument applies more broadly in, for example, Klemperer (1999b, 2002b). See also Gilbert and Klemperer (2000).

28 Similarly others have asserted that the reason the UK planned to include a sealed-bid component in its 3G design if only four licences were available for sale (see below) was because the auction designers (who included me) thought the auction was almost-common values – but publicly-available government documents show that we did not think this was likely.

29 It seems unlikely that the efficiency of the Netherlands auction was much improved by the ascending design.

30 We discuss the UK design below. The design of the US auctions, according to McMillan (1994, pp. 151–2) who was a consultant to the US government, was largely determined by faith in the linkage principle and hence in the revenue advantages of an ascending auction in the presence of affiliation; the economic theorists advising the government judged other potential problems with the ascending design 'to be outweighed by the bidders' ability to learn from other bids in the auction' (McMillan, 1994). (See also Perry and Reny, 1999.) Efficiency was also a concern in the design of the US auctions.

31 There was one entrant who probably did not seriously expect to win a license in an ascending auction – indeed it argued strongly prior to the auction that an ascending auction gave it very little chance and, more generally, reduced the likelihood of entry into the auction. Perhaps it competed in the hope of being bought off by an incumbent by, for example, gaining access rights to an incumbent's network, in return for its quitting the auction early. The Netherlands government should be very grateful that this entrant competed for as long as it did! See Klemperer (2002a) and van Damme (2002) for details.

32 Attracting entry was an even more severe problem in late 2001 than in early summer 2000 when the Netherlands auction was held. By the latter date the dotcom boom was over, European telecoms stock prices at the time of the Danish auction were just one-third the levels they were at in the Dutch auction, and the prospects for 3G were much dimmer than they had seemed previously.

33 I was the principal auction theorist advising the Radiocommunications Agency which designed and ran the UK auction. Ken Binmore had a leading role, including also supervising experiments testing the proposed designs. Other academic advisors included Tilman Börgers, Jeremy Bulow, Philippe Jehiel and Joe Swierzbinksi. Ken Binmore subsequently advised the Danish government on its very successful auction. The views expressed in this chapter are mine alone.

34 With five licenses, the licenses would be of unequal size, which argued for an ascending design. Note that in some contexts an ascending design may promote entry. For example, when Peter Cramton, Eric Maskin and I advised the UK government on the design of its March 2002 auction of reductions in greenhouse gas emissions, we recommended an ascending design to encourage the entry of small bidders for whom working out how to bid sensibly in a discriminatory sealed-bid auction might have been prohibitively costly. (Strictly speaking the auction was a descending one since the auction was a reverse auction in which firms were bidding to sell emissions reductions to

the government. But this is equivalent to an ascending design for a standard auction to sell permits.) (Larry Ausubel and Jeremy Bulow were also involved in the implementation of this design.) See Klemperer *et al.* (forthcoming).

35 For example, in a multi-license US spectrum auction in 1996–97, US West was competing vigorously with McLeod for lot number 378 – a license in Rochester, Minnesota. Although most bids in the auction had been in exact thousands of dollars, US West bid $313,378 and $62,378 for two licenses in Iowa in which it had earlier shown no interest, overbidding McLeod, who had seemed to be the uncontested high-bidder for these licenses. McLeod got the point that it was being punished for competing in Rochester, and dropped out of that market. Since McLeod made subsequent higher bids on the Iowa licenses, the 'punishment' bids cost US West nothing (Cramton and Schwartz, 2000).

36 Although it did not require rocket science to determine the obvious way to divide 12 among six, the largest incumbent, Telekom Austria probably assisted the coordination when it announced in advance of the auction that it 'would be satisfied with just two of the 12 blocks of frequency on offer' and 'if the [five other bidders] behaved similarly it should be possible to get the frequencies on sensible terms', but 'it would bid for a third frequency block if one of its rivals did' (Crossland, 2000).

37 Unlike my other examples this was not a 3G auction; however, it is highly relevant to the German 3G auction which we will discuss.

38 See Jehiel and Moldovanu, 2001, and Grimm, Riedel and Wolfstetter, 2001. Grimm *et al.* argue that this outcome was a non-cooperative Nash equilibrium of the fully-specified game. This is similar to the familiar industrial organization point that oligopolistic outcomes that we call 'collusive' may be Nash equilibria of repeated oligopoly games. But our focus is on whether outcomes look like competitive, non-cooperative, behaviour in the simple analyses that are often made, not on whether or not they can be justified as Nash equilibria in more sophisticated models.

39 Abbink *et al.* write 'The lessons learnt from the experiments are complemented by theoretical strategic considerations'. Indeed, auctions policy advice should always, if possible, be informed by both theory and experiments.

40 In the UK's ascending auction, the fact that bidders were each restricted to winning at most a single object, out of just five objects, ruled out tacit collusion to divide the spoils (provided that there were more than five bidders). More important, the large number of bidders expected (because the UK ran Europe's first 3G auction – see section 9.5) also made explicit (illegal) collusion much less likely (see Klemperer, 2002a), and the fact that the UK retained the right to cancel the auction in some circumstances also reduced bidders' incentive to collude.

41 Doctors are trained to recognise that some types of patients may not take all prescribed medicines or return for follow-up treatment. Pharmaceutical companies have developed one-dose regimens that are often more expensive or less effective than multiple-dose treatments, but that overcome these specific problems. For example, the treatment of chlamydial infection by a single dose of azithromycin is much more expensive and no more effective than a seven-day course of doxycycline; there is a short (two-month) course of preventive therapy for tuberculosis that is both more expensive, and seems to

have more problems with side effects, than the longer six-month course; and the abridged regimen for HIV$^+$ women who are pregnant (to prevent perinatal transmission) is less effective than the longer, more extensive treatment.

42 Two bidders merged the day before the auction was to begin, and a total of five bidders quit in the four days immediately preceding the auction. At least one bidder had quit earlier after hearing from its bidding consultants that because it was a weaker bidder it had very little chance of winning an ascending auction. Furthermore, the regulator investigated rumours that Deutsche Telekom agreed not to participate in the auction in return for subsequently being able to buy into one of the winners.

43 In fact, when the denouement of the auction had become clear, the Swiss government tried to cancel it and re-run it with different rules. But in contrast to the UK auction (see note 40), the designers had omitted to allow themselves that possibility.

The final revenues were 20 euros per capita, compared to analysts' estimates of 400–600 euros per capita in the week before the auction was due to begin. Meeks (2001) shows the jumps in Swisscom's share price around the auction are highly statistically-significant and, controlling for general market movements, correspond to the market believing that bidders paid several hundred euros per capita less in the auction than was earlier anticipated.

44 I am not arguing that an ascending auction plus reserve price is always bad advice, or even that it was necessarily poor advice here. But advisors must make it very clear if success depends on a whole package being adopted, and should think carefully about the likely implementation of their proposals.

Greece and Belgium did set reserve prices that seem to have been carefully thought out, but they were perhaps encouraged to do so by the example of the Swiss auction, and also of the Italian and Austrian auctions which also had reserve prices that were clearly too low, even if not as low as Switzerland's.

45 In Hong Kong, unlike in the Netherlands and Denmark, there were actually more incumbents than licences. But not all Hong Kong's incumbents were thought strong. Furthermore, it is much more attractive for strong firms to form joint ventures or collude with their closest rivals prior to a standard ascending auction (when the strengthened combined bidder discourages entry) than prior to a standard sealed-bid auction (when reducing two strong bidders to one may attract entry). So even though the difference in strength between the likely winners and the also-rans seemed less dramatic in Hong Kong than in the Netherlands and Denmark, a standard ascending auction still seemed problematic. So there was a very serious concern – well-justified as it turned out – that a standard ascending auction would yield no more bidders than licences.

46 In a simple model, if a winning bidder suffers 'embarrassment costs' which are an increasing function of the difference between his payment and the lowest winning payment, then bidders are no worse off in expectation than in an auction which induces no embarrassment costs, but the auctioneer suffers. This is a consequence of the Revenue Equivalence Theorem: under its assumptions, mechanisms that induce embarrassment costs cannot affect bidders' utilities (it is irrelevant to the bidders whether the 'embarrassment costs' are received by the auctioneer or are social waste), so in equilibrium

winning bidders' expected payments are lower by the expected embarrassment costs they suffer. See Klemperer (2003b, Part I).

47   I had no direct involvement with this auction but, embarrassingly, I am told this 'solution' was found in a footnote to Klemperer (2000b) that pointed out this method of running a strategically equivalent auction to the uniform fourth-price auction, and that it might (sometimes) be more politically acceptable. See also Binmore and Klemperer (2002).

48   The lobbyists also successfully ridiculed the original design, calling it the 'dark auction', arguing that it 'perversely' hid information when 'everyone knows that transparent markets are more efficient', and claiming it was an 'unfair tax' since bidders 'paid more than if they had all the information'.

49   The highly sophisticated security arrangements that had been made to ensure secrecy of the dropouts (removal of bidding teams to separate top-secret locations in army camps and so on) were not altered, even though they had become much less relevant; there was no need to lobby against these.

50   It is rumoured that a single bidder's budget for economic advice for lobbying against the design exceeded the UK government's expenditure on economic advice during the entire three-year design process; the lobbying effort included hiring two Nobel Prize winners in the hope of finding arguments against the design. See Binmore and Klemperer (2002) for details of the two versions of the design.

51   When it became possible to offer an additional fifth licence in the UK the design changed – as had been planned for this circumstance – to a pure ascending one, see section 9.3.1.

52   See van Damme, 1999. This auction also illustrates the potential importance of bidders' errors: although high stakes were involved (the revenues were over 800 million euros) it seems that the outcome, and perhaps also the efficiency of the licence allocation, was critically affected by a bidder unintentionally losing its eligibility to bid on additional properties later in the auction; it has been suggested that the bidder's behaviour can only be explained by the fact that it happened on 'Carnival Monday', a day of celebrations and drinking in the south of the Netherlands where the bidder is based (van Damme, 1999)! (The German 3G auction described below provides another example of the large role that bidder error can play.)

53   According to the *Financial Times*, 'One operator has privately admitted to altering the last digit of its bid ... to signal to other participants that it was willing to accept a small licence.' 3 November 2000, p. 21.

54   It seems that another reason why Mannesman expected the firms to coordinate by T-Mobil reducing demand first in response to Mannesman's signals was that Mannesman saw itself as the leading firm in the market. However, T-Mobil may not have seen Mannesman as the leading firm – the two firms were closely matched – and this seems to have contributed to the problem.

55   In particular, the firms might have been concerned about their relative performances. See also Grimm *et al.* (2002), Jehiel and Moldovanu (2002), and Ewerhart and Moldovanu (2001).

56   Furthermore, the number (6) achieved in the second auction (Netherlands) was perhaps lowered by the peculiarly incompetent design; the number (5) achieved in the last auction (Denmark) was raised by its design, which was very skilful except in its timing – see section 9.3.1.

Of course, other factors, in particular the fall in the telecoms stock price index, may have contributed to the fall in the number of entrants.

57 Klemperer (2002a) develops the arguments in this paragraph in much greater detail.

58 Some of the incumbent bidders, by contrast, may possibly have had a clearer understanding. In an interesting example of the importance of political pressures, the Dutch operators successfully lobbied to delay the Netherlands auction and the clear gap that was thereby created between the British and Dutch auctions may have been a contributory factor to the Dutch fiasco.

59 Klemperer (2002d) gives another illustration of how a real-world context that was non-obvious to outsiders was important to the UK 3G auction.

60 Klemperer (2003a) uses the other main piece of the received auction theory – the Revenue Equivalence Theorem – to solve a war of attrition between several technologies competing to become an industry standard in, for example, 3G (see also Bulow and Klemperer, 1999) and to compute the value of new customers to firms when consumers have switching costs as they do for, for example, 3G phones (see also Bulow and Klemperer, 1998). Klemperer (2003a) also uses auction theory to address how e-commerce (and likewise M-commerce) affects pricing.

61 The US Federal Trade Commission has held hearings on this issue, and the European Commission is currently studying it. Amazon has admitted charging different prices to different consumers.

62 Thisse and Vives (1988), Ulph and Vulkan (2001), and Esteves (forthcoming), for example, have developed similar results.

63 Of course, there are more important reasons why 3G is no longer thought as valuable as it once was (see Klemperer, 2002a).

64 In this case, while a firm may raise prices against consumers who particularly value its product, in a competitive environment it will also lower prices to other consumers who like it less – and other firms will then have to respond.

65 For example, the analysis shows that even though it may be no bad thing for consumers if different firms learn different pieces of information about them, the result depends on firms learning the same amount of information about any given consumer. It probably is costly for a consumer to 'lose his privacy' to only one firm, just as having asymmetrically informed bidders may be a bad thing for an auctioneer. Furthermore, even when firms learn the same amount of information about consumers' tastes, this information may sometimes lead to inefficient price-discrimination which reduces total welfare, in which case consumers may be made worse off even though firms' profits are lowered, just as inefficient auctions may be bad for both auctioneers and bidders. Learning information may also affect firms' abilities to collude, and the ease of new entry.

66 Furthermore, it is often only the process of thinking through the sophisticated graduate theory that puts the elementary undergraduate theory in proper perspective.

Conclusion

Colin Jennings and Iain McLean

In the Introduction, we drew attention to the distinctions between Keynesian and neo-classical approaches to macroeconomic policy; and between public finance and public choice. How do these theoretical debates relate to the chapters in the book?

It used to be the case that economists agreed among themselves as to microeconomics, while continuing to disagree about macroeconomics. Two of our chapters – those by Christopher Foster and Paul Klemperer – mostly concern microeconomic policy; the chapter by Iain McLean deals equally with both; the others mostly concern macroeconomic policy. In transport policy, as both Martin Wolf and Christopher Foster have said in this book, there is little dispute among economists as to what works. Road pricing (including its variant, congestion charging) works; most other transport policies that have been tried in the UK over the forty years that Foster has been actively observing it have failed. Policy makers have failed to follow through on the economic advice they have received. The result is the distortions described in Foster's chapter. Since it, and our Introduction, were written, there is more somewhat depressing news. In a referendum in February 2005, the voters of Edinburgh threw out a congestion charge scheme there. This was embarrassing not only because Edinburgh has an acute congestion problem to which charging is the only viable solution, but because it is the home of both the UK's Secretary of State for Transport in the 2001–05 government (Alistair Darling, Edinburgh born and bred, and a former convener of Lothian Council Transport Committee) and the chair of that government's Commission on Integrated Transport (David Begg, Edinburgh born and bred, and a former convener of Lothian Council Transport Committee). And just before the 2005 General Election, road hauliers and farmers were again threatening to blockade the highways, as they did in 2000, in protest against the price of diesel. This again implies that pricing traffic off the road by taxation is a policy dead end. Meanwhile, as recorded in Foster's chapter, the railways are eating up the lion's share of the UK transport budget although they deliver only a small proportion of the UK's transport.

Yet these are political failures, not failures of policy advice. Voters do not face a budget constraint. They would like to be able to travel anywhere by car, and would like not to pay the resulting congestion costs. Oh, and by the way they do not want any new roads in their backyards. And they would like petrol and train fares to be cheaper. In some policy areas, politicians have succeeded in reminding citizens of the constraints of the real world. Prime Minister Jim Callaghan's speech to the 1976 Labour Party Conference, quoted by both Alan Budd and Peter Jay in their chapters, told some home truths that have stuck: *We used to think that you could spend your way out of a recession and increase employment by cutting taxes and boosting government spending. I tell you in all candour that that option no longer exists.* No Callaghan of transport has yet comparably succeeded in getting the equivalent truths home.

Why was the auction of spectrum space described by Paul Klemperer so much more successful than any transport policy? Probably because unlike transport policy it was not something on which every citizen has an opinion. Also, because it was being done for the first time, there was no coalition of vested interests lined up to prevent it.

The 'new social democracy' described by McLean covers both micro and macro policy developments. On the micro side, the Labour Party since Neil Kinnock has been shaking off the vested interests that founded and financed the party from the outset, namely the trade unions. This has been painful and difficult. Trade unions are a perfectly legitimate vested interest group, and for nearly a century UK politics was in rough balance, where suppliers of capital (companies and trade associations) financed the Conservative Party and suppliers of labour financed the Labour Party. Neither of these remains true. On the Conservative side, the main change has come from below: lobbies for capital have deserted the party since 1992 because it has no longer seemed like an election winner. A rational lobby group concentrates its efforts on lobbying parties in power or close to it. On the Labour side the main change has come from above: Kinnock, Smith, Blair and Brown have all decided to varying degrees that increasing the efficiency of the supply side of the UK economy takes priority over protecting the producer interests of the Labour Party's founding interest group.

Turning to macroeconomic policy, what strikes us first is the extent to which the macro-based chapters of this book agree – even though their authors probably disagree widely in politics and ideology. Economists agree far more closely on what works in macroeconomic policy than they did in the days of Ricardo, or Marx, or Keynes. Critics of Keynes had two related complaints. One was that Keynesian macroeconomics lacked microfoundations; the other, that it assumed that actors in the polity were altruistic, while actors in the economy (a superset of the same people) were self-interested. As to the first, they complained that manipulating the level of demand in an economy by adjusting fiscal or monetary policy was, literally, incredible. No rational economic actor could believe that incumbent politicians would not manipulate the economy in the way bested suited to help their re-election – specifically by letting rip before a general election and closing down after it. They had been doing so for 200 years, after all. To believe that politicians would cease behaving like this was to believe that people in politics would not act according to their private interests; whereas economic theory is built on the assumption that people in economic life do act according to their private interests.

The dialectic of debate between the *public finance* vs *public choice* approaches has paved the way for an increasingly accepted new political economy. The seminal work by Kydland, Prescott, Barro and others that has been frequently mentioned in this book supplied the missing microfoundations. They proved that it was in the long-term interest of all actors that monetary and fiscal policy should be governed by *rules rather than discretion*. If politicians have the discretion to alter them, it is not credible that they would refrain from doing so. The three chapters of this book that deal with monetary policy approach it from different per-spectives, reflecting the respective roles of Ed Balls, Christopher Allsopp, and Mark Robson in monetary policy. But they all share a 'rules rather than discretion' framework, and they all describe how UK monetary institutions work better under a rule-based framework than under the older discretionary framework. The implication of all these chapters is that we cannot place a naïve faith in the good intentions of politi-cians. This would seem to be a victory for the public choice approach. The Treasury documents mentioned in the Introduction show that the Treasury was thinking along these lines at least as early as 1988, when it put up the Ricardian (or Kydlandite) idea that the monetary authority should be rule-bound and independent of the chancellor to Chancellor Nigel Lawson. His imperious prime minister Margaret Thatcher would have none of it. If she had accepted the idea in 1988, she might have saved the Conservative Party from its 1992 disaster which continues to haunt it. Equally, if the modern (but in a sense really very old) macroeconomics had been understood in the 1960s and 1970s, the disasters that overtook both Labour governments (see Peter Jay's chapter) and Conservative governments (see Alan Budd's chapter) might have been avoided.

An interesting section of Ed Balls' discussion concerns whether fiscal policy should also be outsourced. Should there, or could there, be a Fiscal Policy Committee? If so, of what body should it be a committee? Balls concludes that fiscal policy is too close to the heart of politics to be ready for the same treatment as monetary policy. Perhaps that idea's time will come. For now, however, the fact that there seems little appetite for such a committee could be interpreted as a sign that trust in the good intentions of politicians is not completely dead and this would seem to be a victory for the public finance approach. In this way modern political economy synthesizes public finance and public choice by warning against possible abuses by politicians and considering the role for rules to protect society. However, the possibility of abuse does not make it inevitable and there is an awareness that the design of such rules is unnecessary in those areas where we have more reason to trust politicians with discretionary power.

Note that we have just explained that the new macroeconomics says that it is in the *long-term* interest of all that monetary policy, and perhaps fiscal policy, should be politician-proof. This does not explain how politician-proofing can ever come into force. To revert to Le Grand's knights and knaves, political institutions must lie somewhere between those designed for knaves at one end and for knights at the other. Designers of institutions should create incentives to turn knaves into knights, while recognising that knavery is part of life. But these designers must have something of the knight about themselves. The public choice theory of constitutional design has for many years concerned itself with the sorts of political institutions that would be good for this purpose. It has completely failed to explain how such institutions could ever come into being in the first place. James Madison is, deservedly, a hero to the constitutional political economists. But in his amazing political efforts from the summoning of a constitutional convention in 1786 until the ratification of the US Constitution and Bills of Rights, completed in 1791, he was truly a knight, and a highly altruistic one at that. He and the other designers of the US Constitution, and the voters who ratified, created the first stable, and yet supple, constitution the world has yet seen. Those who designed the UK's new monetary institutions – and this book shows that they have been numerous – are perhaps the Madisons of our day. In terms of the welfare of the nation these developments in theory are positive to the extent that the means of policy are less disputed, even if the goals may differ widely. It is interesting that economic analysis associated with sceptics of beneficial government intervention has been implemented by a government with redistributive goals requiring substantial government intervention. It is just that the modern Labour governments seem to realize that discretion may not be as good as rules in providing the sound macroeconomic base necessary to achieve those goals.

References

Abbink, K., Irlenbusch, B., Rockenbach, B., Sadrieh, A., and Selten, R. (2002). 'The Behavioural Approach to the Strategic Analysis of Spectrum Auctions: the Case of the German DCS-1800 Auction'. Working Paper, Universities of Nottingham, Erfurt, Tilburg, and Bonn.

Affuso, L., Masson, J., and Newbery, D. (2003). 'Comparing Markets in New Transport Infrastructure: Road vs Railways'. *Fiscal Studies*, 24(3), 235–315.

Alesina, A., Blanchard, O., Galí, J., Giavazzi, F., and Uhlig, H. (2001). 'Defining a Macroeconomic Framework for the Euro Area'. *Monitoring the European Central Bank* 3. London: Centre for Economic Policy Research.

Allsopp, C. (2001). 'Economic Imbalances and UK Monetary Policy'. *Bank of England Quarterly Bulletin*, 41(3), 484–94.

Allsopp, C. (2002). 'The Future of Macroeconomic Policy in the European Union'. External MPC Unit Discussion Paper No. 7.

Allsopp, C. (2004). *Review of Statistics for Economic Policymaking: Final Report*. HM Treasury, December 2003 and March 2004.

Allsopp, C., and Vines, D. (2000). 'The Assessment: Macroeconomic Policy'. *Oxford Review of Economic Policy*, 16(4), 1–32.

Ausubel, L., and Schwartz, J. (1999). 'The Ascending Auction Paradox'. Working Paper, University of Maryland.

Ball, L. (1999). 'Policy Rules for Open Economies'. In J.B. Taylor (ed.), *Monetary Policy Rules*. Chicago: University of Chicago Press, pp. 127–44.

Balls, E. (2001). 'Delivering Economic Stability'. Oxford Business Alumni Annual Lecture, Merchant Taylors' Hall, London, 12 June.

Balls, E., and O'Donnell, G. (eds) (2001). *Reforming Britain's Economic and Financial Policy*. Basingstoke: Palgrave – now Palgrave Macmillan.

Barker, K. (2004) *Review of Housing Supply: Final Report – Recommendations. Delivering Stability: Securing our future Housing Needs*. London: HM Treasury.

Barro, R. (1986). 'Reputation in a Model of Monetary Policy with Incomplete Information'. *Journal of Monetary Economics*, 17(1), 3–20.

Barro, R., and Gordon, D. (1983a). 'Rules, Discretion, and Reputation in a Model of Monetary Policy'. *Journal of Monetary Economics*, 12(1), 101–21.

Barro, R., and Gordon, D. (1983b). 'A Positive Theory of Monetary Policy in a Natural Rate Model'. *Journal of Political Economy*, 91(4), 589–610.

Batini, N., and Haldane, A. (1999). 'Forward-Looking Rules for Monetary Policy'. In J. Taylor (ed.), *Monetary Policy Rules*. Chicago: University of Chicago Press, pp. 157–92.

Bayliss, D., and Muir Wood, A. (2002). *Measures to Mitigate the Effects of Increasing Road Capacity in Line with Demand*. London: RAC Foundation for Motoring.

Bean, C. (1998a). 'The New UK Monetary Arrangements: A View from the Literature'. *Economic Journal*, 108(451), 1795–809.

Bean, C. (1998b). 'Monetary Policy under EMU'. *Oxford Review of Economic Policy*, 14(3), 41–53.

Bean, C., and Jenkinson, N. (2001). 'The Formulation of Monetary Policy at the Bank of England'. *Bank of England Quarterly Bulletin*, 41(4), Winter, 434–41.

Begg, D., Canova, F., Fatas, A., De Grauwe, P., and Lane, P. (2002). 'Surviving the Slowdown'. *Monitoring the European Central Bank*, 4. London: Centre for Economic Policy Research.

Bernanke, B., and Gertler, M. (1999). 'Monetary Policy and Asset Price Volatility.' In *New Challenges for Monetary Policy: A Symposium Sponsored by the Federal Reserve Bank of Kansas City*. Kansas City: Federal Reserve Bank of Kansas City.

Bernanke, B., and Mishkin, F. (1997). 'Inflation Targeting: A New Framework for Monetary Policy?' *Journal of Economic Perspectives*, 11(2), 97–116.

Bikhchandani, S. (1988). 'Reputation in Repeated Second-price Auctions'. *Journal of Economic Theory*, 46, 97–119.

Binmore, K., and Klemperer, P. (2002). 'The Biggest Auction Ever: the Sale of the British 3G Telecom Licences'. *Economic Journal*, 112(478), C74–C96.

Black, D. (1958). *The Theory of Committees and Elections*. Cambridge: Cambridge University Press.

Blinder, A. (1998). *Central Banking in Theory and Practice*. Cambridge, MA: MIT Press.

Bordo, M.D., and Eichengreen, B. (eds) (1993). *A Retrospective on the Bretton Woods System: Lessons for International Monetary Reform*. Chicago: University of Chicago Press.

Bordo, M., and Jeanne, O. (2002). 'Boom–Busts in Asset Prices, Economic Instability and Monetary Policy'. CEPR Discussion Paper No. 3398. London: Centre for Economic Policy Research.

Bordo, M., and Jonung, L. (1999). 'The Future of EMU: What does the History of Monetary Unions Tell Us?' Working Paper 7365, National Bureau of Economic Research.

Borio, C., and Lowe, P. (2002). 'Asset Prices, Financial and Monetary Stability: Exploring the Nexus'. BIS Working Paper No. 114, Bank for International Settlements.

Bradley, F. (1876). *Ethical Studies*. London: H. S. King.

Brittan, S. (1971). *Steering the Economy: The Role of the Treasury*. Harmondsworth: Penguin Books.

Brittan, S. (1996). *Capitalism with a Human Face*. London: Fontana Press.

Brown, G. (1994). 'John Smith's Socialism: His Writings and Speeches'. In Brown and Naughtie (1994), pp. 61–103.

Brown, G. (2003). 'State and Market: Towards a Public-Interest Test'. *Political Quarterly*, 74(3), 266–84.

Brown, G., and Naughtie, J. (eds) (1994). *John Smith: Life and Soul of the Party*. Edinburgh: Mainstream.

Brusco, S., and Lopomo, G. (2002a). 'Collusion via Signalling in Simultaneous Ascending Bid Auctions with Heterogeneous Objects, With and Without Complementarities'. *Review of Economic Studies*, 69, 407–36.

Brusco, S., and Lopomo, G. (2002b). 'Simultaneous Ascending Auctions with Budget Constraints'. Working Paper, Stern School of Business, New York University.

Buchanan, J., and Musgrave, R. (2001). *Public Finance and Public Choice: Two Contrasting Views of the State*. Cambridge, MA: MIT Press.

Buchanan, J., and Tullock, G. (1962). *The Calculus of Consent*. Ann Arbor: University of Michigan Press.

Buiter, W.H., and Grafe, C. (2002) *Anchor, float or Abandon Ship: Exchange Rate Regimes for Accession Countries*. London: Centre for Economic Policy Research.

Bulow, J., Huang, M., and Klemperer, P. (1999). 'Toeholds and Takeovers'. *Journal of Political Economy*, 107, 427–54. (also reprinted in Biais, B. and Pagano, M. (eds) (2002). *New Research in Corporate Finance and Banking*. Oxford: Oxford University Press, pp. 91–116).

Bulow, J., and Klemperer, P. (1996). 'Auctions vs. Negotiations'. *American Economic Review*, 86(1), 180–94.

Bulow, J., and Klemperer, P. (1998). 'The Tobacco Deal'. *Brookings Papers on Economic Activity: Microeconomics*, 323–94.

Bulow, J., and Klemperer, P. (1999). 'The Generalized War of Attrition'. *American Economic Review*, 89, 175–89.

Bulow, J., and Klemperer, P. (2002). 'Prices and The Winner's Curse'. *Rand Journal of Economics*, 33(1), 1–21.

Bulow, J., and Klemperer, P. (forthcoming) 'Privacy and Pricing'. Discussion Paper, Nuffield College, Oxford University.

Butler, D., and Stokes, D. (1974). *Political Change in Britain*, 2nd edn. London: Macmillan.

Butler, D., and Kavanagh, D. (1980). *The British General Election of 1979*. London: Macmillan.

Cagan, P. (1956). 'The Monetary Dynamics of Hyperinflation'. In M. Friedman (ed.), *Studies in the Quantity Theory of Money*. Chicago: University of Chicago Press.

Callaghan, J. (1987). *Time and Chance*. London: Collins.

Carlyle, T. (1853). *Occasional discourse on the nigger question*. London: Reprinted from Fraser's Magazine.

Cecchetti, S. (2000). 'Making Monetary Policy: Objectives and Rules'. *Oxford Review of Economic Policy*, 16(4), 43–59.

Cecchetti, S., Genberg, H., Lipsky, J., and Wadhwani, S. (2000). *Asset Prices and Central Bank Policy*. Geneva Report on the World Economy 2. London: Centre for Economic Policy Research and International Centre for Monetary and Banking Studies.

Cecchetti, S., Genberg, H., and Wadhwani, S. (2002). 'Asset Prices in a Flexible Inflation Targeting Framework'. NBER Working Paper No. 8970. Cambridge, MA: National Bureau of Economic Research.

Central Statistical Office (CSO) (1996). *CSO Economic Trends Annual Supplement*. London: HMSO.

Chrystal, K., and Mizen, P. (2001) 'Goodhart's Law: Its Origins, Meaning and Implications for Monetary Policy', paper for Festschrift in honour of Charles Goodhart, 15–16 November 2001 at the Bank of England, at http://www.cass.city.ac.uk/faculty/a.chrystal/files/Goodharts_Law.pdf.

Clarida, R., Galí, J., and Gertler, M. (1998). 'Monetary Policy Rules in Practice: Some International Evidence'. *European Economic Review*, 42, 1033–67.

Clarida, R., Galí, J., and Gertler, M. (2001). 'Optimal Monetary Policy in Open versus Closed Economies: An Integrated Approach'. *American Economic Review (Papers and Proceedings)*, 91(2), 248–52.

Clark, C. (1939). *The Conditions of Economic Progress*. Brisbane, Australia.

Committee on Stabilisation Policy (2002). *Stabilisation Policy in the Monetary Union*. Swedish Official Government Report, 12 March.

Cramton, P., and Schwartz, J. (2000). 'Collusive Bidding: Lessons from the FCC Spectrum Auctions'. *Journal of Regulatory Economics*, 17(3), 229–52.

Cramton, P., Gibbons, R., and Klemperer, P. (1987). 'Dissolving a Partnership Efficiently'. *Econometrica*, 55, 615–32.

Crewe, I., and King, A. (1995). *SDP: The Birth, Life, and Death of the Social Democratic Party*. Oxford: Oxford University Press.

Crick, M. (1984). *Militant*. London: Faber & Faber.

Crossland, D. (2000). 'Austrian UMTS Auction Unlikely to Scale Peaks'. Reuters. 31 October. Available at ⟨http://www.totaltele.com⟩.

Department of Transport (1989). *Roads for Prosperity*. Cm 693. London: Department of Transport.

Department of the Environment, Transport and the Regions (1998). *A New Deal for Transport: Better for Everyone*. Cm 3950. London: HMSO.

Department of Transport (2004a). *The Future of Transport: a Network for 2030*. Cm 6234. London: Department of Transport, July.

Department of Transport (2004b). *The Future of Rail*. London: Department of Transport, July.

Department of Transport (2004c). *Transport Trends*. London: Department of Transport.

Department of Transport (2004d). *Feasibility Study of Road Pricing in the UK: A Report to the Secretary of State for Transport*. London: Department of Transport: July.

Dodge, D. (2002). 'The Interaction between Monetary and Fiscal Policies'. Donald Gow Lecture, School of Policy Studies, Queens University, Kingston, Ontario, 26 April.

Dornbusch, R. (1989) 'Ireland's Disinflation'. *Economic Policy*, 8, 173–209.

Dornbusch, R. (1999). 'Commentary: Monetary Policy and Asset Price Volatility'. In *New Challenges for Monetary Policy: A Symposium Sponsored by the Federal Reserve Bank of Kansas City*. Kansas City: Federal Reserve Bank of Kansas City. 129–35.

Dow, J.C.R. (1998). *Major Recessions, Britain and the World, 1920–1995*. Oxford: Oxford University Press.

Dow, J.C.R. (1964). *The Management of the British Economy, 1945–1960*. Cambridge: Cambridge University Press.

Eichengreen, B. (1993). 'Labor Markets and European Monetary Unification'. In P. Masson and M. Taylor (eds), *Policy Issues in the Design of Currency Unions*. Cambridge: Cambridge University Press.

Engel, C. (2002). 'The Responsiveness of Consumer Prices to Exchange Rates and the Implications for Exchange-Rate Policy: A Survey of a Few Recent New Open-Economy Macro Models'. NBER Working Paper No. 8725. Cambridge, MA: National Bureau of Economic Research.

Engelbrecht-Wiggans, R. (1987). 'Optimal Reservation Prices in Auctions'. *Management Science*, 33, 763–70.

Engelbrecht-Wiggans, R. (1993). 'Optimal Auctions Revisited'. *Games and Economic Behaviour*, 5, 227–39.

Engelbrecht-Wiggans, R., and Khan, C. (1998). 'Low Revenue Equilibria in Simultaneous Auctions'. Working Paper, University of Illinois.

Esteves, R. (forthcoming). 'Targeted Advertising and Price Discrimination in the New Media'. Forthcoming, DPhil thesis, Oxford University.

European University Institution (2000). 'Euro Spectator: Implementing the Euro 1999 Swedish/UK/ Synthesis Reports'. EUI Working Paper LAW No 2000/9. Florence: European University Institution.

Ewerhart, C., and Moldovanu, B. (2001). 'The German UMTS Design: Insights from Multi-Object Auction Theory'. *ifo Studien*, 48(1), 158–74.

FitzGerald, G. (1991). *All in a Life*. London: Macmillan.

Foster, C. (2001). 'Transport Policy'. In A. Seldon (ed.), *The Blair Effect*. London: Little Brown.

Foster, C. (2005) *British Government in Crisis*. Oxford: Hart Publishing.

Foster, C., and Castles, C. (September 2004). 'Creating a Viable Railway for Britain – what has gone wrong and how to fix it. A response to the 2004 White Paper'. To be published Bath: Centre for the study of Regulated Industries.

Friedman, M. (1953). *Essays in Positive Economics*. Chicago: University of Chicago Press.

Friedman, M. (1967). 'The Monetary Theory and Policy of Henry Simons'. *Journal of Law and Economics*, 10(2), 1–13. Reprinted in M. Friedman (1969). *The Optimum Quantity of Money and Other Essays*. Chicago: Aldine, pp. 81–96.

Friedman, M. (1968). 'The Role of Monetary Policy'. *American Economic Review*, 58, March, 1–17.

Gamble, A. (1994). *The Free Economy and the Strong State: the Politics of Thatcherism*, 2nd edn. Basingstoke: Macmillan – now Palgave Macmillan.

Giavazzi. F., and Giovannini, A. (1989). *Limiting Exchange Rate Flexibility: the European Monetary System*. Cambridge: MIT Press.

Giddens, A. (1998). *The Third Way: the Renewal of Social Democracy*. Cambridge: Polity Press.

Gilbert, R., and Klemperer, P. (2000). 'An Equilibrium Theory of Rationing'. *Rand Journal of Economics*, 31(1), 1–21.

Glaister, S. (2004). *Competition Destroyed by Politics: British Rail Privatisation*. Bath: Centre for the Study of Regulated Industries.

Goldman, L. (2004). 'Richard Henry Tawney' in *Oxford Dictionary of National Biography*, online at http://www.oxforddnb.com.

Graham, D., and Marshall, R. (1987). 'Collusive Bidder Behavior at Single-Object Second-Price and English Auctions'. *Journal of Political Economy*, 95, 1217–39.

Graham, D., Marshall, R., and Richard, J.-F. (1990). 'Differential Payments within a Bidder Coalition and the Shapley Value'. *American Economic Review*, 80, 493–510.

Greenspan, A. (2002a). 'Chairman's Remarks: Transparency in Monetary Policy'. *Federal Reserve Bank of St. Louis Review*, 84(4), 5–6.

Greenspan, A. (2002b). 'Economic Volatility'. Speech given at the Federal Reserve Bank of Kansas City Symposium on 'Rethinking Stabilization Policy', Jackson Hole, Wyoming. 30 August.

Grimm, V., Riedel, F., and Wolfstetter, E. (2001). 'Low Price Equilibrium in Multi-Unit Auctions: The GSM Spectrum Auction in Germany'. Working Paper, Humboldt Universität zu Berlin.

Grimm, V., Riedel, F., and Wolfstetter, E. (2002). 'The Third Generation (UMTS) Spectrum Auction in Germany'. *ifo Studien*, 48(1), 123–43.

Haile, P. (1996). 'Auctions with Resale Markets'. PhD dissertation. Northwestern University.

Haines, J. (2003). *Glimmers of Twilight*. London: Politico's.

Hall, P., and Soskice, D. (eds) (2001). *Varieties of Capitalism: the Institutional Foundations of Comparative Advantage*. Oxford: Oxford University Press.

Halpern, D., Wood, S., White, S., and Cameron, G. (eds) (1996). *Options for Britain: a Strategic Policy Review*. Aldershot: Dartmouth.

Hansen, R.G. (1986). 'Sealed Bids versus Open Auctions: The Evidence'. *Economic Inquiry*, 24, 125–42.

Harstad, R. (1990). 'Alternative Common Values Auction Procedures: Revenue Comparisons with Free Entry'. *Journal of Political Economy*, 98, 421–9.

Hendricks, K., and Porter, R. (1989). 'Collusion in Auctions'. *Annales D'Économie et de Statistique*, 15/16, 217–30.

Hendricks, K., Porter, R., and Tan, G. (1999). 'Joint Bidding in Federal Offshore Oil and Gas Lease Auctions'. Working Paper, University of British Columbia.

Hendry, D., and Mizon, G. (2000). 'Reformulating Empirical Macroeconomic Modelling'. *Oxford Review of Economic Policy*, 16(4), 138–59.

HM Treasury (1944). *Employment Policy*. Cmd 6527. London: HMSO.

HM Treasury (1997). *Fiscal Policy: Learning the Lessons from the Last Economic Cycle*. London: HMSO.

HM Treasury (2002). *2002 Spending Review: Public Service Agreements 2003–2006*, cited from http://www.hm-treasury.gov.uk/media/B3039/psa02_ch4t.pdf, consulted 10.01.05.

HM Treasury (2002). *Budget 2002*. London: Stationery Office.

HM Treasury (2003). *Fiscal Stabilisation and EMU: a Discussion Paper*. London, June 2003, at http://www.hm-treasury.gov.uk./media/909/CC/adhereford03_exec_96.pdf.

HM Treasury (2004). *2004 Spending Review: Public Service Agreements 2003–2006*. Cm 6238. London: TSO.

Hicks, J. (1967). *Critical Essays in Monetary Theory*. Oxford: Clarendon Press.

House of Commons Treasury Committee (1997–8). *Seventh Report*, at http://www.publications.parliament.uk/pa/cm199798/cmselect/cmtreasy/993/99303.htm

Hume, D. (1738/1911) *A Treatise of Human Nature*, Everyman edn, 2 vols. London: Dent.

Hume, D. (1741/1994). *Political Essays*. Ed. by K. Haakonssen. Cambridge: Cambridge University Press.

Hutton, W. (1995). *The State We're In*. London: Cape.

Jay, P. (1976). 'Employment, Inflation and Politics'. *IEA Occasional Paper*, 46. London: Institute of Economic Affairs.

Jehiel, P., and Moldovanu, B. (2001). 'The UMTS/IMT-2000 License Auctions'. Working Paper, University College London, and University of Mannheim.

Jehiel, P., and Moldovanu, B. (2002). 'An Economic Perspective on Auctions'. Working Paper, University College London, and University of Mannheim.

Jenkins, P. (1970). *The Battle of Downing Street*. London: Charles Knight.

Joumard, I., and Kongsrud, P. (2003). 'Fiscal Relations across Government Levels'. *OECD Economic Studies*, No. 36.

Kagel, J., and Roth, A. (eds) (1995). *The Handbook of Experimental Economics*. Princeton: Princeton University Press.

Kara, A., and Nelson, E. (2002). 'The Exchange Rate and Inflation in the UK'. Manuscript, Bank of England.

Keegan, W. (2003). *The Prudence of Mr Gordon Brown*. Chichester: Wiley.

Keller, H. (2004). *The European Central Bank: History, Role and Functions*. Frankfurt: European Central Bank.

Kenen, P. (2002). 'Currency Unions and Policy Domains'. In D.M. Andrews, C.R. Henning and L.W. Pauly (eds). *Governing the World's Money*. Ithaca: Cornell University Press.

Kennedy, J., and Smith, A. (2004). 'Assessing the Efficient Cost of Sustaining Britain's Rail Network'. *Journal of Transport Economics and Policy*, 38, 2.

Keynes, J. (1933). *Essays in Biography*. London: Macmillan and Co., Ltd.

Keynes, J. (1936). *The General Theory of Employment, Interest and Money*. London: Macmillan.

King, M. (1996). 'How Should Central Banks Reduce Inflation? – Conceptual Issues'. In *Achieving Price Stability: A Symposium Sponsored by the Federal Reserve Bank of Kansas City*. Kansas City: Federal Reserve Bank of Kansas City, pp. 53–91.

King, M. (1997a). 'The Inflation Target Five Years On'. *Bank of England Quarterly Bulletin*, 37(4), November, 434–42.

King, M. (1997b). 'Changes in UK Monetary Policy: Rules and Discretion in Practice'. *Journal of Monetary Economics*, 39(1), 81–97.

King, M. (2002). 'The Monetary Policy Committee Five Years On'. *Bank of England Quarterly Bulletin*, 42(2), Summer, 219–27.

Klein, M.W. (1998). 'European Monetary Union'. *New England Economic Review*, March/April, 3–12.

Klemperer, P. (1998). 'Auctions with Almost Common Values'. *European Economic Review*, 42(3–5), 757–69.

Klemperer, P. (1999a). 'Auction Theory: A Guide to the Literature'. *Journal of Economic Surveys*, 13(3), 227–86. (Also reprinted in S. Dahiya (ed.) (1999), *The Current State of Economic Science*, 2, 711–66.)

Klemperer, P. (1999b). 'Applying Auction Theory to Economics'. Invited Lecture to Eighth World Congress of the Econometric Society, at www.paulklemperer.org.

Klemperer, P. (ed.) (2000a). *The Economic Theory of Auctions*. Cheltenham: Edward Elgar.

Klemperer, P. (2000b). 'What Really Matters in Auction Design'. May 2000 version, at www.paulklemperer.org.

Klemperer, P. (2002a). 'How (Not) to Run Auctions: the European 3G Telecom Auctions'. *European Economic Review*, 46(4–5), 829–45.

Klemperer, P. (2002b). 'What Really Matters In Auction Design'. *Journal of Economic Perspectives*, 16(1), 169–89.

Klemperer, P. (2002c). 'Some Observations on the German 3G Telecom Auction'. *ifo Studien*, 48(1), 145–56.

Klemperer, P. (2002d). 'Some Observations on the British 3G Telecom Auction'. *ifo Studien*, 48(1), 115–20.

Klemperer, P. (2003a). 'Why Every Economist Should Learn Some Auction Theory'. In M. Dewatripont, L. Hansen, S. Turnovsky (eds), *Advances in Economics and Econometrics: Invited Lectures to Eighth World Congress of the Econometric Society*. Cambridge: Cambridge University Press.

Klemperer, P. (2003b). *Auctions: Theory and Practice*. Published 2004, Princeton: Princeton University Press.

Klemperer, P. *et al.* (forthcoming). 'Auctions for Environmental Improvements: the UK ETS Auction'. Working Paper, Nuffield College, Oxford, and www.paul.klemperer.org.

Klemperer, P., and Pagnozzi, M. (2003). 'Advantaged Bidders and Spectrum Prices: An Empirical Analysis'. Forthcoming at www.paulklemperer.org.

Kohn, D. (1999). 'Comment: Forward-Looking Rules for Monetary Policy'. In J. Taylor (ed.), *Monetary Policy Rules*. Chicago: University of Chicago Press, pp. 192–9.

Kohn, D. (2000). 'Report to the Non-Executive Directors of the Court of the Bank of England on Monetary Policy Processes and the Work of Monetary Analysis'. 18 October. Reprinted in *Bank of England Quarterly Bulletin*, 41(1), Spring 2001, 35–49.

Krueger, A. (1974). 'The Political Economy of the Rent-Seeking Society'. *American Economic Review*, 64, June, 291–303.

Krugman, P. (2002). 'Passing the Buck'. *New York Times*, 3 September.

Kydland, F., and Prescott, E. (1977). 'Rules Rather than Discretion: The Inconsistency of Optimal Plans'. *Journal of Political Economy*, 85, 473–90.

Lane, P. (1999). 'Disinflation, Switching Nominal Anchors and Twin Crises: the Irish Experience'. Trinity College Dublin and Centre for Economic Policy Research, April.

Law Commission (1988). 'The Rules against Perpetuities and Excessive Accumulations'. Report No. 251, March.

Lawson, Nigel (1992). *The View from No. 11*. London: Bantam.

Le Grand, J. (2003). *Motivation, Agency, and Public Policy*. Oxford: Oxford University Press.

Levin, D., Kagel, J., and Richard, J.-F. (1996). 'Revenue Effects and Information Processing in English Common Value Actions'. *American Economic Review*, 86(3), 442–60.

Levin, D., and Smith, J. (1994). 'Equilibrium in Auctions with Entry'. *American Economic Review*, 84, 585–99.

Levy, D., and Peart, S. (2001). 'The Secret History of the Dismal Science: Economics, Religion and Race in the 19th Century' in *Library of Economics and Liberty, Contributors' Forum* at http://www.econlib.org/library/Columns/LevyPeartdismal.html, consulted 07.05.05.

Lucas, Robert E., Jr (1976) 'Econometric Policy Evaluation: A Critique' In K. Brunner and E. Melzer (eds), *The Phillips Curve and Labour Markets*, Carnegie-Rochester Conference series on Public Policy, Vol. 1, 19–46.

Maasland, E. (2000). 'Veilingmiljarden Zijn een Fictie (Billions from Auctions: Wishful Thinking)'. *ESB* June 9: 479 and translation available at www.paulklemperer.org.

Macdonald, R., and Hallwood, P. (2004). 'The Economic Case for Fiscal Federalism in Scotland'. Allander Series, University of Strathclyde.

Machlup, F. (1946). 'Marginal Analysis and Empirical Research'. *American Economic Review*, 36 (Sept.), 519–54.

Mailath, G., and Zemsky, P. (1991). 'Collusion in Second Price Auctions with Heterogeneous Bidders'. *Games and Economic Behavior*, 3, 467–86.

Marshall, A. (1890). *Principles of Economics*. London: Macmillan & Co., Ltd.

Marshall, A. (1906). Letter to A. L. Bowley, February 27, in A.C. Pigou (ed.) (1925). *Memorials of Alfred Marshall*. London: Macmillan, pp. 427–8.

Maskin, E., and Riley, J. (1984). 'Optimal Auctions with Risk Averse Buyers'. *Econometrica*, 52, 1473–518.

Maskin, E., and Riley, J. (2000). 'Asymmetric Auctions'. *Review of Economic Studies*, 67, 413–39.

Matthews, S. (1983). 'Selling to Risk Averse Buyers with Unobservable Tastes'. *Journal of Economic Theory*, 3, 370–400.

Matthews, S. (1984). 'Information Acquisition in Discriminatory Auctions'. In M. Boyer and R. Kihlstrom (eds), *Bayesian Models in Economic Theory*. New York: North-Holland, pp. 181–207.

McAfee, R., and McMillan, J. (1987). 'Auctions with Entry'. *Economics Letters*, 23, 343–47.

McAfee, R., and McMillan, J. (1988). 'Search Mechanisms'. *Journal of Economic Theory*, 44, 99–123.

McAfee, R., and McMillan, J. (1992). 'Bidding Rings'. *American Economic Review*, 82, 579–99.

McCallum, B. (1995). 'Two Fallacies Concerning Central-Bank Independence'. *American Economic Review*, 85(2), 207–11.

McKibbin, W., and Sachs, J. (1991). *Global Linkages: Macroeconomic Interdependence and Cooperation in the World Economy*. Washington DC: Brookings Institution Press.

McLean, I. (1999). *The Legend of Red Clydeside*, 2nd edn. Edinburgh: John Donald.

McLean, I. (2001a). *Rational Choice and British Politics*. Oxford: Oxford University Press.

McLean, I. (2001b). 'Scotland: Towards Quebec – or Slovakia?' *Regional Studies*, 35, 637–44.

McLean, I. (2002). 'Fiscal Federalism in Australia'. Working Paper 2002-W28, Nuffield College, Oxford University.

McLean, I. (2003). 'Fiscal Federalism in Canada'. Working Paper 2003-W17, Nuffield College, Oxford University.

McLean, I., and McMillan, A. (2003). 'The Distribution of Public Expenditure across the UK Regions'. *Fiscal Studies*, 24(1), 45–71.

McMillan, J. (1994). 'Selling Spectrum Rights'. *Journal of Economic Perspectives*, 8, 145–62.

Mead, W., and Schneipp, M. (1989). 'Competitive Bidding for Federal Timber in Region 6, An Update: 1983–1988'. Santa Barbara CA: Community and Organization Research Institute, University of California.

Meade, J. (1951). *The Theory of International Economic Policy, Volume 1: The Balance of Payments*. Oxford: Oxford University Press.

Meeks, R. (2001). 'An Event Study of the Swiss UMTS Auction'. Research Note, Nuffield College, Oxford University.

Meltzer, A. (1977). 'Anticipated Inflation and Unanticipated Price Change'. *Journal of Money, Credit, and Banking*, 9(1), 182–205.

Menezes, F. (1996). 'Multiple-unit English auctions'. *European Journal of Political Economy*, 12, 671–84.

Menezes, F., and Monteiro, P. (1997). *Auctions with Endogenous Participation*. Mimeo, Australian National University and Instituto de Matematica Pura e Aplicada.

Meyer, L. (2002). 'Rules and Discretion'. Speech at the Owen Graduate School of Management, Vanderbilt University, Nashville, Tennessee, 16 January.

Miles, D. (2004) *The UK Mortgage Market: Taking a Longer-Term View*. London: HM Treasury.

Milgrom, P. (1987). 'Auction Theory'. In T. Bewley (ed.), *Advances in Economic Theory: Fifth World Congress*. Cambridge: Cambridge University Press.

Milgrom, P., and Weber. R. (1982). 'A Theory of Auctions and Competitive Bidding, II'. *Econometrica*, 50, 1089–122.

Milgrom, P., and Weber, R. (2000). 'A Theory of Auctions and Competitive Bidding'. In P. Klemperer (ed.), *The Economic Theory of Auctions*. Cheltenham: Edward Elgar, II, pp. 179–94.

Morgan, K. (1997). *Callaghan – A Life*. Oxford: Oxford University Press.

Mueller, D. (2003). *Public Choice III*. Cambridge: Cambridge University Press.

Mundell, R. (1961). 'The Theory of Optimal Currency Areas'. *American Economic Review*, 51, 509–17.

Myerson, R. (1981). 'Optimal Auction Design'. *Mathematics of Operations Research*, 6, 58–73.

Naughtie, J. (1994). 'A Political Life Observed' in Brown and Naughtie, 1994, pp. 21–55.

Nellthorp, J., and Mackie, P. (2000). 'The UK Roads Review: a Hedonic Model of Decisionmaking'. *Transport Policy*, 17, 127–38.

Nelson, E., and Nikolov, K. (2001). 'UK Inflation in the 1970s and 1980s: The Role of Output Gap Mismeasurement'. Bank of England Working Paper No. 148 and Centre for Economic Policy Research Discussion Paper No. 2999.

Newbery, D. (forthcoming). 'Road User and Congestion Charges' in S. Cnossen (ed.), *Taxes on Pleasure*. Oxford: Oxford University Press.

Office of the Deputy Prime Minister (2004). *Balance of Funding Review – report*, July.

Olson, M. (1965). *The Logic of Collective Action*. Cambridge, MA: Harvard University Press.

Olson, M. (1982). *The Rise and Decline of Nations*. New Haven: Yale University Press.

Opie, R. (1972). *Economic Planning and Growth in the Labour Government's Economic Record 1964–1970*. Ed. by W. Beckerman. London: Duckworth.

Orphanides, A. (2000). 'The Quest for Prosperity without Inflation'. ECB Working Paper No. 15. Frankfurt: European Central Bank.

Paarsch, H. (1991). 'Empirical Models of Auctions and an Application to British Columbian Timber Sales'. University of British Columbia Discussion Paper.

Parsons, W. (1989). *The Power of the Financial Press*. Aldershot: Edward Elgar.

Patinkin, D. (1969). 'The Chicago Tradition, the Quantity Theory, and Friedman'. *Journal of Money, Credit, and Banking*, 1(1), 46–70.

Perry, M., and Reny, P. (1999). 'The Failure of the Linkage Principle in Multi-Unit Auctions'. *Econometrica*, 67(4), 895–900.

Persico, N. (1997). 'Information Acquisition in Auctions'. Working Paper, UCLA.

Phillips, A. (1958). 'The Relation Between Unemployment and the Rate of Change of Money Wage Rates in the United Kingdom 1861–1957'. *Economica*, 25, 283–99.

Plowden Report (1961). *The Control of Public Expenditure*. Cmnd 1432. London: HMSO.

Pollitt, M., and Smith, A. (2002). 'The Restructuring of British Rail'. *Fiscal Studies*, 23(4), 463–502.

Posen, A. (1993). 'Why Central Bank Independence Does Not Cause Low Inflation: There Is No Institutional Fix for Politics'. In R. O'Brien (ed.), *Finance and the International Economy. Volume 7. The Amex Bank Review Prize Essays: In Memory of Richard Marjolin*. Oxford: Oxford University Press, pp. 41–54.

Rees-Mogg, W. (1974). *The Reigning Error: The Crisis of World Inflation*. London: Hamish Hamilton.

Riley, J., and Li., H. (1997). 'Auction Choice: A Numerical Analysis'. Mimeo, University of California at Los Angeles.

Riley, J., and Samuelson, W. (1981). 'Optimal Auctions'. *American Economic Review*, 71, 381–92.

Robbins, L. (1932). *An Essay on the Nature and Significance of Economic Science.* London: Macmillan.

Robinson, M. (1985). 'Collusion and the Choice of Auction'. *Rand Journal of Economics*, 16, 141–5.

Rogoff, K. (1985). 'The Optimal Degree of Commitment to an Intermediate Monetary Target'. *Quarterly Journal of Economics*, 100(4), 1169–89.

Rose, A. (2000). 'One Money, One Market: Estimating the Effects of Common Currencies on Trade'. *Economic Policy*, 30, 9–33.

Rose, A., and Engel, C. (2000). 'Currency Unions and International Integration'. NBER Working Paper 7872, National Bureau of Economic Research.

Rose, A., and Glick, R. (2002). 'Does a Currency Union affect Trade? The Time-Series Evidence'. *European Economic Review*, 46, 1125–51.

Roth, A. (2002). 'The Economist as Engineer: Game Theory, Experimentations, and Computation as Tools for Design Economics'. *Econometrica*, 70(4), 1341–78.

Rothkopf, M., and Engelbrecht-Wiggans, R. (1993). 'Misapplications Reviews: Getting the Model Right – The Case of Competitive Bidding'. *Interfaces*, 23, 99–106.

Rotemberg, J., and Woodford, M. (1997). 'An Optimization-Based Econometric Framework for the Evaluation of Monetary Policy'. *NBER Macroeconomics Annual*, 12, 297–346.

RAC Foundation for Motoring (2002). *Motoring Towards 2050.* London: RAC Foundation for Motoring.

Royal Swedish Academy of Sciences (1986). *Press Release: The Sveriges Riksbank (Bank of Sweden) Prize in Economic Sciences in Memory of Alfred Nobel for 1986.* At http://nobelprize.org/economics/laureates/1986/press.html, consulted 11.01.05.

Sargent, T. (1999). *The Conquest of American Inflation.* Princeton: Princeton University Press.

Schonhardt-Bailey, C. (2003). 'Ideology, Party and Interests in the British Parliament of 1841–47'. *British Journal of Political Science*, 33, 581–605.

Sills, D. (ed.) (1968). *International Encyclopedia of the Social Sciences.* New York: Macmillan Company and The Free Press, vol. 10.

Simons, H. (1948). *Economic Policy for a Free Society.* Chicago: University of Chicago Press.

Smeed, R. (1964). *Road Pricing: The Economic and Technical Possibilities.* Ministry of Transport Panel. London: HMSO.

Smith, A. (1759/2002). *The Theory of Moral Sentiments.* Ed. by K. Haakonssen. Cambridge: Cambridge University Press.

Smith, A. (1776/1976). *An Inquiry into the Nature and Causes of the Wealth of Nations.* Glasgow edn., 2 vols. Oxford: Oxford University Press.

Smith, A. (2004). 'Are Britain's Railways Costing Too Much? Perceptions based on TRP Comparisons with British Rail, 1963–2002'. Leeds: University of Leeds Institute of Transport Studies.

Stewart, W. (1921). *J. Keir Hardie: a Biography.* London: Keir Hardie Memorial Committee.

Stuewe, H. (1999). 'Auktion von Telefonfrequenzen: Spannung bis zur letzten Minute'. *Frankfurter Allgemeine Zeitung*, October 29.

Svensson, L. (1997). 'Inflation Forecast Targeting: Implementing and Monitoring Inflation Targets'. *European Economic Review*, 41(6), 1111–46.

Svensson, L. (2002). 'What Is Wrong with Taylor Rules? Using Judgment in Monetary Policy through Targeting Rules'. Manuscript, Princeton University.

Tawney, R. (1922/1938). *Religion and the Rise of Capitalism*. First published 1922; cited from Penguin edn, Harmondsworth, 1938.

Tawney, R. (1921). *The Acquisitive Society*. London: G. Bell & Sons.

Taylor, J. (1993). 'Discretion versus Policy Rules in Practice'. *Carnegie-Rochester Conference Series on Public Policy*, 39(1), 195–214.

Taylor, J. (1997). 'America's Peacetime Inflation: The 1970s. Comment'. In C. Romer and D. Romer (eds), *Reducing Inflation: Motivation and Strategy*. Chicago: University of Chicago Press, pp. 276–80.

Taylor, J. (1999). 'The Robustness and Efficiency of Monetary Policy Rules as Guidelines for Interest Rate Setting by the European Central Bank'. *Journal of Monetary Economics*, 43(3), 655–79.

Taylor, J. (2000). 'Alternative Views of the Monetary Transmission Mechanism: What Difference Do They Make for Monetary Policy?' *Oxford Review of Economic Policy*, 16(4), 60–73.

Taylor, J. (2001). 'The Role of the Exchange Rate in Monetary-Policy Rules'. *American Economic Review (Papers and Proceedings)*, 91(2), 263–7.

Taylor, R. (2004). 'John Smith' in *Oxford Dictionary of National Biography* online at http://www.oxforddnb.com.

Thisse, J., and Vives, X. (1988). 'On the Strategic Choice of Spatial Price Policy'. *American Economic Review*, 78, 122–37.

Thom, R., and Walsh, B. (2002). 'The Effect of a Currency Union on Trade: Lessons from the Irish Experience'. Department of Economics Working Paper, University College Dublin, March.

Tiebout, C. (1956). 'A Pure Theory of Local Expenditures'. *Journal of Political Economy*, 64(5), 416–24.

Titmuss, R. (1963). *Essays on the Welfare State*, 2nd edn. London: Allen & Unwin.

Titmuss, R. (1970). *The Gift Relationship: From Human Blood to Social Policy*. London: Allen & Unwin. Citations from Penguin edition, Harmondsworth, 1973.

Ulph, D., and Vulkan, N. (2001). 'E-Commerce, Mass Customisation and Price Discrimination'. Mimeo, UCL and University of Bristol.

van Damme, E. (1999). 'The Dutch DCS-1800 Auction'. In F. Patrone, I. Garcia-Jurado and S. Tijs (eds), *Game Practise: Contributions from Applied Game Theory*. Boston: Kluwer Academic Publishers, pp. 53–73.

van Damme, E. (2002). 'The European UMTS Auctions'. *European Economic Review*, 45(4–5), 846–58.

Vickers, J. (1998). 'Inflation Targeting in Practice: The UK Experience'. *Bank of England Quarterly Bulletin*, 38(4), November, 368–75.

Vickers, J. (1999). 'Monetary Policy and Asset Prices'. *Bank of England Quarterly Bulletin*, 39(4), November, 428–35.

Vickers, J., and Yarrow, G. (1988). *Privatization: an Economic Analysis*. Cambridge, MA: MIT Press.

Vickrey, W. (1961). 'Counterspeculation, Auctions, and Competitive Sealed Tenders'. *Journal of Finance*, 16, 8–37.

Vines, D., Maciejowski, J., and Meade, J. (1983). *Stagflation, Vol. 2: Demand Management*. London: George Allen and Unwin.

Walsh, C. (1995). 'Optimal Contracts for Central Bankers'. *American Economic Review*, 85(1), 150–67.

Waterson, M. (1984). *Economic Theory of the Industry*. Cambridge: Cambridge University Press.

Weber, R. (1997). 'Making More from Less: Strategic Demand Reduction in the FCC Spectrum Auctions'. *Journal of Economics and Management Strategy*, 6(3), 529–48.

Westaway, P. (2003). *Modelling the Transition to EMU*. London: Stationery Office.

Wilson, R. (2002). 'Architecture of Power Markets'. *Econometrica*, 70(4), 1299–340.

Wood, S. (1997). 'Capitalist Constitutions: Supply-Side Reforms in Britain and West Germany 1960–1990'. PhD dissertation, Department of Government, Harvard University.

Wood, S. (2000). 'Why Indicative Planning Failed: British Industry and the Formation of the National Economic Development Council (1961–65)'. *Twentieth-Century British History*, 11(4), 431–59.

Wood, S. (2001). 'Labour Market Regimes under Threat? Sources of Continuity in Germany, Britain, and Sweden'. In P. Pierson (ed.), *The New Politics of the Welfare State*. Oxford: Oxford University Press, pp. 368–409.

Wood, S. (2002). 'Business, Government, and Patterns of Labor Market Policy in Britain and the Federal Republic of Germany'. In Hall and Soskice, 2002, pp. 247–74.

Woodford, M. (2003). *Interest and Prices*. Princeton: Princeton University Press.

World Bank (1993). *The East Asian Miracle: Economic Growth and Public Policy*. Oxford: Oxford University Press.

Wren-Lewis, S. (2000). 'The Limits to Discretionary Fiscal Stabilization Policy'. *Oxford Review of Economic Policy*, 16(4), 92–105.

Wrigley, C. (2004). 'Ernest Bevin' in *Oxford Dictionary of National Biography* online at http://www.oxforddnb.com.

Index